"From classroom examp[les] African American stude[nts] [and insights from] pre-service and in-service elementary, middle, and high school teachers, Boutte's argument is clear: Teachers, teacher educators, educational researchers—all of us who care about teaching—must believe in "the humanity and teachability of Black children." This book comes at an important time as the push for "one size fits all" educational reforms is at an all-time high, and when debates over the relevance of standardized curricula and testing, especially for African American students, continue to cast a shadow over what teachers already know how to do—teach!"

—**Valerie Kinloch**, Professor, Literacy Studies and Director, EHE Office of Diversity and Inclusion, Ohio State University, USA

"This book compels educators to reexamine, reimagine, and revise the ways in which we perceive African American children and others who are perpetually underserved in schools across the United States. A thought-provoking, accessible, poignant, and moral call to all of us—educators, parents, researchers, policymakers, and politicians—this book shepherds us into posing an essential question in all the work we do: And How Are the Children? This book educates as it enlightens!"

—**H. Richard Milner IV**, Helen Faison Professor of Urban Education, University of Pittsburgh, USA

"Gloria Boutte enlightens practitioners and scholars alike to look beyond the popular arguments around educating African American students. She takes readers through the historical frames that have shaped the ways in which African American students have been marginalized in educational systems. More importantly, she offers a wealth of knowledge toward how we can responsively and competently educate African American students."

—**Dalisha Williams**, Middle School Math Teacher, Columbia, SC, USA

"This is a vitally important and powerful book for those charged with the responsibility of educating African American children. A beautiful dissection of how theory can inform practice, Dr. Boutte provides us with an uncannily reflective and instructive book that can potentially play a pivotal place in the educational salvation of African American children."

—**Jerome E. Morris**, Professor of Education and Research Fellow at the Owens Institute for Behavioral Research, The University of Georgia, USA

EDUCATING AFRICAN AMERICAN STUDENTS

Focused on preparing educators to teach African American students, this straight-forward and teacher-friendly text features a careful balance of published scholarship, a framework for culturally relevant and critical pedagogy, research-based case studies of model teachers, and tested culturally relevant practical strategies and actionable steps teachers can adopt. Its premise is that teachers who understand Black culture as an asset rather than a liability and utilize teaching techniques that have been shown to work can and do have specific positive impacts on the educational experiences of African American children.

Each chapter begins with one to three key propositions or ideas and includes foundational knowledge and insights that effective teachers use to guide their teaching. The propositions make chapter themes explicit and are handy if readers want to find something quickly in the book. The text addresses major elements shown to be useful for effectively educating African American students—wisdom from existing knowledge bases, educators' dispositions, instructional strategies and curricular transformations—and emphasizes four major teaching strategies: critical literacy, counternarratives, culturally relevant teaching, and contrastive analysis. Culturally relevant teaching exemplars for African American students from different content areas and grade levels are presented, along with commentaries about related issues to consider. A Companion Website provides additional resources.

Gloria Swindler Boutte is a Professor at the University of South Carolina, USA.

Visit the Companion Website for instructors at www.routledge.com/cw/boutte for PowerPoint slides; sample culturally relevant teaching lessons; activities (Culturally Relevant Rhythms) to help teachers think about their practices; and multimedia examples from teachers.

EDUCATING AFRICAN AMERICAN STUDENTS

And How Are the Children?

Gloria Swindler Boutte

Routledge
Taylor & Francis Group

NEW YORK AND LONDON

First published 2016
by Routledge
711 Third Avenue, New York, NY 10017

and by Routledge
2 Park Square, Milton Park, Abingdon, Oxon OX14 4RN

Routledge is an imprint of the Taylor & Francis Group, an informa business

Library of Congress Cataloging-in-Publication Data
A catalog record for this book has been requested

ISBN: 978-1-138-89231-6 (hbk)
ISBN: 978-1-138-89232-3 (pbk)
ISBN: 978-1-315-70923-9 (ebk)

Typeset in Bembo and Stone Sans
by Florence Production Ltd, Stoodleigh, Devon, UK

CONTENTS

FOREWORD

Among the myriad scholarly work—a veritable cottage industry—that offers absolutely necessary "how-to" guides for successfully teaching those "failing urban kids" (e.g., "at-risk" inner-city African American children) comes this soon-to-be classic culturally authoritative, empirically informed publication for education professionals. It shows us that one of the things that academics can do better is to make our scholarly work accessible to wider audiences—especially to K–12 educators. *Educating African American Students: And How Are the Children?* accomplishes much more than this: It is a paradigm-shifting exception. The book is intended to mobilize and inspire K–12 teachers and teacher educators to engage in informed action: transformative teaching on behalf of African American students—transformative, liberating, pedagogical action. Engaging readers with an allegory based on the traditional greeting among the Masai people of Kenya, the book poses the question, "And how are the children?"—denoting that, when the children of a society are well, then peace and prosperity will prevail. This deeply rooted African–African American cultural ideal can and should inform teacher preparation and pedagogy.

Presenting numerous social and academic indicators that show the extent to which Black children *are not faring well in schools*, for reasons not inherent in themselves, their culture, or communities, this book provides opportunities for discussion on decolonizing conceptual frameworks and strategies such as critical literacy, diaspora literacy, and contrastive analysis, which can be transformative for Black children, educators, and schools. The strategies and activities provided in this book are not prescriptive but are certainly powerful alternatives to the still-prevalent deficit mindset that pervades schools and universities, and the basic tenets are elastic enough to be applied to different content areas and grade levels.

Using compelling arguments and examples for teachers who are successful teaching African American students, Gloria Swindler Boutte invites educators to move beyond conventional approaches that have not been effective with Black children and encourages them to teach in an emancipatory manner that is liberating for students and teachers alike. These examples include liberating approaches for classroom management, parent engagement, and critical thinking. Knowing that the vast majority of K–12 teachers want to make a difference in the lives of the children whom they teach, Dr. Boutte asks teachers to step outside their comfort zones on behalf of the children. Acknowledging that many African American students are in uncomfortable educational and social spaces for most of their school careers, she lovingly explains that educators, who seek to protect the children, nurture their cultural well-being, and ensure their success, can certainly be uncomfortable as they discuss difficult issues.

This book provides enough examples that teachers can immediately extrapolate and tailor to their classrooms. This book will also be instructive for teaching *all* children in liberating, humanizing ways. Indeed, the goal that most of us have as educators is to ensure that the students in our respective educational spaces are well. Doing so will contribute to the humanity of all of us.

Joyce E. King, Ph.D.
Benjamin E. Mays Endowed Chair for Urban Teaching,
Learning and Leadership, Georgia State University, and
President, The American Educational Research Association

PREFACE

This book focuses on preparing teachers to teach African American students. It is written in straightforward, teacher-friendly language and makes theoretical and research information accessible to educators in K–12 schools and teacher educators. The larger goal of this book is to *activate and energize* educators so that they will view teaching African American students as exhilarating and rewarding, rather than as problematic and laborious. Additionally, the book seeks to help educators develop proficiency using culturally relevant pedagogy and other effective educational strategies for teaching African American students. It provides examples from classrooms of teachers who are effective in teaching African American students.

This book goes beyond recounting the well-known and oft-cited problems and provides case studies and sample lessons that showcase teachers who are committed to effectively teaching African American children. It draws from the experiences of a cadre of teachers who served as "model teachers" for the Center of Excellence for the Education and Equity of African American Students (CEEEAAS).[1] These teachers are/were committed[2] to the quest for effective teaching of African American students.

As part of the orientation for the CEEEAAS model teachers, they completed a course titled, "Educating African American Students." The course was typically taught on site at an urban school and has been offered to more than 100 teachers since 2003. Many aspects of the course have been adapted for this book. In addition to building on the examples from CEEEAAS's teachers' classes, this book also draws from my professional expertise as a scholar who has studied and taught about issues relating to African American students for more than 30 years. This book also draws from the extensive body of academic literature on the topic, as well as from teachers whom I have worked with in other capacities. Additional information on CEEEAAS and the teachers can be found in Chapter 5.

Classrooms, lessons, inquiry units, and other examples provided in this book are intended to be elastic and can readily be extrapolated to different grade levels and content areas. Although this book intentionally focuses on African American students, the basic tenets can be adapted to other culturally and linguistically diverse (CLD) groups.

This book makes the needs of African American students explicit by illuminating the interplay between structural inequities and the identities and experiences of Black children, families, and communities. Most importantly, this book illustrates the inherent beauty, strengths, and humanity of Black children and invites educators to view them using these lenses. This is an ambitious and noble task, but a possible one. I have witnessed teachers from various ethnic groups, content areas, and grade levels transform their disbeliefs and disenchantment regarding African American students into a strong belief in the humanity and teachability of Black children.

Finally, it is important to note that the chapters in this book will be useful for pointing interested educators in a transformative direction. The book is not intended to be exhaustive or formulaic, and it is expected that teachers will make adaptations, extensions, revisions, and extrapolations for their specific contexts. Additionally, it is hoped that readers will consult some of the many resources and readings listed throughout the book, so that they can continue to build their knowledge bases and apply new information in their classrooms and schools that will lead to transformations in instruction, curriculum, and assessment practices.

Overview of Chapters

Each chapter in this book presents between one and three key propositions or key ideas, as well as foundational information and insights. These propositions represent the larger themes for the chapters and are embedded throughout, rather than in one specific section. The propositions are presented at the beginning of each chapter. Each chapter also contains reflective activities and resources. Key points are summarized at the end of each chapter.

Chapter 1: And How Are the Children? Seeing Strengths and Possibilities

Chapter 1 provides the foundation on which Chapters 2–7 build. It includes a focus on the welfare of Black children, reflective guidelines for processing the information in the book, terms and definitions, an overview of the current educational and societal landscape, a discussion of Black culture, implications for teachers, and a preview of major strategies discussed in the book.

Chapter 2: Liberty and Justice for All? Breaking the Code

This chapter provides the conceptual framework of the book and draws from decolonizing theories (e.g., Fanon, 1952/2008; Freire, 1970/1999). Making a distinction between individual and institutional acts of discrimination, it allows educators to see how anyone (even well-meaning teachers and teacher educators) can unknowingly contribute to oppression. This chapter sensitively, but poignantly, helps educators name and dissect oppression, so that they can detect it in school structures and practices. Recommendations for interrupting countering oppression are offered.

Chapter 3: Critical Literacy: Providing Mirrors and Windows for African American Students

This chapter presents information on *Diaspora literacy*, *liberation literature*, and guidelines for detecting biases in books, media, and other texts. It also provides information on assembling book collections in K–12 classrooms. Emphasis is placed on counternarratives and multiple perspectives. Reflective activities are included. Key concepts include providing reflections of African American culture in book collections (mirrors), as well as windows to the larger, global society. It is stressed that books alone, without accompanying ideological understanding and changes in instructional practices, are insufficient for effectively educating African American students.

Chapter 4: Loving the Language (African American Language)

The importance of viewing Standard English/Mainstream American English and African American Language as co-equal language systems is a key premise of this chapter. Consideration is given to the pervasive misconceptions about African American Language. A discussion of the structure and rules of African American Language is presented. Educational implications for educators are provided. Recommended strategies that have been shown to be particularly successful for developing Standard English proficiency (without denigrating or eradicating African American Language) are presented. Examples of code-switching and code meshing will be shared. Sample activities are included.

Chapter 5: Culturally Relevant Teaching: Views from Classrooms

This chapter provides an overview of the basic tenets of culturally relevant teaching. Culturally relevant teaching focuses on: (a) academic excellence that is not based on cultural deficit models of school failure, (b) cultural competence that locates excellence within the context of the students' community and cultural identities, and (c) critical consciousness that challenges inequitable school and societal structures (Ladson-Billings, 2002). This chapter provides examples of culturally relevant teaching from elementary, middle, and secondary classrooms, in different content areas. Emphasis is on recognizing opportunities to teach skills in a relevant manner and expose students to global perspectives beyond their own worldviews.

Chapter 6: Families and Communities: Looking with Different Lenses

This chapter focuses on ways to learn about and *from* African American families. Stressing variation among African American families, tips for locating funds of knowledge (e.g., cooking, church activities, sewing, fishing) during daily routines are provided. This chapter provides guidelines for educators to engage in micro-ethnographies and study of African American communities and culture. Insight is provided into recognizing the "sages" in the homes and communities, as well as immersion in aspects of Black culture (e.g., music, magazines, movies, cultural events, television). It includes a provocative discussion about missionary efforts that attempt to "save" African American children from themselves and their culture and reconsideration of typical home visits.

Chapter 7: Revisioning the Teaching of African American Students

This chapter recaps and helps readers consider how key concepts from this book can be used in their respective settings. Dialogic questions are posed, and a culminating activity is designed to help teachers activate their power to teach for liberation. The emphasis is on moving beyond lamenting past problems and mistakes and focusing on future trajectories and plans. A reminder of the collective impact of teachers and strategies for making infrastructural changes are given. Following the guidance, *when we know better, we do better*, educators can move beyond guilt about what they have or have not done toward transformational teaching.

Companion Website

The companion website for this book (www.routledge.com/cw/boutte) provides additional resources:

- PowerPoint slides to accompany each chapter, with sample culturally relevant teaching lessons;
- descriptions of activities (Culturally Relevant Rhythms) to help teachers think about their practices; and
- multimedia examples from teachers.

Notes

1. The CEEEAAS was initially funded by the South Carolina Commission of Higher Education.
2. The use of the past tense is not intended to imply that the teachers are no longer committed to the effective education of African American students. The teachers were affiliated with the CEEEAAS for four years. The teachers who are still teaching continue to be committed to the effective education of African American students.

References

Fanon, F. (1952/2008). *Black skin, White masks*. New York: Grove Press.

Freire, P. (1970/1999). *Pedagogy of the oppressed*. New York: Continuum Publishing.

Ladson-Billings, G. (2002). I ain't writin' nuttin: Permissions to fail and demands to succeed in urban classrooms. In L. Delpit (Ed.), *Skin that we speak* (pp. 107–120). New York: The New Press.

ACKNOWLEDGMENTS

The initial funding for the CEEEAAS was made possible by the South Carolina Commission on Higher Education. A special thanks is extended to Dr. Joann Thompson, who skillfully served as Project Director, and to CEEEAAS's model teachers, who continue to believe in the "Possibility of the Black Child." Appreciation is also expressed to the other teachers whose work is featured in this book.

Thanks to the reviewers for your insightful comments and guidance and for seeing the promise of this important work. A special shout out to Dr. Rich Milner, who stayed on my case to make sure that I finished the book. Much love to Susi Long and Valerie Kinloch, for their supportive reviews of earlier versions of this work.

Without my mother, Mildred Shelton, my scholarship would not be possible. Thank you for teaching me *how* to write in a way that people will want to read it. I'll never forget your revision of my first submission for publication to *Readers Digest* when I was 14 years old. Also, thanks for always believing in the possibility of *this* Black child.

To my husband, Dr. George L. Johnson, Jr., thank you for believing in the possibility of this noble work that we do together on behalf of humanity and for holding our home together as I wrote. The inviting fires and delicious meals were especially appreciated, as was the time that you spent entertaining and educating the grandkids.

To my children (Stephanie and Jonathan Boutte, and McKenzee Johnson) and grandchildren (Jaliyah and Janiyah Ware, Carter Archie, and Layla Johnson): Thank you for supporting me as I spent endless hours at the computer while you were engaging in family time. And yes, Miss Jaliyah, you can also have your book published! Because of all of you, this work is particularly important. I believe in the unlimited potential of each of you! #Blacklivesmatter

1

AND HOW ARE THE CHILDREN?

Seeing Strengths and Possibilities

Proposition 1.1 There is a need to illuminate the existing strengths of African American children, families, communities, and schools and to disrupt the prevailing discourse of Black inferiority.

Proposition 1.2 Black culture is an asset and source of strength.

Proposition 1.3 Equity, not equality, is the goal.

In light of the seemingly perpetual and alarming statistics about African American students, educators need to know that our work matters more than we can imagine. Black students will not succeed without us, and we are their lifelines to a better future (Delpit, 2012). Nevertheless, as educators, we can also be complicit in the process of students' nonsuccess, albeit often unintentionally or because we are unaware of the larger implications and influence of our actions and practices. In order for changes to occur in the pervasive, negative trends faced by Black children, doing nothing is not an option for educators who care about Black children and want to contribute to improving the education process on their (students') behalf. Acknowledging the inherent strengths, beauty, and humanity of Black students and their communities, each of us must find ways to make a positive and impactful difference and to teach for the liberation of African American students, such that optimistic educational and economic opportunities are not foreclosed for them.

This chapter, then, provides an overview of foundational ideas that will be explained in more detail in subsequent chapters. Although many educators will want to delve into "solutions" and strategies immediately, the intent of this book is to provide a comprehensive conceptualization, instead of a shallow recipe and "quick fix." Hence, some background on the issues facing African American students is necessary. Because African and African American cultures have a rich and strong storytelling tradition, I seek to honor that tradition by beginning with a story. This story has been passed down over the generations and across cultures, and its guiding question serves as the key theme of the book. It is my hope that this story and its guiding question will direct educators' attention to the need to prioritize the care of children and, in this case, of African American students.

And How Are the Children?[1]

Among the most accomplished and fabled groups of warriors were the mighty Masai warriors of eastern Africa. No tribe was considered to have warriors more fearsome or more intelligent than the mighty Masai. It is perhaps surprising, then, to learn that the traditional greeting that passed between Masai warriors was "*Kasserian Ingera*," which means, "And how are the children?" Even warriors with no children of their own would give the traditional answer, "All the children are well," which indicated that, when the priorities of protecting the young and the powerless are in place, peace and safety prevail.

This is still the traditional greeting among the Masai people of Kenya. It acknowledges the high value that the Masai place on their children's well-being. The Masai society has not forgotten its reason for being, its proper functions and responsibilities. "All the children are well" means that life is good. It means that the daily struggles for existence do not preclude proper caring for their young.

Gleaning insight from the Masai, we may ask how our own consciousness about our children's welfare might be affected if we took to greeting each other with this daily question: "And how are the children?" I wonder whether, if we heard that question and passed it along to each other a dozen times a day, it would begin to make a difference in the reality of how children are thought of or cared about in our own country. What if every adult among us, parent and nonparent alike, felt an equal responsibility for the daily care and protection of all the children in our community, in our town, in our state, in our country, and in our world?

Imagine what it would be like if heads of government (e.g., presidents, governors, mayors) began every press conference, every public appearance, by asking and answering the question: "And how are the children?" Envision beginning every faculty or school meeting with the same greeting. It would be interesting to hear their answers. I wonder if they could truly say, without any hesitation, "The children are well. Yes, all the children are well." (And how are the children, 2013).

Indeed, in some settings, the answer to this compelling question may actually be "The children are well." However, if we asked, "And how are the *Black* children in America?", the answer would not likely be a promising one in most schools and would more likely be a resounding, "The children are *not* well," in most cases.

Sustained interest in the welfare of Black children is rarely seen outside circles of Black families, communities, and professional groups. Would we, as a country, tolerate the same dismal trends that Black children face for White children?

Early in their lives, many Black children hear (and learn) the message that they are devalued (Perry, Steele, & Hilliard, 2003). For example, I am reminded of the children's chant:

> If you're white, you're alright
> If you're brown, stick around
> If you're yellow you're mellow
> But if you're black, get back.

I have found it difficult to engage a sustained and non-deficit interest in Black children from people outside Black communities—and sometimes, even within the community. Metaphorically, my efforts have been like those of a doctor trying to convince a person to diet or exercise for their own health benefits. In either case, the person has to give up something that he or she likes (unhealthy food) and has to exert more energy. In the long run, however, the benefits outweigh the sacrifices. In the case of transforming schools to meet the needs of Black children, educators will have to relinquish aspects of white privilege or internalized racism in order to retool and transform their teaching. Nevertheless, the end result will be beneficial to them, as teaching African American students will be viewed as rewarding rather than cumbersome, and the *children will be well*. Indeed, if we are to build a just and equitable world, we must begin with the children, as they are the key to our survival and the barometer of how we are doing as a society.

What Does All of This Mean for Educators?

So how does all of this translate to changes in the classroom? What do teachers need to effectively teach African American students? In order for African American students' negative performance trends to change, educators typically need to make adjustments in their (a) existing knowledge bases, (b) dispositions, (c) instructional strategies, and (d) curriculum. Recommendations for addressing the four components shown in Figure 1.1 will be included in each chapter. A brief description of each component follows.

- *Knowledge bases*: This book makes much of the substantive existing body of knowledge accessible to teachers and teacher educators. This includes frameworks for thinking about teaching African American students that demonstrate how to engage aspects of Black culture as an asset versus a liability.
- *Dispositions*: In order to effectively teach African American students, we educators often have to reframe what we think about the students and their homes, as well as how we view ourselves, our social identities, and our roles in this process. Because of endemic racism in schools and society, many educators may have difficulty seeing existing strengths among African Americans. An explanation and accompanying exercises in Chapter 2 will make this point

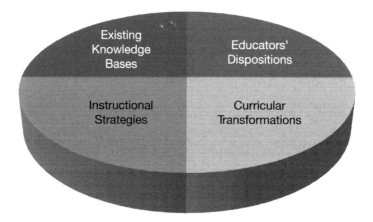

FIGURE 1.1 Key Areas of Change.

clearer. Additionally, understanding how one's own cultural perspectives, experiences, and preferences influence teaching and learning is essential.

- *Instructional strategies*: This book explores instructional strategies—some conventional and some nonconventional—that have been shown to be effective. The role of teachers is pivotal, as the relationships that they have with students, families, and communities are important parts of this process. Recommended strategies in this book are elastic enough so that they can be adapted for educators' respective classrooms and educational spaces.
- *Curriculum*: This book demonstrates ways to make the curriculum relevant to African American students. An emphasis will be placed on, not only building on what students know, but extending their perspectives, knowledge bases, and worldviews as well. A case is made that, by providing multiple and global perspectives, educators will meet and exceed existing standards. It will be important for educators to recognize and understand that curriculums and standards are not neutral or culture-free. Typically, standards are "culturally relevant" to White, mainstream students, as most of the content is Eurocentric in nature (Banks, 2006; Boutte, 2002b). Hence, it is not surprising that performance trends favor students from mainstream and/or White ethnic groups and disadvantage African American students.

Focusing on what we, as educators, need to change is not intended to romanticize Black students and communities, or to not contend with problematic elements that may exist (Paris & Alim, 2014). Rather, as there has been an overemphasis on what is *wrong* with Black students and communities and what *they* need to change, the intent is to focus on *what we as educators can change* and *what strengths already exist that we may build on.*

Guidelines for Processing Information and Activities in This Book

It is impossible to discuss educating Black children without talking about race. Acknowledging the provocative and sensitive nature of discussing issues of race and other types of oppression, it is useful to set guidelines. Educators may find the following suggestions to be helpful (Hardiman, Jackson, & Griffin, 2007).

1. Be willing to tolerate some discomfort while reading this book. Keep in mind that discomfort/disequilibrium is a part of the growth and transformation process. It may be helpful to remember that many African American students experience discomfort for most of their school experiences. So, *on behalf of the children*, I am asking that educators remain open to trying to process and understand the issues presented in this book. If Black children have been experiencing long-term discomfort, surely we, as educators, can tolerate discomfort on their behalf during the short time that it takes to read this book.

2. If you find yourself withdrawing or resisting information, recognize that you may be on a learning edge and poised to learn something new. It is helpful to know that you may experience strong feelings when you are on a learning edge, such as annoyance, anger, anxiety, surprise, confusion, and defensiveness. If you retreat at this point, you may lose an opportunity to expand your understanding. Again, keep in mind your reason for doing this (for the children) and perhaps seek support and guidance from others who are engaged in this process.

3. Be alert to words or phrases that serve as triggers for you. Triggers are instantaneous responses without accompanying conscious thought. If something triggers you, try to reflect on why it is a trigger for you. A few examples of triggers for me are included in Table 1.1, along with accompanying explanations for why they are triggers for me and what I have to do to move past them. After reading them, write down examples of some of your triggers and how you may process them, so that you will not be deterred in your quest to become an excellent teacher of African American students. It is also important to realize that some of your comments may trigger others.

4. Lastly, in terms of guidelines, I urge educators to see issues beyond their own experiences and to see things from the perspective of what schooling is like for far too many African American students. Recognize that, as educators, we cannot do everything, but we can change what is done in our own classrooms. Continuing to do the same things that have been shown to be unsuccessful will lead to the same results. As educators, we have to accept the roles that we play in continuing negative social and academic trends, albeit unintentionally at times. Educators are encouraged to "Believe in the possibility of the Black child" and determine what is possible within our sphere(s) of influence (e.g., classrooms).

TABLE 1.1 Examples of Triggers for Me

Triggers	Commentary	How I temper my response and move forward
Black parents don't care about their children *or* Black parents should just be more involved in their children's lives	This is a trigger for me because this does not reflect my lived experience. In fact, as an African American parent, I feel sure that my children's teachers would say that I care *too much* about my children	I recognize that many educators/people are influenced by the pervasive discourse that intimates that Black parents do not care about their children and are uninvolved in their lives. To temper this and to keep the dialogue open, I share my own experiences and explain or share readings or examples that demonstrate that Black parents do care about their children. I may also point out that caring takes many forms other than the conventional ones prescribed by schools
I am African American, and my children did well in school	This is a trigger for me because I am familiar with the enormous body of literature to the contrary. I recognize that, although my children may have fared well in school, most African American students do not. I also recognize that, even when social class is held constant, there are racial differences between Black and White students on achievement tests and other indices	I temper this by recognizing that I have the advantage of being familiar with the academic literature and national testing trends. I try to share this information and also discuss inequities in practices and policies that disprivilege African American students and privilege White students
Teachers have to teach all children	It's the word *all* that triggers me. I see this as a deflection strategy that is often brought up when there is an attempt to focus on Black children. I have not noticed this phrase used for children from other social groups. This does not mean that I focus only on Black children; however, in order to address the unique needs of Black children, efforts targeted at them must be made. Their needs cannot simply be aggregated into the needs of *all* children	I try to point out the unique, pervasive, and persistent educational and social trends faced by Black children. I also try to appeal to educators' desire to make a difference in the lives of *all* children—including Black children

Terms and Definitions

- The terms *African American* and *Black* will be used interchangeably.
- The terms "children" and "students" will be used interchangeably. These terms refer to children in PreK–12 grades.
- I use the term *educators* to refer to teacher educators and to PreK–12 educators. At times, I will use the term "we" to pointedly emphasize that I include myself in this definition and, as such, I can choose to either be a part of the larger problem or a part of the solution.
- *Structural inequities* refer to unfair differences that exist in societal institutions such as schools, businesses, government, media, and the like. These structural, institutional, systemic, and/or foundational differences are reflected in existing customs, practices, policies, and laws/rules that systematically reflect and produce racial inequities in the US and privilege some groups while disadvantaging others. This concept will be discussed in detail in Chapter 2.
- *Racism* (this may be one of those words that is a trigger for some people): In this book, reference will be made to *institutional* versus *individual* levels of racism. *Institutional racism* refers to "established laws, customs, practices that systematically reflect and produce racial inequities in American society" (Jones, as cited in Koppelman & Goodhart, 2005, p. 179). Institutional racism represents a social system in which race is the major criterion of role assignment, role rewards, and socialization. In the US, institutional racism refers to a system that privileges Whites over people of color. Whereas individuals can and do commit racist acts (e.g., calling a person a racial epithet), the institutional level of racism is more concerned with systemic polices and practices that maintain systems of inequity.
- *Equity and equality*: The book focuses primarily on *equity* versus *equality*. Equity assumes that diversity among people exists; therefore, there is sometimes a need to do *different* things for groups that are marginalized in order to give them a fair chance. "An example using gender is presented to illuminate this point. Since there is an underrepresentation of women in administrative positions in schools (e.g., superintendent's positions), women may be recruited to apply for such positions in an effort to bring parity to the situation" (Boutte, 1999, p. 289). Issues of equity affect educational access, outcomes, and resources (Kahle, 1994). Sample questions about equity are presented below.

  1. *Equity in access*: Issues of equity in access examine who studies what—for example: Do African American students have access to high-level courses (Berry, 2008; Darling-Hammond, 2000)? Do African American students have access to highly trained and successful educators?
  2. *Equity in outcomes*: Equity can be examined in terms of how schooling affects student outcomes. Sample questions that can be posed include: What is the impact of culturally relevant pedagogy on student outcomes (King, 2005)? Why have traditional educational systems been unable to

effectively teach African American students? Do alternative programs/ approaches better educate African American students (King, 2005)? Why are African American children not achieving to their fullest potentials? How might the "achievement gap" be closed and eliminated (King, 2005; Young, 2001)? How do the educational outcomes of African American students impact their communities and life experiences? What professional development models are powerful enough to change teachers' dispositions and instructional practices in schools for African Americans (King, 2005)?

3.   *Equity in resources*: Sample questions that probe the role of equity in allocation of resources include: Do African American students have optimal and *equal* facilities, resources, and other types of support? What are the resources needed for African American students to obtain an equitable education?

What Percentage of School Populations Is African American?

African American students represent the second largest ethnic group in U.S. schools, comprising 17 percent of the student enrollment (U.S. Department of Education, 2014). In some locales, the percentages of African American students are significantly higher. As reported in *A New Diverse Majority* report (2014), beginning in 2009, for the first time in the nation's history, children of color comprised the majority of students enrolled in the South's public schools. On average, African American students make up 27 percent of the school populations in the South, representing the largest group of students of color. With the exception of Florida and Texas, African Americans are the largest group of students of color in each of the 15 southern states, as has been the case for well over 140 years (*A New Diverse Majority*, 2014). In addition to southern states, the majority of African American students are enrolled in urban schools nationally (Lewis, James, Hancock, & Hill-Jackson, 2008; U.S. Department of Education, National Center for Education Statistics, 2007–2008).

In contrast to the increasing numbers of students of color in public schools, the majority of the teaching profession is and will continue to be comprised of White teachers. Currently, 83 percent of the teaching population is White, 7 percent is Black, 7 percent is Latino, and less than 2 percent is made up of other ethnic groups (U.S. Department of Education, National Center for Education Statistics, 2007–2008). Given the demographic reality of a majority White teaching force in the US, the informed involvement of White teachers is pivotal in the education of African American students (Milner, 2008a). The effort to gain the interest of primarily White teachers on behalf of Black children is a noble and daunting task. It is not that most White teachers are uninterested in teaching African American students, *nor that most teachers of color are*. Indeed, it is also important to note that there are many White teachers who have accepted the challenge to effectively teach Black children (Ladson-Billings, 1994/2009). However, most teacher education programs have not included a focus on African American students; thus, teachers often graduate from programs underprepared and unprepared (Boutte & Johnson, 2013; Ladson-Billings, 2000).

The goals of this book are: (a) to engage and enlist the interest of teachers from all ethnic groups in Black children's well-being; (b) to facilitate educators' understanding of some of the forces that have contributed to the pervasive, negative images of Black children; and (c) to provide strategies for effectively teaching African American children. In order to interrupt and reverse the lingering trends and to ensure that *Black children are well*, there is a pressing need for educators to engage in collective efforts aimed at doing so across racial and cultural groups.

Why Do We Need a Book or Course(s) About African American Students?

One of the questions that I ask students who take my course on "Educating African American Students" is, "Do we need a course like this one?" Among the 100 and more graduate students and 15 undergraduate students who have taken the course, the response has consistently been a resounding *Yes!* Many educators cite problems and issues that they have encountered teaching African American students, in the academic literature that they have read, or at conferences/ professional development sessions that they have attended. Typically, they give an array of reasons that include achievement trends such as the ones in Figures 1.2–1.4.[2] Although it is not my intent to spend an extensive amount of time on the well-publicized achievement and social trends that have been deliberated for decades, it is important to briefly reflect on the existing landscape. Before reading further, examine the three figures and take a few minutes to think about the questions in Box 1.1.

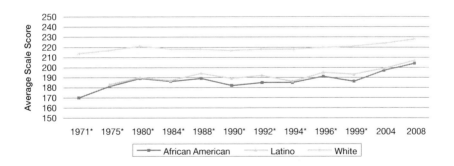

FIGURE 1.2 NAEP Fourth-Grade Reading.

Source: NAEP 2008 Trends in Academic Progress, NCES

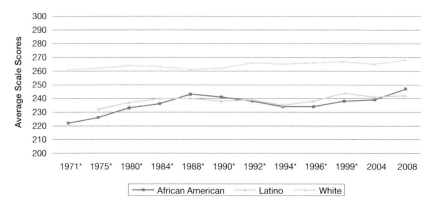

FIGURE 1.3 NAEP Eighth-Grade Reading.

Source: NAEP 2008 Trends in Academic Progress, NCES

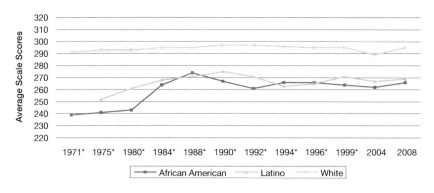

FIGURE 1.4 NAEP 12th-Grade Reading.

Source: NAEP 2008 Trends in Academic Progress, NCES

Box 1.1 Reflecting on African American Students' Performance

- Why do African American students typically perform less well than their White counterparts?
- How do you explain the "achievement gap"?
- What role do educators play in the "achievement gap"?
- How effective are conventional methods with African American students?
- What role, if any, does socioeconomic status play in academic achievement of African American students?
- How do African American students view themselves academically?

When I ask educators why they think the achievement trends in Figures 1.2–1.4 exist, and why African American students perform at the bottom—even below Latino and Native American students on the average, most offer explanations such as low socioeconomic status, "economically disadvantaged" home environments, uncaring/uninvolved parents, or cultural differences (Boutte & Johnson, 2013). Although the first three responses will be examined in this book, rarely is the role of educators or schools considered in their responses.

A familiar mantra is that families must change or need to do more at home with their children. Although not debating this, and while acknowledging that it would be ideal, this alternative effectively frees schools from the responsibility of educating all children. That is, this position advocates for students who come to school essentially knowing everything that schools are supposed to teach (or for only teaching students who have parents who can teach the children what they need to know). It begs the question, "Is this really what teaching should be?" As educators, we must figure out how to teach children from many different backgrounds—even those whom we mistakenly *think* do not have the requisite skills and dispositions. If we truly teach *all* students (as the rhetoric goes), we should ask ourselves, "Why are there differential patterns of performance among ethnic groups in my class?", "Given what I know about this child's home, culture, and community context, how can I best educate this child within my educational space?", and "What can I learn from others who have been successful teaching students from the same demographic backgrounds?"

Acknowledging that many factors contribute to these trends, this book focuses specifically on the role that educators and school play in the equation. Teacher education programs typically pay little attention to the existing knowledge bases on teaching diverse populations in general, and African Americans specifically. Consider the hypothetical test question below.

Hypothetical Test Question

African American students consistently and pervasively perform less well than any other ethnic group in the US. Therefore, teachers and teacher educators should:

A   continue using the same methodologies and strategies;
B   familiarize themselves with the knowledge base about effective methodologies and strategies;
C   blame the students and their families;
D   none of the above.

Although answer (B) seems obvious, too many education programs behave as if A, C, and D are the correct answers and continue on a predictable collision course with failure, for themselves and their African American students. Many educators and non-educators alike do not view African Americans as a distinct cultural group, and the academic teacher education literature rarely expressly addresses effective education of Black students (Ladson-Billings, 2000). Given this state of affairs, it is not surprising that most teachers have not been adequately prepared to teach African American students, through no fault of their own (educators).

What Are the Educational and Social Landscapes for African American Students?

For a number of complex, structural reasons, not inherent to the children, families, and communities themselves, the needs of African American children are not being met. Because of the persistent and pervasive differential achievement trends between White and Black students, many scholars argue that African Americans are the ethnic group whose academic needs are least likely to be met in U.S. schools (Hammond, Hoover, & McPhail, 2005). As Perry (2003) explained, there is no other group for whom there has there been such a persistent, well-articulated, and unabated ideology about their mental incompetence. Consequently, despite decades of school reforms, African American students continue to fare poorly in school (Baugh, 1999; Delpit, 2012; McDermott & Rothenberg, 2000). On virtually every measure, they consistently perform significantly lower on standardized achievement tests, drop out of school at higher rates, and are disproportionately placed in remedial or special education programs, as compared with their White counterparts (Delpit, 2012; Delpit & Dowdy, 2002; McDermott & Rothenberg, 2000). Although some gains have been made in the achievements of African American students, these increases are sporadic and inconsistent (Grigg, Donahue, & Dion, 2007). As shown in the 37 years of data presented in Figures 1.2–1.4, the gap between Blacks and Whites may occasionally decrease, but not significantly or continuously. For example, according to the National Assessment of Educational Progress (NAEP), the score gaps between White and African American students and White and Latino students in reading have been relatively unchanged since 1992 (Grigg et al., 2007). As conclusively noted by the former Secretary of Education, Margaret Spelling, "Too many African American students have been shortchanged by our nation's schools" (U.S. Department of Education, 2010).

A primary factor in the continued existence of such inequities is a pervasive and rarely examined deficit perspectives used to judge children of color in schools (Boutte, 2002a; Milner, 2008b; Volk & Long, 2005). Because the culture of African American students is delegitimized, they are often treated as if they are corruptions of White culture. The consequences of such perceptions (e.g., tracking in low placements; overidentification in special education classes; disproportionality in disciplinary actions, suspensions, and expulsions) affect how students are treated and contribute to negative performance trends in school and later inequities in life (Perry, 2003).

> ## Box 1.2 Differential Status Held by the Six Major Ethnic Groups in the US
>
> Rank the six major ethnic groups in the US in terms of their status, where 1= most status and 6= least status.
>   Six major ethnic groups (listed alphabetically):
>
> - African American
> - Asian American
> - Biracial American
> - European American
> - Latino American
> - Native American.
>
> Provide examples to support your responses by reflecting on different institutions, such as education, health services, media, legal system, government, employment (e.g., Which ethnic group holds the most positions in the government? Which ethnic group earns more money? Which ethnic group earns the least amount of money?)

Schools are a microcosm of society, and the existence of Black people is continuously influenced by *structural inequities* in society. The reality is that we live in a racially stratified society, and these structures mediate what it means to be Black. The activity in Box 1.2 can be used to reflect on this. A recommended DVD (older, but well done, and still relevant) that drives this point home is *True Colors* (Lukasiewicz & Harvey, 1991/2005), an 18-minute documentary featuring Diane Sawyer as she follows a Black man and a White man as they try to purchase a car, go shopping, apply for a job, find housing, and request assistance with car trouble; it is useful in opening the discussion on structural inequities.

Although the term *status* may have conjured up different meanings (e.g., economic, educational, social, political), European Americans (as a group) unequivocally hold the highest status in all of these dimensions in the US. The ethnic groups holding the least amount of status may vary depending on geographic contexts. Typically, African, Latino, and Native Americans are ranked at the bottom. Asian Americans typically are ranked second after European Americans. Biracial Americans (as a group) may be ranked next, but this depends on their racial lineage. The key point is that some groups are privileged, and others are not. Our social identities predispose us to unequal roles in the dynamic system of oppression, as will be discussed in Chapter 2. So the question is, "How can we interrupt and *counter* the prevailing negative beliefs about African Americans?"

Racism will not disappear by the ignoring of social realities of race that position Black people in an inferior position. Valuing Blackness, then, is essential to the education of Blacks and others (hooks, 1995; King, 2005). It is important to note that pro-Black is not synonymous with anti-White or anti-other ethnic groups (Delgado & Stefancic, 2001; Helms, 2008). The point is that African Americans, like other groups, are a central part of humanity.

Moving Beyond Limited Views and Negative Stereotypes: Seeing Brilliance and Strengths

In order to see the humanity in Black children, it is important to think beyond the incredibly dismal backdrop of pervasive, negative statistics about African American students. One way of doing so is *not* to regard Black children as if they are *other people's children* (Delpit, 1995). As we educators begin this dialogic exploration about Black students, we can think about them as if they were our family members—our sons, daughters, nephews, and so forth. In many instances, this will require that educators adjust their lenses in order to see beyond typical negative portrayals of Black students. Before reading any further, complete the reflection activity in Box 1.3 and reflect on the strengths that Black students bring to school.

Box 1.3 Strengths and Stereotypes of Black Children

1. Take a few minutes to write down as many strengths/assets as you can think of that African American students possess.

2. Next, write down as many stereotypes—positive or negative—as you can think of about Black students, families, and communities. You do not have to believe them, but just write down the ones that you know or have heard.

3. Based on your list of strengths, what strategies can you use to effectively teach African American students?

4. Do you think that most Black students would recognize the strengths that you listed? If not, how can we help students recognize their strengths?

5. How do you think that the students' perceptions of their strengths compare with yours?

6. What are some of the reasons why educators do not recognize and/or build on students' strengths?

7. Write down any other thoughts that you have about Black students as learners.

My experience with educators' reflections on strengths that African American students have is that the list usually comprises social and physical characteristics such as: *They are very athletic. They can sing well.* Although these are certainly cultural strengths that have yet to be fully realized and valued in the general population (King, 2005), seldom do educators and the general public view Black students academically *or* see the *social* and *physical* strengths as academic possibilities. Most educators are overly familiar with the barrage of *negative* stereotypes about Black students, families, and communities (Brown & Donnor, 2011; Ladson-Billings, 2011). The narrow focus on the all-too-familiar statistics about Black students seems to carry inherent indictments against the students and obscure possibilities for effectively teaching them. When I probe educators about why they do not begin their instruction by starting with the strengths that Black students bring, they typically say things like:

1.   I have to focus on meeting the standards.
2.   I have to start with what the students do not know (weaknesses) and try to remediate.
3.   I have to follow the textbook/curriculum.

Without doubt, these are all valid issues, but, given that these approaches have not worked to improve Black students' achievement, it seems wise to consider other possibilities that may work. Each one of these explanations is problematic. For instance, not only is teaching narrowly about "standards" (or strictly following the textbook/curriculum) limiting, but, if teachers were actually *effectively teaching the standards*, then *students would learn*, and we would not see the negative, pervasive, and persistent low-performance trends among African American students. In other words, conventional approaches are obviously not working. Additionally, much of the K–12 curriculum is incomplete and contains inaccuracies regarding Black people (King & Swartz, 2014).

Contrary to the dominant storyline that society and schools put forth, African American students are just as brilliant as any other ethnic group. Delpit and Dowdy (2002) questioned:

> What happens . . . when we convince them (children) that they come from brilliance, when we encourage them to understand their amazing potential? When they recognize that we believe in them, then they come to trust us, to accept us, to identify with us, and to emulate us.
>
> (p. 46)

Although many educators may not always recognize the existing strengths that African American students have, this book seeks to make these strengths readily apparent. This simple, but powerful, proposition *that African American culture is an asset* undergirds other tenets in this book.

Effectively teaching African American students often requires reconceptualizing what we educators do in our classrooms, rather than dreaming of changing families and home contexts (over which we have no control) or insisting that students have particular prerequisite skills or dispositions for being able to be taught (instead of figuring out *how* students can learn what is necessary). The reality is that we can only change what is within our power to do and learn to see the strengths that children do bring rather than what they do not have. Part of this recognition is that virtually all students have informal and cultural knowledge that can be used as a link to academic skills.

Advancing the thesis that African Americans have a long tradition of excellence in education, socialization, and mastery of their environment and circumstances (Hilliard, 2002; King, 2005; Perry et al., 2003), this book invites educators to consider wisdom from African American communities when seeking *best practices*.

Drawing parallels between the biblical city of Nazareth and prevailing scholarly and public portrayals of African American students, schools, and communities, Jerome Morris (2004) profoundly and poetically posed the question, "Can anything good come from Nazareth?" Like the people in Nazareth and their beliefs about Jesus Christ's hometown, many educators have misconceptions about Black students, families, and communities. This book reframes this focus to one of looking at possibilities, using real examples from schools and classrooms to demonstrate that African American students, like other groups, possess brilliance that needs to be tapped. It is written to activate educators to work on behalf of Black children and to see their possibilities, instead of seeing them as problems. When this transformation happens, Black children will no longer be viewed as having a language deficit, but educators will clearly see their language dexterity and flexibility instead. Black children will no longer be viewed as "disadvantaged"; rather, the complex levels of intelligence that the children possess will be readily apparent to educators, as evidenced by their astute abilities to navigate two often decidedly different terrains (schools and homes/communities).

How Many Models of Successful Schools Do We Need to See Before We Are Convinced that Black Children Can Succeed?

More than three decades ago, Dr. Ronald Edmonds, then Director of the Center for Urban Studies at Harvard University and founder of the effective schools movement, posed a resoundingly haunting question that should be revisited as we think about the stagnant progress of urban schools today:

> How many effective schools would you have to see to be persuaded of the educability of . . . children? If your answer is more than one, then I submit that you have reasons of your own for preferring to believe that pupil

performance derives from family background instead of school response to family background.

(Edmonds, 1979, pp. 22–23)

Although not widely reported and circulated, the Education Trust (2011) continually documents examples of schools that are successful in reducing and alleviating Black–White and other academic gaps in public school settings—(e.g., Atlanta, Georgia; Louisville, Kentucky; Aldine, Texas; Raleigh, North Carolina; Boston Public Schools; Long Beach, California; South Carolina). These substantive efforts, aimed at improving urban schools, do not narrowly define success by test scores, although they certainly are directed toward increasing the overall academic performance and long-term success of children whose academic needs have remained unmet in schools.

Exemplars of schools that have been successful in educating African American students despite incredible odds are encouraging and provide insights into particular teacher competencies that are effective. For instance, Morris's (2004, 2009) account of his 3-year involvement with African American, low-income urban elementary schools—one in St. Louis, Missouri, and the other in Atlanta, Georgia—represents an example of this. Despite racial and social class inequalities that undermined their schools, educators and family members collectively worked to meet the children's social and educational needs. Morris concluded that the interpersonal relationships between the teachers and families, as well as the teachers' valuing and building on African American culture, were essential elements of the schools' success over time. Unlike many educators who teach African American children, teachers in both schools were connected—culturally, psychologically, and proximally—to the children in the school. Hence, they understood the children's lives beyond school. Distinct from teachers in many schools, most of the teachers remained at the school and were highly committed to the children's academic and social achievements. Such examples represent only a preview of the large range of promising possibilities in urban schools. These efforts can be amplified and emulated, *if we believe in the possibility of the Black child.*

What Is African American Culture?[3]

In order to ensure that African American students achieve, educationally and socially, to their fullest potential, educators need sufficient in-depth understanding of students' cultural backgrounds to make education meaningful and transformative (King, 1994). Mainstream ways of acquiring school competencies do not offer universally applicable models of development (King, 1994, 2005). Part of the difficulty in teaching African American students is that many educators: (a) do not understand and/or respect Black culture; (b) do not view Black students' behaviors as cultural, despite the existence of a substantial knowledge base; (c) erroneously define Black culture narrowly (e.g., limited to hip-hop culture or people living in poverty); and (d) believe that content taught in school is neutral or culture-free.

When teaching students of color, it is important to study and consult the knowledge base on respective cultural groups (Hilliard, 1992). The complexity of simultaneously understanding that culture is too important to be overlooked while, at the same time, being careful about overgeneralizing cultural information must be realized by educators (Boutte & DeFlorimonte, 1998). The importance of holding both of these concepts in mind is stressed. The point is that African Americans are not monolithic, but, at the same time, we share a collective history (King, 2005), and social constructions of race affect Black people in many sociopolitical ways (e.g., "Driving While Black" (Hale, 2001). This will mean that teachers will have to become astute at noticing cultural nuances that may be unique to communities or to children and families.

In this book, culture is broadly defined as the sum total of who we are, which includes both implicit (attitudes, beliefs) and explicit (e.g., language, dress, religious rituals) aspects (Boutte & DeFlorimonte, 1998). Culture can be defined as the "particular ways in which a social group lives out and makes sense of its 'given' circumstances and conditions of life" (McLaren, 2007, p. 201). Importantly, culture is dynamic and always evolving, which makes discussions on any cultural group a bit tricky, as it is important both to *see culture* and to *not overgeneralize it*, as well as recognizing changes and shifts in culture with each generation (Paris & Alim, 2014) and also *within* each generation, as no generation is monolithic.

I will focus specifically on aspects of Black culture that have been documented by research. Notwithstanding the caveat regarding overgeneralizations about cultural groups, a significant body of research has demonstrated general cultural strengths and legacies among people of the African diaspora (Boykin, 1994; Hale, 2001; Hale-Benson, 1986; Hilliard, 1992; King, 2005; Shade, 1997). Instead of adopting the common deficit-based beliefs (e.g., "What's wrong with the students?", "They don't know anything," "They don't want to learn," or "We have got to fix them"), educators would benefit from using students' cultural strengths as starting points for instruction. Box 1.4 provides a summary of some of the major dimensions of Black culture that have been cited in the literature. Ultimately, the vision is for schools to integrate these (or other emerging or existing) cultural strengths as part of the nucleus of the curriculum and instruction, instead of merely using them as a bridge to learning Eurocentric content. Examples for doing so will be included in Chapters 3–6. A detailed discussion of the deconstruction of current school culture, curriculum, instruction, and values will be discussed in this book.

Readily acknowledging that there are variations within Black culture, and not intending to "essentialize" or convey that it is monolithic, I accept that, "racial realities are so complex that no one set of experiences can serve as a representative reality for all individuals of a particular racial group" (Howard, 2010, p. 109).

Box 1.4 Dimensions of African American Culture

- *Spirituality*: an approach to life as being essentially vitalistic rather than mechanistic, with the conviction that nonmaterial forces influence people's everyday lives.
- *Harmony*: the notion that how one fares is interrelated with other elements in the scheme of things, so that humankind and nature are harmonically conjoined.
- *Movement*: an emphasis on the interweaving of movement, rhythm, percussiveness, music, and dance, all of which are taken as central to psychological health.
- *Verve*: a propensity for relatively high levels of stimulation and for action that is energetic and lively.
- *Affect*: an emphasis on emotions and feelings, together with a specific sensitivity to emotional cues and a tendency to be emotionally expressive.
- *Communalism/collectivity*: a commitment to social connectedness, which includes an awareness that social bonds and responsibilities transcend individual privilege.
- *Expressive individualism*: the cultivation of a distinctive personality and proclivity for spontaneous, genuine personal expression.
- *Oral tradition*: strengths in oral/aural modes of communication, in which both speaking and listening are treated as performances, and cultivation of oral virtuosity—the ability to use alliterative, metaphorically colorful, graphic forms of spoken language. This does not mean that strengths do not exist in written and other literacy traditions as well.
- *Social time perspective*: an orientation in which time is treated as passing through a social space rather than a material one, and in which time can be recurring, personal, and phenomenological.
- *Perseverance*: the ability to maintain a sense of agency and strength in the face of adversities.
- *Improvisation*: substitution of alternatives that are more sensitive to Black culture.

(Sources: Boykin, 1994; Hale, 2001; Hale-Benson, 1986; Hilliard, 1992; King, 2005; King & Swartz, 2014; Shade, 1997)

Without a doubt, Black people have multiple identities, and there are many different ways to be Black. At the same time, we have a collective present, as well as historical experiences and memories that cannot be overlooked or undermined. Moreover, when Black children are "aggregated" under the "all children" umbrella amid the unrelenting and omnipresent academic indices, such as high dropout rates, disproportionality in special education, and high incarceration rates, it is difficult to focus on the specific and often unique needs of African American students. The book will try to make these needs explicit by illuminating the interplay between structural inequities and the social identities and experiences of Black children in school.

Dr. Joyce King, 2014–2015 president of the American Educational Research Association, perceptively noted that a caveat regarding the contemporary concern about, and preoccupation with, essentializing Black culture is that it implies that we cannot talk about our (Black) people (personal communication, September 28, 2013). Yet, our experiences are a part of a larger Black experience (King, personal communication, September 27, 2014), even if they operate unconsciously (King & Swartz, 2014). As with indigenous people who have experienced systemic and systematic ethnicide and linguicide (McCarty & Lee, 2014), African Americans have been and continue to be subjected to the same processes in schools and in society. Hence, it will be important not to prematurely foreclose on the telling of our stories. In his book, *There Was a Country* (Achebe, 2012), Chinua Achebe advised:

> My position, therefore, is that we must hear all the stories. That would be the first thing. And by hearing all the stories we will find points of contact and communication, and the world story, the Great Story, will have a chance to develop. That's the only precaution I would suggest—that we not rush into announcing the arrival of this international, the great world story, based simply on our knowledge of one or a few traditions.
>
> (pp. 60–61)

> We did not make the world, so there is no reason we should be quarreling with the number of cultures there are. If any group decides on its own that its culture is not worth talking about, it can stop talking about it. But I don't think anybody can suggest to another person, Please drop your culture; let's use mine. That's the height of arrogance and the boast of imperialism. . . . It is up to the owners of any particular culture to ensure it survives, or if they don't want to survive, they should act accordingly, but I am not going to recommend that.
>
> (p. 60)

To say that there is a Black culture is similar to saying that humans share much in common. Neither position assumes that all individuals within the respective group are the same. We are both similar and dissimilar, simultaneously. That is, we share some collective experiences that unite us, while also having unique experiences that make us different (Boutte & DeFlorimonte, 1998). But we may ask ourselves, what might we lose by *not* seeing culture? Black students, like all students and humans, are not acultural and, hence, are influenced by how the people around them construct culture.

Drawing from the American Research Education Association's *Commission on Research in Black Education* [*CORIBE*] 10 Vital Principles of Black Education/ Socialization, I conclude this section by sharing the first principle: "We (Black people) exist as African People, an ethnic family. Our perspective must be centered in that reality" (King, 2005, p. 20). My advice for readers of this book is to use the cultural legacies of Black culture as an important guide for obtaining insight into the ontological essence of Black students, while understanding, at the same time, that there may be other influences that outweigh the influence of Black culture.

What Major Instructional Strategies and Approaches Are Stressed in This Book?

The book assumes that effective teachers of African American students need:

1. deep content knowledge—that is, to be experts in their content areas (e.g., science, early childhood education, English);
2. strong pedagogical content knowledge—that is, the necessary instructional skills to deliver the content. Here the focus is on, not only knowing the content, but also how to effectively deliver it; and
3. culturally relevant pedagogy—that is, how teachers make school content relevant to various cultural groups—in this case, African American students (Martin, 2007).

The focus of this book is on the third area—culturally relevant pedagogy (CRP) or culturally relevant teaching. As shown in Figure 1.5, four other major strategies and/or approaches will be integrated throughout the book, in concert with the larger focus on CRP. Each is briefly discussed.

Culturally Relevant Pedagogy

Many educators misinterpret CRP as meaning focusing only on affirmation of children's culture. Although that is certainly a key element, the primary goal is to help students achieve. Using Ladson-Billings's conception (1994/2009), there are three major dimensions of CRP:

1. academic excellence that is not based on cultural deficit models of school failure;

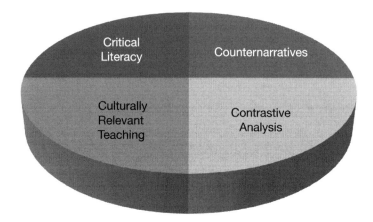

FIGURE 1.5 Four Major Strategies and Instructional Approaches in This Book.

2. cultural competence that locates excellence within the context of the students' community and cultural identities; and
3. critical consciousness that challenges inequitable school and societal structures (Ladson–Billings, 2002).

Acknowledging the new iterations of CRP (e.g., *culturally sustaining pedagogy* (Paris, 2012), I decided to focus on CRP, because it is foundational to evolutions that follow and because there is a gap between theory and practice. That is, although conversations about culturally relevant pedagogy 2.0 (culturally sustaining pedagogy) (Ladson–Billings, 2014) are occurring in teacher education programs, it is not widely practiced in schools.

As schools are clearly not meeting the needs of African American students, acknowledging students' strengths cannot be sidestepped. At the same time, culturally relevant teachers can and should pay careful attention to the diversity among African American students. CRP's focus on building on students' assets also allows for flexibility within cultural groups, as it emphasizes using funds of knowledge within the community, as well as connections between their national and global identities (Ladson–Billings, 1994/2009). Therefore, as Milner (2010) advises, it is important for educators to start where they are, but not stay there. A natural progression from CRP will be what Paris refers to as "culturally sustaining pedagogy," which supports multilingualism and multiculturalism as a part of the democratic goal of society.

As Joyce King (2014–2015 president of the American Association of Education Research) recommended from her study of Mao Tse Tung, teachers should:

"Pull from both ends toward the middle." And I say to my students: "We don't all have to do the same thing." So I value the ground we each are standing on and I truly believe it takes all of us working together to move forward. I talk to so many people who are "in the fire"—but there are many fires.

(Personal communication, April 11, 2014)

Dr. King's wisdom allows educators to lovingly reconcile different and complementary approaches to complex issues, such as educating African American students. One such approach parallels the process that McCarty and Lee (2014) propose for Native American students—*culturally sustaining/revitalizing pedagogy*. This pedagogy would be designed to address the sociohistorical and contemporary contexts of schooling for African American students. The three dimensions of CRP represent a nice beginning and can also be generative as well.

CRP is more of a pedagogical approach than a strategy per se. The next three strategies and/or approaches can be considered to be important and concrete components of CRP classrooms.

Critical Literacy

Like CRP, critical literacy is more of a way of thinking and teaching rather than an instructional strategy. Critical literacy focuses on examining how discrimination is produced and reproduced in books, media, and other texts. The book seeks to assist educators in understanding issues of voice and power as they relate to schooling and society. A focus is placed on identifying ideologies in texts (e.g., books, world experiences, media) and developing critical multicultural literature collections. A discussion on providing multiple perspectives will be included. Teachers must recognize and question the values and cultures being promoted in their classrooms; otherwise, they socialize their students to accept the uneven power relations of society along lines of race, class, gender, and ability (Segura-Mora, 2008).

Counternarratives

Counternarratives are continuous and planned actions to counter the dominant ideology regarding the intellectual capacities of African Americans (Perry et al., 2003). Counternarratives can be thought about as complements to the "cultural competence" dimension of CRP, which needs to be omnipresent. That is, as a part of efforts to develop cultural competence, it is essential to develop diaspora literacy in African and African American culture. As explained by Dr. Joyce King (personal communication, January 13, 2014), "Diaspora Literacy starts within our own experience/cultural reality, whereas counternarratives and Critical Race Theory start as a response to 'them' [dominant White narrative] and 'what has been done to us' [Black people]—and as such is really about 'them.'"

This books shares sample lessons using counternarratives. For example, text sets that counter the dominant negative discourse about African Americans are presented.

Contrastive Analysis

This strategy helps educators explicitly compare and contrast the applicable rules for African American children as they become increasingly more bicultural, bilingual, and biliterate (Boutte & Johnson, 2012, 2013; Delpit, 1995; Wheeler & Swords, 2006). Contrastive analysis (explicit comparison and contrast of the communication styles of mainstream and nonmainstream language systems) has been shown to be effective in increasing children's use of Mainstream American English, while maintaining students' home language (Wheeler & Swords, 2006). Oral and written activities will be suggested for code-switching between two language systems (African American Language (AAL) and Mainstream American English (MAE)). Although contrastive analysis will be explained, and examples will be shared in the chapter on language (Chapter 4), the general strategy can be used in other areas as well, to help African American students successfully navigate between two cultures (Black culture and mainstream culture).

Conclusion

Defying the prevailing negative perceptions about Black children's achievement and school performance, this book puts forth its belief in the "possibility of the Black child." In spite of an incredibly pessimistic backdrop, there are substantive examples of educators who have fundamentally reversed the negative legacies bequeathed to Black students and who have countered the accompanying disbeliefs about their potential to succeed in school and society. African Americans have a long tradition of excellence in education, socialization, and mastery of their environment and circumstances, and educators can consider wisdom from African American communities when seeking *best practices* (Hilliard, 2002; Perry et al., 2003).

Although no one book or resource contains everything needed to effectively teach African American students, this book provides the necessary foundation to begin transforming school experiences of Black students and their teachers. It invites educators to be *powers of good on behalf of Black children*. We can do so by asking ourselves, "And how are the Black children doing in my classroom, my school, my state, and my nation?" I firmly believe and have seen that most educators are committed to teaching African America children, but need additional tools and information to do so. Maya Angelou (2010) advised, "Do the best you can until you know better. Then when you know better, do better" (no pagination). I am hopeful that this book can help more educators enthusiastically respond, "The Black children in my class are well."

Key Points From the Chapter

1. The guidelines for processing issues in this book can be used to help readers move out of their comfort zones, so that they can address sensitive and complex issues surrounding the education of African American students. It is also helpful to remember that addressing and rethinking issues are done on behalf of the welfare of African American students.
2. Several key terms have been introduced, such as distinctions between equity and equality and institutional and individual levels of racism.
3. African American students are the second largest ethnic group in U.S. schools.
4. The social and academic needs of African American students are not being met in schools.
5. There are models of successful teachers and schools that can be instructive to educators who want to effectively educate African American students.
6. African American culture is too important to overlook, but, at the same time, should not be overgeneralized.
7. In order to reverse negative educational trends for African American students, educators will need to make changes in their knowledge bases, dispositions, instruction, and curriculum.
8. Four major strategies/approaches will be presented in this book: CRP, critical literacy, counternarratives, and contrastive analysis.

Activities

1. Make a list of the strengths of African American students in your class. Ask the students to make a list of their strengths. Compare the two lists. Note the categories of the strengths in both lists (e.g., academic, creative, or social skills).
2. View an African American television show or movie. Look for examples of the dimensions of Black culture that are provided in Box 1.4. Be sure to look for both commonalities and variations. View the DVD *Black Is, Black Ain't*,[4] a documentary about Black identities. Producer Marlon Riggs uses gumbo as a metaphor for the rich diversity among Black people and explores the complexities of Black culture using song, interviews, historical clips, and a variety of other media.
3. After viewing the video, identify some of the Black cultural dimensions, as well as the wide array of variations within Black culture.

Resources

1. National Black Child Development Institute (NBCDI) (www.nbcdi.org/): A professional organization whose goals focus on the welfare of Black

students. The organization offers an annual conference as well as other resources.

2. Institute for the Study of the African American Child (ISAAC) (https://isaac. wayne.edu/about.php): ISAAC offers a free online journal, *African American Learners*, that addresses issues facing African American students, a biennial conference (Conference on Research Directions), and other resources.

Notes

1. Adapted from a well-known African allegory. Retrieved March 16, 2014 from www.kidsgrowth.com/resources/articledetail.cfm?id=1089
2. Typical trends can be seen in other content areas (e.g., mathematics, science, and social studies). The reading test results are used for illustrative purposes only.
3. This section is excerpted and adapted from Boutte & Hill, 2006. Used with the permission of Taylor & Francis.
4. Marlon Riggs & Nicole Atkinson (Co-Producers). 1995. *Black Is, Black Ain't* [DVD]. Available from California Newsreel (http://newsreel.org/video/BLACK-IS-BLACK-AINT) (87 minutes runtime).

References

Achebe, C. (2012). *There was a country. A personal history of Biafra.* New York: The Penguin Press.

A new diverse majority: Students of color in the South's public schools. (n.d.) Retrieved March 10, 2014 from www.luminafoundation.org/publications/latino_student_success/New_Diverse_Majority.pdf

Angelou, M. (2010). Maya Angelou quotes. Retrieved May 10, 2010 from www.good reads.com/quotes/show/197836

Banks, J. A. (2006). *Cultural diversity and education: Foundations, curriculum, and teaching.* Boston, MA: Pearson/Allyn & Bacon.

Baugh, J. (1999). *Out of the mouths of slaves/African American language and educational malpractice.* Austin, TX: University of Texas Press.

Berry, R. Q. III (2008). Access to upper-level mathematics: The stories of successful African American middle school boys. *Journal for Research in Mathematics Education, 39*(5), 464–488.

Boutte, G. (1999). *Multicultural education. Raising consciousness.* Atlanta, GA: Wadsworth.

Boutte, G. S. (2002a). *Resounding voices: School experiences of people from diverse ethnic backgrounds.* Needham Heights, MA: Allyn & Bacon.

Boutte, G. S. (2002b). The critical literacy process: Guidelines for examining books. *Childhood Education, 78*(3), 147–152.

Boutte, G. S., & DeFlorimonte, D. (1998). The complexities of valuing cultural differences without overemphasizing them: Taking it to the next level. *Equity and Excellence in Education, 31*(3), 54–62.

Boutte, G. S., & Hill, E. (2006). African American communities: Implications for educators. *New Educator, 2,* 311–329.

Boutte, G. S., & Johnson, G. (2012). Do educators see and honor biliteracy and bidialectalism in African American Language speakers? Apprehensions and reflections of two grandparents/professional educators. *Early Childhood Education Journal*. DOI 10.1007/s10643–012–0538–5.

Boutte, G. S., & Johnson, G. (2013). Who CAN TEACH African American students? Preservice teachers' perceptions about their preparation to teach African American students. *African American Learners Journal, 2*(2). Retrieved May 14, 2015 from https://isaac.wayne.edu/research/journal/article.php?newsletter=191&article=3291.

Boykin, A. W. (1994). Afrocultural expression and its implications for schooling. In E. Hollins, J. King, & W. Hayman (Eds.), *Teaching diverse populations: Formulating a knowledge base* (pp. 243–273). Albany, NY: State University of New York Press.

Brown, A. L., & Donnor, J. K. (2011). Toward a new narrative on Black males, education, and public policy. *Race Ethnicity and Education, 14*(1), 17–32.

Darling-Hammond, L. (2000). New standards and old inequalities: School reform and the education of African American students. *Journal of Negro Education, 69* (4), 263–287.

Delgado, R., & Stefancic, J. (2001). *Critical race theory. An introduction.* New York: New York University Press.

Delpit, L. (1995). *Other people's children: Cultural conflicts in the classroom.* New York: The New Press.

Delpit, L. (2012). *"Multiplication is for White people." Raising expectations for other people's children.* New York: The New Press.

Delpit, L., & Dowdy, J. K. (2002). *The skin that we speak. Thoughts on language and culture in the classroom.* New York: The New Press.

Edmonds, R. (1979). Effective schools for the urban poor. *Educational Leadership, 3*(1), 15–27.

Education Trust. (2011). Success stories. Dispelling the myth. Retrieved August 1, 2011 from www.edtrust.org/dc/resources/success-stories.

Grigg, W., Donahue, P., & Dion, G. (2007). *The nation's report card: 12th-grade reading and mathematics 2005* (NCES 2007-468). U.S. Department of Education, National Center for Education Statistics. Washington, DC: U.S. Government Printing Office.

Hale, J. (2001). *Learning while black: Creating educational excellence for African American children.* Baltimore, MD: Johns Hopkins University Press.

Hale-Benson, J. E. (1986). *Black children: Their roots, culture, and learning styles* (Rev. ed.). Baltimore, MD: Johns Hopkins University Press.

Hammond, B., Hoover, M. E. R., & McPhail, I. P. (Eds.). (2005). *Teaching African American learners to read: Perspectives and practices.* Washington, DC: International Reading Association.

Hardiman, R., Jackson, B., & Griffin, P. (2007). Conceptual foundations for social justice education. In M. Adams, L. A. Bell, & P. Grant (Eds.), *Teaching for diversity and social justice* (2nd ed., pp. 35–66). New York: Routledge.

Helms, J. (2008). *A race is a nice thing to have: A guide to being a white person or understanding the white people in your life* (2nd ed.). Hanover, MA: Mircrotraining Associates.

Hilliard, A. G. (1992). Behavioral style, culture, and teaching, and learning. *Journal of Negro Education, 61*(3), 370–377.

Hilliard, A. G. (2002). *African power. Affirming African indigenous socialization in the face of the culture wars.* Gainesville, FL: Makare.

Howard, T. C. (2010). *Why race and culture matter in schools: Closing the achievement gap in America's classrooms.* New York: Teachers College Press.

hooks, b. (1995). *Killing rage. Ending racism.* New York: Henry Holt.

Kahle, J. B. (1994). Ohio's statewide systemic initiative: Lessons from the trenches. Building the system: Making science education work. National Science Foundational National Invitational Conference. Washington, DC.

King, J. E. (1994). The purpose of schooling for African American children. In E. R. Hollins, J. E. King, & W. C. Hayman (Eds.), *Teaching diverse populations/Formulating a knowledge base* (pp. 25–56). New York: SUNY Press.

King, J. E. (2005). *Black education: A transformative research and action agenda for the 21st century.* Mahwah, NJ: Lawrence Erlbaum.

King, J. E., & Swartz, E. E. (2014). *"Re-membering" history in student and teacher learning. An Afrocentric culturally informed praxis.* New York: Routledge.

Koppelman, K. L., & Goodhart, R. L. (2005). *Understanding human differences: Multicultural education for a diverse America.* Boston, MA: Pearson.

Ladson-Billings, G. (1994/2009). *The dreamkeepers. Successful teachers of African American children.* San Francisco, CA: Jossey-Bass.

Ladson-Billings, G. (2000). Fighting for our lives. Preparing teachers to teach African American students. *Journal of Teacher Education, 51*(3), 206–214.

Ladson-Billings, G. (2002). I ain't writin' nuttin: Permissions to fail and demands to succeed in urban classrooms. In L. Delpit (Ed.), *Skin that we speak* (pp. 107–120). New York: The New Press.

Ladson-Billings, G. (2011). Boyz to men? Teaching to restore Black boys' childhood. *Race Ethnicity and Education, 14* (1), 7–15.

Ladson-Billings, G. (2014). Culturally relevant pedagogy 2.0: A.K.A. the remix. *Harvard Educational Review, 84*(1), 74–84.

Lewis, C., James, M., Hancock, S., & Hill-Jackson, V. (2008). Framing African American students' success and failure in urban settings: A typology for change. *Urban Education, 43*(2), 127–153.

Lukasiewicz, M. (Producer), & Harvey, E. (Director). (1991/2005). *True colors* [DVD video]. United States: CorVision.

Martin, D. B. (2007). Beyond missionaries or cannibals: Who should teach mathematics to African American children? *The High School Journal, 91*(1), 6–28.

McCarty, T. L., & Lee, T. S. (2014). Critical culturally sustaining/revitalizing pedagogy and indigenous education sovereignty. *Harvard Educational Review, 84*(1), 101–124.

McDermott, P., & Rothenberg, J. (2000). Why urban parents resist involvement in their children's elementary education. *The Qualitative Report, 5*(3 & 4), 1–14.

McLaren, P. (2007). *Life in schools: An introduction to critical pedagogy in the foundations of education* (5th ed.). Boston, MA: Pearson Education.

Milner, H. R. (2008a). Critical race theory and interest convergence as analytic tools in teacher education policies and practices. *Journal of Teacher Education, 59*(4), 332–346.

Milner, H. R. (2008b). Disrupting deficit notions of difference: Counter-narratives of teachers and community in urban education. *Teaching and Teacher Education, 24*(6), 1573–1598.

Milner, H. R. (2010). *Start where you are but don't stay there: Understanding diversity, opportunity gaps, and teaching in today's classrooms.* Cambridge, MA: Harvard Education Press.

Morris, J. E. (2004). Can anything good come from Nazareth? Race, class, and African-American schooling and community in the urban South and Midwest. *American Educational Research Journal, 41*(1), 69–112.

Morris, J. E. (2009). *Troubling the waters: Fulfilling the promise of quality public schooling for Black children.* New York: Teachers College Press.

Paris, D. (2012). Culturally sustaining pedagogy: A needed change in stance, terminology, and practice. *Educational Researcher, 41*(3), 93–97.

Paris, D., & Alim, H. S. (2014). What are we seeking to sustain through culturally sustaining pedagogy? *Harvard Educational Review, 84*(1), 85–100.

Perry, T. (2003). Up from the parched earth: Toward a theory of African-American achievement. In T. Perry, C. Steele, & A. G. Hilliard III. (Eds.), *Young, gifted, and Black. Promoting high achievement among African-American students* (pp. 1–10). Boston, MA: Beacon Press.

Perry, T., Steele, C., & Hilliard, A. III. (2003). *Young, gifted, and Black. Promoting high achievement among African-American students.* Boston, MA: Beacon Press.

Segura-Mora, A. (2008). What color is beautiful? In A. Pelo (Ed.), *Rethinking early childhood education* (pp. 3–6). Milwaukee, WS: Rethinking Schools.

Shade, B. J. (1997). *Culture, style, and the educative process: Making schools work for racially diverse students* (2nd ed.). Springfield, IL: Charles T. Thomas.

U.S. Department of Education. (2010). How no child left behind benefits African Americans. Retrieved April 5, 2010 from www2.ed.gov/nclb/accountability/achieve/nclb-aa.html

U.S. Department of Education. (2014). Racial/ethnic enrollment in public schools. Retrieved March 1, 2014 from http://nces.ed.gov/programs/coe/indicator_cge.asp

U.S. Department of Education, National Center for Education Statistics. (2007–2008). Schools and Staffing Survey (SASS), "Public School Teacher, BIE School Teacher, and Private School Teacher Data Files," 2007–08. Retrieved May 14, 2015 from http://nces.ed.gov/pubs2009/2009324/tables/sass0708_2009324_t12n_02.asp

Volk, D., & Long, S. (2005). Challenging myths of the deficit perspective. *Young Children, 60*(6), 12–19.

Wheeler, R. S., & Swords, R. (2006). *Code-switching. Teaching Standard English in urban classrooms.* Urbana, IL: National Council of Teachers of English.

Young, L. J. (2001). Border crossings and other journeys: Re-envisioning the doctoral preparation of education researchers. *Educational Researcher, 30*(5), 3-5.

2

LIBERTY AND JUSTICE FOR ALL?

Breaking the Code

Proposition 2.1 An understanding of oppression is necessary to teach for social justice and equity.

Proposition 2.2 Although racism is permanent and endemic, most people try to live decent and good lives and can fight to interrupt it and diminish its power.

Proposition 2.3 An essential part of a decolonizing curriculum is naming the oppression.

> And the day came when the risk to remain tight in a bud was more painful than the risk it took to blossom.
>
> (Anaïs Anin, 2014)[1]

Although I realize that readers are eager to read about strategies for educating African American students, this chapter provides a conceptual framework that will be useful for comprehensively understanding the rationale for the four broad strategies and approaches presented in this book (critical literacy, counternarratives, CRP, and contrastive analysis). As a reminder of the guidelines presented in Chapter 1 for addressing issues surrounding race and other issues of diversity and equity, readers should pay attention to their thoughts and reactions when processing the information presented in this chapter on oppression. Recall that moving out of comfort zones provides opportunities to learn new information. So, be prepared to ride the learning curve on behalf of the children. The information provided in this chapter will help educators build and extend their *knowledge bases* and *dispositions* regarding educating African American students. It will point educators toward strategies to use in the classroom, which will be elucidated in Chapters 3–6.

So What Is a Conceptual Framework?

A conceptual framework provides the logic and assumptions that are made when one thinks about a topic. The conceptual framework makes it clear how the topic is being thought about and situates it (the topic) within one or more schools of thought. It helps all parts of the discussion cohere or hang together. For example, in this book, the ideas and strategies that are presented are based on the following interrelated and organizing assumptions:

- Oppression exists in institutions (e.g., educational, economic, health, and political systems) and affects the experiences and academic and social outcomes of Black students.
- In order to interrupt oppression, the systems, practices, and policies that support oppression must be identified and named.
- School practices and strategies must be emancipatory in nature. That is, they should engage the voices, perspectives, and worldviews of Black students.
- Educators and students are both teachers *and* learners in the educational process. That is, educators will need to position themselves as learners and recognize that there are things that can be learned from students.
- Reflective actions on behalf of the educators that involve collaboration with others are likely to offer the most promise for interrupting oppression and reversing the current negative academic and social outcomes experienced by African American students.
- Educators should focus on individual levels of oppression as well as institutional levels.

It may be helpful to think of the conceptual framework using a metaphor such as a foundation for a house. The foundation is the most important component of any building, be it a house or a high-rise apartment. Simply put, the foundation is what all parts of the building rests on. So, getting the foundation right will go a long way toward having a solid and stable building for many years. Indeed, it is impossible to build a solid house without a strong foundation. In order to decide on the type of foundation, many factors, including the condition of the soil and the type of climate, must be considered. For example, some types of foundation do not perform well in flooding or cold temperatures. Homes that are built on poor soil conditions may require a deep foundation, whereas most homes only require shallow foundations. A structural engineer is usually consulted to discuss which type of foundation is best for the building that is being constructed. A potential builder may have windows, sheetrock, doors, and other necessary materials, but the placement of everything must be carefully planned and connected to the foundation. Moreover, the foundation is made in such a way that not just any materials will fit. They must match the specifications. When the concrete is poured for the foundation, it must be strong enough to support each part of the house. Steel reinforcing bars are added, but the house cannot be built until the concrete sets. Likewise, the conceptual framework for this book helps make all the parts of the topic cohesive. For example, Chapter 1 presented many different details about educating African American students, and readers may not yet be able to see how they fit together and/or why other strategies and approaches will not work with the conceptual framework. Yet, it was noted that much of the thinking and conceptualizing about educating African American students has been based on deficit conceptions. Deficit foundations will not lead to a strong house or to the effective education of African American students. That is, starting by focusing on *what's wrong* with Black students is foundationally flawed. Conversely, starting by understanding the "soil" and "climate" surrounding educating Black students and focusing on their strengths and humanity will result in a stronger foundation and stronger academic and social outcomes.

So, what are the "soil" and "climate" like for Black students? In Chapter 1, the activity in Box 1.2, which asked readers to rank the six major ethnic groups in terms of status held in the US, helps us to understand the unique psychological, social, and cognitive competencies that Black students may be required to achieve in school (Perry, Steele, & Hilliard, 2003). As Theresa Perry (2003) (aka structural engineer for the education of Black students) explained, school achievement for African American students may be more complicated, for some of the reasons listed below.

1. Being a member of a racial caste group automatically brings with it some challenges for making an ongoing commitment to achievement (p. 105).
2. This influences effort optimism.
3. Society's ideology of intellectual inferiority also fundamentally affects commitment to achievement over time.
4. "For no other group has there been such a persistent, well-articulated, and unabated ideology about their mental incompetence" (p. 105).
5. Schools do not have spaces that are intentionally organized to forge identities of African American students as achievers.
6. Schools do not provide spaces that intentionally buffer African American students from the day-to-day experience of racism in the school or from the explicit and subtle impact of the ideology of Black intellectual inferiority.
7. Schools are not likely to have a narrative that is counter to the narrative of "openness and opportunity," which talks about Black achievement in the face of constraints and limits.
8. Schools make few attempts to systematically organize occasions to create desire, to inspire hope, and to develop and sustain effort optimism or to socialize students to the behaviors that are necessary for them to be achievers.
9. There is little to no discussion about how racism in and out of schools affects effort optimism.

10. African American parents may not have figured out how to navigate schooling in schools in a racially integrated society.

Given these considerations, the conceptual framework and thinking about educating Black children must be comprehensive and reflective of issues on the macro (societal) and micro (school, child, home, community) levels. Hence, the framework presented in this chapter is twofold. As shown in Figure 2.1, the two dimensions included in the conceptual framework are: (1.) a focus on the social identities of students and educators; and (2.) an understanding of oppression and structural inequities. Structural inequities refer to systems of discrimination that manifest themselves in everyday structures (e.g., schools), policies, and practices. Both (social identities and structural inequities) of these interlocking dimensions will be discussed in the following sections.

This chapter provides the framework that shows how all the pieces of this book fit together. My hope is that it will also help readers understand why some of the existing conceptual frameworks and thinking about educating African American students contribute to the current dismal predicament that many African American students face in school. Although two dimensions are presented, the conceptual framework for this book is not intended to be prescriptive or formulaic or exhaustive. I am not suggesting that the framework presented in this chapter is the only viable one. Yet, it provides general tenets and is broad enough to be used across grade levels and content areas. Finally, it will be useful in helping educators figure out how to normalize high achievement for African American students. The expectation is that, as educators continue to develop their knowledge bases on the topic, other possible and related frameworks may emerge.

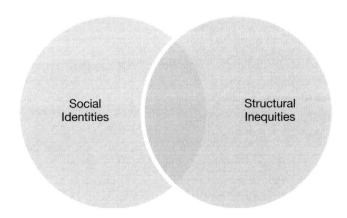

FIGURE 2.1 Two-Fold Framework for Thinking About Oppressive Cycles.

Levels of Oppression

Each semester, typically whenever there is a prolonged discussion about race in my courses, undergraduate and graduate students alike express discomfort, either verbally or nonverbally. A normally animated and engaging conversation about perceived *neutral* or *safe* topics such as child development theory or literacy strategies suddenly turns cold when race or oppression is injected into the discussion. One of the discomforts many educators have with discussing issues surrounding race, class, gender, and other forms of oppression is that they fear that they will be personally implicated (Harro, 2000a; Howard, 2006). In the quest for social justice, many White educators experience emotions such as denial, guilt, shame, confusion, fear, and anger (Helms, 2008; Howard, 2006). This range of emotions is a normal part of the process and learning curve. Likewise, educators of color experience a range of emotions that vary, depending on degrees of assimilation. Some educators of color also experience discomfort, denial, and fear when discussing these issues. Many educators from all ethnic groups have viewed racism and other forms of discrimination on an individual level and have not thought about how oppression exists in systems, policies, and practices. Therefore, the discussion moves them out of their comfort zones. It is hoped that, after reading this chapter, educators will be able to distinguish between individual and institutional acts of oppression, in order to understand that *good* people can and do contribute to oppression. Throughout the process, educators will have to reflect on the difference between being a *good person* and being a *good teacher* (Stan Karp, as cited in Salas, Tenorio, Walters, & Weiss, 2004). Hence, it will be necessary to maintain a critical distance to reflect on situations and to avoid internalizing or personalizing everything. Readers are encouraged to pause after reading major sections to reflect on how they are feeling and to write down their thoughts. If there is discomfort, tension, and other strong emotions, it may be useful to reread the guidelines for processing this information that were provided in Chapter 1.

I begin the discussion of the two dimensions of the conceptual framework (social identities and structural inequities) with a definition of oppression. Oppression is "a system that maintains advantage and disadvantage based on social group memberships and operates, intentionally or unintentionally, on individual, institutional, and cultural levels" (Hardiman, Jackson, & Griffin, 2007, p. 58). Most teacher preparation programs focus narrowly on students in isolation and do not address larger systems that affect schooling; therefore, readers may not see the immediate relationship to educating African American and other minoritized students. However, the relevance of understanding oppression will be apparent soon. Table 2.1 shows the three levels of oppression and examples of each one. Each level is explained in the subsequent sections.

TABLE 2.1 Levels and Types of Oppression

Individual	Institutional	Societal/Cultural
Attitudes	Housing	Values, norms, needs
Beliefs	Employment	Language
Socialization	Education	Standards of beauty
Interpersonal interactions	Health services (physical/ emotional)	Holidays
Individual behaviors	Religion Media Government/laws Legal system	Sex roles Logic system Societal expectations

Source: Hardiman et al., 2007

Individual Level of Oppression

Individual oppression includes intentional and unintentional acts of prejudice, ignorance, and hatred. The individual level of oppression refers to an act that *one* person is doing. So, as individuals, any of us can commit an act of prejudice or hatred. Additionally, we may have been socialized to believe stereotypes about other groups that are reflected in our individual interactions and preferences. That is, we may limit ourselves to interacting with only people from the same ethnic group, may fear other cultural groups, and/or call another person a racial epithet, for example. However, although our individual actions are ethically questionable and hurtful to the person(s) they are directed at, in general, they affect the targeted individual, but not necessarily his/her livelihood or policies in a person's place of work or residence (though they may and sometimes do). As explained by critical theorist Derrick Bell, in his classic book, *Faces at the Bottom of the Well*, "racial policy is the culmination of thousands of these individual practices" (1992, p. 7). This revelation helps us think in terms of institutional structures and patterns, rather than people's individual acts.

Institutional Level of Oppression (Structural Inequities)

In contrast to the individual level of oppression, *institutionalized oppression* refers to established laws, practices, rules, norms, and customs that systematically reflect and produce racial inequities (Hardiman et al., 2007; Koppelman & Goodhart, 2005). Focusing on a specific type of oppression, *institutional racism* represents a social system in which race is the major criterion of role assignment, role rewards, and socialization. It is a *system* that privileges Whites in the US over people of color. As seen on Table 2.1, structural or systemic racism, then, refers to a system of social structures or institutions that produces cumulative, durable, race-based inequalities in housing, employment, education, health services, religion, media, government/laws, and the legal system (Hardiman et al., 2007).

If we distinguish between institutional and individual levels of racism, it becomes evident that racialized outcomes do not require racist actors. This realization is pivotal in understanding that even well-intentioned educators can inadvertently harm the very students they are seeking to help. This will be explained more when we examine the misconception that schools are neutral and objective places in which all children have an equal chance of succeeding. In order to change the current landscape in schools that do not work for most African American and other minoritized students, it will be important for educators to collaboratively move past the *I love all children* mode and to be open to seeing and addressing issues of structural racism in relation to teaching and learning practices, polices, preferences, and curricula.

Societal/Cultural Level

The *societal/cultural* level of oppression refers to the "social norms, roles, rituals, language, music, and art that reflect and reinforce the belief that one social group is superior to another" (Hardiman et al., 2007). These societal values and beliefs are often reflected in standards of beauty (who we think is beautiful or not), holidays (which holidays are centered and valued in the mainstream—e.g., Christmas, Kwanzaa), logic systems (which ways of thinking we value—e.g., linear versus circular), and other values that we have acquired through socialization, without thinking about the subtextual meanings and implications.

Intentional and Unintentional Oppression

It is important to note that actions at any of the three levels of oppression can be intentional or unintentional. That is, a good person may engage in an oppressive act without intending to be discriminatory. For example, on an individual level, a teacher may call on White students three times more than she calls on African American students. The teacher may do so unintentionally and because of familiarity with White culture, unconscious differential teacher expectations for Black and White students, habit, or for a number of other reasons. The point is that her intent is not to discriminate against the students, though her actions are discriminatory and may escape her notice without careful reflection. Institutionally, schools (or other institutions) may celebrate Christmas holidays and close schools, but do not do the same for other religious holidays such as Ramadan. At the societal level, beauty standards that value blond hair, blue eyes, and fair skin may cause people to devalue African American students with natural hairstyles, brown eyes, and dark skin. So, a key part of thinking about education is to consciously reflect on actions (even minute ones in classroom settings). Box 2.1 provides an exercise to help readers understand that schools are microcosms of society, and that societal/cultural values, norms, and beliefs often result from what we experienced during our socialization in a society that is racially stratified.

Social Identities

Although the focus of the book is on Black students, as educators, we must also reflect on our social identities and how they may interact with those of our students, as we are an important part of the schooling equation. The conceptual framework of this book includes educators' understanding of their social identities and positions in society, as well as systems of oppression, and how the two dimensions interact with each other.

In terms of social identities, all of us have memberships in multiple social groups. That is, we can be described by our gender, race, sexual orientation, religion, socioeconomic status, age, ability, and so forth (Hardiman et al., 2007). The social system of oppression uses the social identity structure to assign dominant and subordinate status to all individuals and groups in society. As shown in Table 2.2, we are each born with a specific set of social identities, and these social identities predispose us to unequal roles in the dynamic system of oppression (Harro, 2000a).

As readers reflect on their own social identities, it is import to remember the earlier distinction between individual and institutional levels of oppression. This will make it clear the focus is on the institutional or system level. Individually, we can all experience discrimination, but, on institutional and societal/cultural levels, systems, policies, practices, norms, and mores privilege some groups and disprivilege others. If we keep the focus on African American students, African Americans are likely to experience structural inequities in society. As we all have a variety of social identities (some privileged; some not), it may be useful for educators to better understand that, although some African American students may be privileged in terms of, say, socioeconomic status, religion, etc., being a member of what Perry (2003) described as a racial caste group influences school experiences for many of them. Hence, just as it is important to see and understand Black culture, as mentioned in Chapter 1, it is also important to see and understand how institutional racism impacts the schooling of Black students.

The reflection activity in Table 2.3 allow readers to reflect on various social identity groups in terms of subconscious and conscious messages that they learned during childhood. For each group, write down messages that you received about the respective social groups. These messages may have been covert or overt and could have come from a variety of sources, including books. This reflection activity will help educators think about how classroom practices (e.g., who is called on and who is not) can contribute to cycles of oppression. It also helps make positive and negative stereotypes about various groups apparent. Understanding how oppressive processes began, and, importantly, what can be done about them, will be discussed in the following sections.

Box 2.1 Envisioning a Different World

Reflect on the three parts of this exercise. Fill in the blank below with the choices that follow.

1. What if all the _____ were African American?

    • Presidents of the US
    • teachers (88 percent currently White)
    • doctors
    • CEOs
    • university professors
    • artists
    • greeting cards
    • mainstream dance styles (African vs. ballet)
    • products (dolls, action figures, pictures on products, e.g., paper towels)
    • magazines
    • radio stations
    • TV news anchors
    • TV shows
    • telephone operators and recording systems
    • colleges
    • faces on currency
    • real-estate owners
    • members of the Senate
    • members of the House of Representatives
    • store owners
    • cab drivers
    • famous historical heroes and heroines
    • pupils in academically gifted classes in school
    • school boards
    • PTAs
    • police officers
    • owners of professional sports teams.

2. What if the lower ranks of society were filled with Whites (see examples below)?

    • custodians
    • people who collect garbage
    • people who are incarcerated
    • pupils in remedial classes in schools

- residents of government-supported houses
- cafeteria workers.

3. Assuming an unequal power structure in society, how would:

- Whites feel?
- Other people of color?
- How would your life be different?
- Would you likely be in the same position today?
- Would you dress differently?
- Which hairstyles would be preferred?

TABLE 2.2 Social Identities Matrix

Social identity category	Privileged social groups (institutional level)	Border social groups (may experience privilege or discrimination, depending on the context)	Social groups that are likely to be discriminated against at the institutional level	Type of oppression
Race	White people	Biracial people	Asian, African, Latino, and Native Peoples	Racism
Gender	Males	Transgendered or intersex people	Females	Sexism
Sexual orientation	Heterosexual people	Bisexual people	Lesbian and gay people	Heterosexism
Socio-economic Status statuses	People from upper socio-economic statuses	People from middle socio-economic statuses	People from lower socio-economic	Classism
Ability/ Disability	Temporarily abled-bodied people	People with temporary disabilities	People with disabilities	Ableism
Religion	Protestants	Varies—historically Roman Catholics —could also be Jehovah's Witnesses, Mormons and other groups	Jewish, Islamic, Hindu, Buddhist, etc. people	Religious oppression
Age	Adults	Young adults	Elderly and young people	Ageism/adultism

Source: Hardiman et al., 2007

TABLE 2.3 Childhood Messages

Groups	Messages from your parents/guardians, books, media, and friends	How were they communicated? (e.g., verbally, tacitly, physically)	Messages that you will communicate/have communicated to your own children or your students	How will the messages be communicated to your own children or students, or how were they communicated?
Africans/African Americans				
Americans (USA				
Asians/Asian Americans				
Biracial Americans				
Latinos/Latino Americans				
Indigenous people/Native Americans				
Males				
Females				
Lesbian, bisexual, gay, transsexual, queer				
Lower socioeconomic status				
Middle socioeconomic status				
Upper socioeconomic status				
Other groups (e.g., different religions, immigrants, people from other countries)				

So How Did It Come to Be This Way?

In order to examine how oppression (gender, ethnic, social class, language, religion, etc.) is produced and reproduced in the context of schools and schooling, I direct readers to Table 2.4, which summarizes four models/theories about the colonization (oppression) process. The table should be read linearly, as the number of stages or steps varied among theorists.

I have provided a synopsis of several different models so that readers will get a sense of the key themes and parallels across them. Additionally, I do not want readers to think that they have to be guided by one model, and, hopefully, it will become apparent that the oppressive cycle works similarly across various types of oppression. Although the intent is to focus in a composite manner, using a synthesis of general tenets from the models, I will also expatiate on one of the theories (Freire's antidialogical dimensions of oppression), so that readers can understand the colonization process and how it maintains itself. Additionally, brief summaries of several models provide readers with a preview of the scope of what exists in the academic literature. Interested readers should consult the respective references to continue to increase their knowledge bases. Near the end of the chapter, I will also discuss decolonizing and dialogical models and pedagogies that can be used to interrupt oppressive processes, rather than inadvertently, unintentionally, and unknowingly contributing to them. These and similar models can be studied for better understanding of structural inequities.

Conceptual Frameworks: Models/Theories That Explain Structural Inequities in Schools and Society

Conceptually, this book draws from African American emancipatory, decolonizing, and critical pedagogical perspectives. These frameworks are used to examine how discrimination is produced and reproduced in the context of schools and schooling (Freire, 1970/1999; Lynn, Jennings, & Hughes, 2013). Implicit in this conceptualization is a probe into how theoretical concepts such as diversity and equity are practiced in schools. A basic premise is that:

> There is no such thing as a *neutral* educational process. Education either functions as an instrument that is used to facilitate the integration of students into the logic of the present system and bring about conformity to it, *or* it becomes "the practice of freedom," the means by which students learn to deal critically and creatively in the transformation of their world.
>
> (Shaull, as cited in Freire, 1970/1999, p. 16)

Because classrooms and societies are not neutral spaces, they reflect the ideologies, thoughts, and perspectives of someone or some institution. As Desmond Tutu (as quoted in Quigley, 2003) said, "If you are neutral in situations

TABLE 2.4 Models and Theories of the Colonization Process (Stages/Dimensions of Oppression)

Freire (1970/1999): dimensions of oppression/ antidialogical action	Fanon (1963): stages of colonization	Woodson (1933/ 1990) miseducation of the Negro	Enriquez (1992): six steps of colonization
Conquest: The oppressed develops a colonial mentality—a denigration of self and an aspiration to be like the colonizer	First stage: The colonizer purposefully takes over a country.	Use of physical force and unethical "laws" to control African people who were enslaved and to destroy their humanity. They were not permitted to be educated or to have a functioning family	Denial/withdrawal: The indigenous people are denied the xculture and withdraw from identifying with their culture
Divide and rule: Unification of the people is a serious threat	Second stage: The colonizer exploits, appropriates, and belittles the country's culture	Efforts were made to control the Negro's thinking. When a person's thinking is controlled, the oppressor does not have to worry about his actions	Destruction/ eradication: The physical elements of the indigenous culture are eradicated
Manipulation: Oppressors try to make the masses conform to their objectives	Third stage: The colonizer substitutes the indigenous culture with the dominant culture	Negroes were "trained" and miseducated to glorify European culture, to the detriment of their own	Denigration/ belittlement/insult: The cultural practices of the traditional culture are treated as criminal
Cultural invasion: The oppressed become inauthentic and view selves with the invaders' outlook rather than their own	Fourth stage: The colonizer justifies colonialism in the name of nobility and the uplifting of 'uncivilized' people	Psychological enslavement is used to keep African people divided	Surface accommodation/ tokenism: Surviving cultural elements are folkloricized Transformation: Indigenous cultural practice is infused into the dominate culture Exploitation: Indigenous culture is sought for commercial, artistic, and political gain

of injustice, you have chosen the side of the oppressor." In Chapter 3, strategies will be provided to help educators think about ways of detecting these subtexts, which are often covert. Paulo Freire, a critical theorist, stressed that educators must learn to be astute at *reading the world* and discerning oppression in its many disguises. As will be discussed more in the chapter on critical literacy, educators can become adept at *problem posing* and questioning existing structures, policies, practices, and the like. The goal is to learn to take reflexive action (which Freire refers to as *praxis*) in order to teach in an emancipatory manner that liberates, not only Black students and students from other marginalized groups, but educators themselves.

The role of critical, emancipatory, and decolonizing pedagogies is to emancipate people who are oppressed, not just from the oppressor, but also from their own perceptions of themselves in the oppressed state (Freire, 1970/1999). The fundamental issue of power, of whose voice gets to be heard in determining what is best for students, is an issue addressed by critical theory and critical pedagogy.

Because of the diverse ways that oppression is manifested in different contexts and eras, it cannot be simplified. What readers will notice is that a key theme among African American emancipatory pedagogies (Lynn et al., 2013; Woodson, 1933/1990), critical pedagogies, and decolonizing pedagogies (Enriquez, 1992; Fanon, 1963; Freire, 1970/1999; Halagao, 2010; Laenui, 2000; Strobel, 2001) is that the type of oppression (regardless of what it is) must be first identified and named. Like 12-step programs such as Alcoholics Anonymous, the first step is to acknowledge or admit that there is a problem. The focus on structural inequities as a key part of the conceptual framework provides a mechanism for doing so.

Although Paulo Freire's book *Pedagogy of the Oppressed* is widely cited, and some of his earlier ideas have received criticism about sexist language, his conceptions about the dimensions of oppression are useful for examining structural inequities. For decades, Freire's work emphasized methods for teaching students from oppressed groups (Freire, 1970/1999, 1973/1998, 1985). According to Freire's theory of antidialogical action to explain the process of colonization, oppression of all types (e.g., gender, class, religious) has four dimensions that remain constant: (1.) conquest, (2.) divide and conquer, (3.) manipulation, and (4.) cultural invasion. Because oppressive structures exist in schools (e.g., instructional methods, curriculum), even well-intentioned educators can unknowingly contribute to oppression. Each of these dimensions is shown in Figure 2.2 and is discussed in turn. Parallels can be drawn across the other models and theories shown in Table 2.4.

Conquest

In order to conquer a group of people, conquerors present themselves as "authorities" and "prototypes." In this process, the oppressed must be silenced

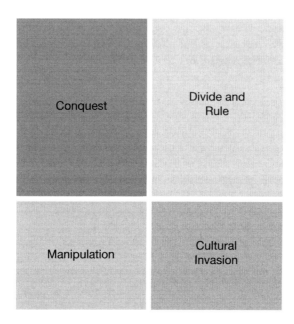

FIGURE 2.2 Freire's Four Dimensions of Oppression.

and controlled in as many arenas as possible (e.g., economically, culturally, educationally). No true dialogue (bidirectional exchange) is permitted or encouraged. Indeed, the process is antidialogical. For example, historically, when the Europeans "colonized" parts of Africa, schooling and religion fell under the jurisdiction of the Europeans, and information was presented from a European versus African perspective. Colonial and postcolonial practices of conquest include: (a) disruption of native cultures and their ways of being; (b) eradication of original languages, religions, and institutions; and (c) imposition of European values and folkways and a racial caste system that codifies White supremacy (Banks, 2006). Banks explains that:

> The system of chattel slavery that was established in the Caribbean, the United States, and Brazil reinforced and institutionalized White supremacy and left a powerful and pernicious legacy of racialization, which these nations have yet to overcome. Racialization affects educators and students in these nations in significant ways today.
>
> (p. xiii)

Similar trends can be seen in many other places around the globe (e.g., Australia, Canada, South Africa) (Banks, 2006).

Relating the concept of conquest to contemporary education, any methods that silence the worldviews of minoritized groups are oppressive and contribute to the colonization process. The role of language and literacy is central to teaching and learning. Each individual has the right, as Freire puts it, to "say his or her own words, to name the world" (1970/1999, p. 15). "In a democracy, people should be educated to tell their stories, to make their own voices heard, and to act together to defend and expand their rights" (Featherstone, 1995, p. 14). In order to become liberated and to participate in the transformation of society toward new possibilities, people must have a voice in the process (Freire, 1970/1999; Greene, 1995). Classrooms that use "banking" or antidialogical processes, in which information flows in one direction—from the teacher to the student—do not allow input from students. Students are viewed as empty vessels or blank slates, and the teacher is viewed as the infallible expert who transmits essential "facts" to students.

Some students come to school with worldviews that are more synchronized with what is valued and considered appropriate in their respective societies. Hence, their cultural tools are more closely represented in textbooks and assessments, and these students tend to fare well (Boutte, 1999; Gallard, 1993). On the other hand, students whose cultural orientations are not synchronized with schools' may not fare well or may even disassociate themselves from their cultural identities in order to succeed (Boutte, 2002; Fordham, 1988, 1996).

In the case of the multiple languages and literacies of indigenous people, little attempt has been made to understand the associated sociopolitical issues or historical contexts. Myths about the language and intellectual capabilities of indigenous people are still prevalent (Perry et al., 2003), as we shall see in Chapter 4, when African American Language (AAL) is discussed. Hence, many educators do not consult the voluminous knowledge bases on indigenous languages and literacies, which are often viewed as aberrations that must be eradicated.

The evolutionary ranking of one culture or language system as superior or inferior to another causes further divisions among minoritized and majoritized people. Hence, mainstream or dominant languages and literacies are deemed to be at the top (e.g., "Standard English") and reign as the only ones that are legitimate. Such inaccurate distinctions not only separate speakers of dialects or "non-mainstream" language from "formal" English speakers, they also create divisions between various students and communities.

Divide and Rule

The second dimension of Freire's theory of antidialogical action is "divide and rule." When groups that are oppressed are divided by ethnicities, languages, religions, skin colors, socioeconomic statuses, and other aspects of their social identities, disharmony exists within and between groups. Hence, focus on contesting one another is centered on intercultural and intra-cultural disagreements, and the reigning power structure is not challenged and remains intact. Such divisions between groups have been shown to be the basis of conflicts worldwide (e.g., British and Irish, Tutsis and Hutus in Rwanda, Croatians and Serbians, Israeli and Palestinians, Asians and Blacks, males and females, Bloods and Crips (gangs), Christians and non-Christians, Republicans and Democrats, to name a few). All of these divisions interfere with prospects of peace and love for humanity, which include respecting differences *and* seeing commonalities.

Manipulation

The third dimension is "manipulation." Central to Freire's pedagogy of the oppressed is the vision of liberated humans who are capable of questioning and thinking critically about information (Freire, 1985). Historically, Eurocentric information has been presented as official stories to impose the will of the dominant culture (Morrison, 1997; Watkins, 2005). Information was also intentionally manipulated and presented inaccurately.

Intentionally or not, schools have done an excellent job of teaching students not to critically question authority (a key part of manipulation). Hence, perspectives presented in books, the media, and other texts are rarely questioned and are often readily accepted as legitimate and official knowledge. As long as information in schools is presented from a primarily Eurocentric perspective and not questioned, other worldviews will be considered illegitimate (Boutte, 1999; Boutte, Hopkins, & Waklatsi, 2008). Likewise, acknowledgment of the voices of people who are minoritized will continue to be on the periphery—or absent in dominant narratives.

It is important to note that manipulation is not limited to educational contexts. It can be legal, economic, religious, social, political, or otherwise. For example, many images that are put forth in the media have been manipulated and are inaccurate, thus falsely pathologizing minoritized groups (Morrison, 1997; Watkins, 2005). Following the tradition of Charles Darwin, who documented that there were no biological differences among various racial groups, Stephen Jay Gould's *The Mismeasure of Man* (1996) documents an array of fallacious biological arguments, in science and other fields, that intended to show that Whites were superior. For instance, images published in 1868 and widely distributed to people studying medicine and science compared the skull of a "Negro" man with that of a Greek man. The skull of the Greek man is shown as upright, and the skull of the Negro has been likened to that of a chimpanzee by false inflation of the chimpanzee's skull. Gould fast-forwards his discussion to similar manipulations such as *The Bell Curve* (Herrnstein & Murray, 1994) to demonstrate contemporary iterations of the same type, in which fraudulent and non-replicable "data" are presented to demonstrate genetic differences between the intelligence of Blacks and Whites. Misinformation such as this has been presented as scientific truisms, even though it has not been validated (King, 2005).

Additionally, the legal system may involve manipulation as well. For example, the mistreatment of minoritized groups and indigenous people around the world has been supported by laws (e.g., chattel slavery in the US, apartheid in South Africa, and treatment of indigenous people in the US, Australia, and New Zealand). Likewise, school policies guide and support inequities such as disproportionality in special education placements, expulsions, and suspensions of minoritized groups, to include students of color and poor children. Numerous other examples can be mentioned, such as funding formulas for schools and differential incarceration sentences for blue- versus white-collar crimes. Such glaring inequities in systems (educational or otherwise) interfere with peace among various groups of people around the globe.

Cultural Invasion

> They saw themselves as others had seen them. They had been formed by the images made of them by those who had the deepest necessity to despise them.
> (James Baldwin, 1955/1983)

The final dimension of Freire's theory of antidialogical action is "cultural invasion." Cultural invasion occurs when marginalized groups internalize the negative messages that the oppressor has put forth about them. The dominant narrative puts forth overt and covert (often by omission) messages about aspects of minoritized peoples' lived experiences. Negative, invasive, and culturally assaulting messages may include, express, or implied messages about minoritized peoples' beauty, names, religions, languages, intelligence, and many other dimensions of their lives. For example, beauty has been widely and pervasively defined for females as comprising blue eyes and long, flowing blonde hair. Examples of some of the culturally invasive messages that prevail are included in Box 2.2.

For cultural invasion to succeed, it is essential that those invaded become convinced of their intrinsic inferiority (Freire, 1970/1999). Historically and currently, this has been done overtly and covertly, via books, curriculum, media, legal decisions, and the like. In the early 1900s, studies on language and culture routinely classified non-European cultures as "underdeveloped," "primitive," or inherently inferior in comparison with Western civilizations (Wolfram & Fasold, 1974). In the US, this ideology has been reinforced legally through laws designating African Americans as inferior and not entitled to the same rights as Whites. Vestiges of the inferiority ideology are factors in the present disproportionate placement of Whites in academically gifted classes, invisibility of Africans/African Americans in the curriculum and media, and a host of other examples that contribute to the belief that African Americans are inferior (Hale, 2001; Perry et al., 2003).

Box 2.2 Examples of Culturally Invasive Messages in Society and Schools About Blacks

- Beauty: Because of preferences for White beauty standards at the cultural/societal level, dark skin and African American hairstyles are typically not defined as beautiful. Additionally, because of a long history of cultural/societal mores that devalue Black beauty, colorism exists among Blacks and others, giving preferences to Black people with lighter skin and Europeanized hair styles (Monroe, 2013).
- Names: Names that are thought of as African American names are often subjected to ridicule, and people with these names are often discriminated against in the job market.[2]
- Intelligence: Black intelligence is continuously under assault, from sources ranging from the yearly reporting of standardized test scores, in which Blacks continuously score least well compared with other ethnic groups, to the disproportional number of Black students placed into special education classes. Negative innuendos about Black intelligence prevail, without the corollary critique of systemic inequities and other variables that contribute to these trends.

Although prevailing beliefs about the inferiority of Blacks, historically and currently, are incorrect, many people (African American and others) have internalized these pervasive messages. In other words, the inherent strengths of Black culture (such as AAL, with its rich historical legacy and systematic and complex linguistic rules) have come to be viewed as liabilities by many people, including African Americans.

How Can Oppression Be Interrupted?

> In a people's rise from oppression to grace, a turning point comes when thinkers determined to stop the downward slide get together to study the causes of common problems, think out solutions and organize ways to apply them.
> (Ayi Kwei Armah, as cited in King, 2005, front matter)

After thinking about the expansiveness of the four dimensions of oppression presented in Freire's theory of antidialogical action, educators may question, "How do we make a dent in something that seems so big?" (Harro, 2000b, p. 463). As shown in Table 2.5, dialogical actions provide the counters to antidialogical actions. Freire explained that education needs to be done *with* the people, for the people. That is, the education process cannot be antidialogical. He recommended dialogue as a fundamental two-way strategy in which the teacher is also student, and the students are also teachers. This will require educators to learn both *about* their students and *from* their students. The educator becomes a provocateur of sorts who engages students in problem-posing education that problematizes the inequities and inequalities in society. As shown in Chapter 3, critical literacy as an avenue to liberation becomes important. When people are liberated, and their voices are not silenced or denied, they are able to become *more fully human* (Freire, 1970/1999) and, thus, enjoy human rights in the manner that they are entitled to do.

In terms of moving toward solutions and informed classroom strategies, several other decolonizing, critical, and African emancipatory theories exist that help educators think about ways to deconstruct negative narratives about African American students and to construct counternarratives. The larger themes from African American emancipatory pedagogies (Woodson, 1933/1990), critical theories (Freire, 1970/1999), and decolonizing theories (Enriquez, 1992; Fanon, 1963; Freire, 1970/1999; Halagao, 2010; Laenui, 2000; Strobel, 2001) can be seen on Table 2.5. Big ideas include:

- naming/identifying the oppression and its constituent components;
- learning one's history;
- imagining possibilities of a better world;
- taking reflective actions to interrupt ongoing oppression;
- organizing and collaborating with others who are seeking to dismantle oppressive structures. Although individual efforts in classrooms and other educational spaces are important, major changes at the institutional and societal/cultural levels will occur through thoughtful action and collaboration. For example, the abolition of slavery in the US or apartheid in South Africa was the result of organized, sustained, and collective efforts of people across racial, ethnic, gender, and other social groups. Likewise, major changes that occurred during the Civil Rights era were the result of collective efforts by Black communities, college students, churches, White allies, and others.

Concrete strategies that demonstrate ways to begin decolonizing classrooms and educational spaces are presented in Chapters 3–5.

Focusing more specifically on African American people, King explained that African Americans are likely to use one of three modes of responses to racism and other forms of hegemony: (1.) adaptation, or adopting what is deemed useful; (2.) improvisation, or substituting or improvising alternatives that are more sensitive to African American culture; and (3.) resistance, or resisting that which is destructive and not in the best interests of African Americans (King, 2005). Returning to the twofold conceptual framework, which includes considering the roles that social identities and structural inequities play in the process of effective education of African American students, educators will notice a variety of possible perspectives and behaviors among their students. The commonalities and variations

TABLE 2.5 Decolonizing Models and Theories

Freire's theory of dialogical action (1970/1999)	Strobel's process of decolonization (2001)	Halagao's decolonizing curriculum (2010)	Woodson's education of the Negro (African emancipatory pedagogy) (1933)	Laenui's process of decolonization (2000)
Cooperation: There is a need to communicate with the oppressed to bring about equity	Naming the oppression and articulating its impact on one's identity—that is, loss of "cultural memory," and "loss of language"—are the first steps to healing	(1.) A decolonizing curriculum requires deep and critical thinking about one's history and culture within a multicultural and global context so as to see how concepts such as diversity, multiculturalism, imperialism, oppression and revolution, and racism are universal	The education of any people should begin with the people themselves. Black people should learn their history and claim their humanity	(1.) Rediscovery/recovery
Unity for liberation: Unity of the revolutionary leaders and the oppressed to engage in praxis (reflective action). Oppressed must divest selves of myths that bind them to the world of oppression	Reflecting: looking deeply and thinking critically about one's position. But, unless moved to action, the reflection stage can be self-consuming and nonproductive	(2.) A decolonizing curriculum must be feeling-based, with activities that promote love of self, empathy and perspective-taking, and stir up anger. Mixed emotions of mourning, dreaming, confusion, struggle, excitement, passion, and empathy are natural feelings to encounter and discuss openly, and help	Black people should resist culturally invasive negative messages about themselves	(2.) Mourning (of what was taken from them)

Organization: The oppressed organize among themselves and with revolutionary leaders in order to establish a new, fair, and equitable reality

Cultural synthesis: The oppressed and revolutionary leaders work in communion in their praxis

Acting: becoming a leader and giving back to one's cultural community by ongoing questioning and spreading one's story

students move forward in the decolonization process

(3.) A decolonizing curriculum needs to create an academic and social space for formerly colonized people to gather, unite, and fight systems of oppression

(4.) A decolonizing curriculum teaches life skills such as critical thinking, public speaking, and social interaction that enhance one personally and professionally

(5.) A decolonizing curriculum must have a social action component that develops leadership, models activism, produces empowerment and self-efficacy, and inspires one to carve one's own niche in giving back to the community to effect social change

(3.) Dreaming (imagining a world free of denigration)

(4.) Commitment

(5.) Action

that are observed result from a complex interplay of students' social identities and the particular structural inequities that they are facing. In turn, this means that educators must become astute at critically considering these factors and tailor their educational strategies accordingly. The strategies presented in the next three chapters, therefore, should be thought of as guides and possibilities that should be tweaked and adapted for particular settings. The conceptual framework presented in this chapter has provided insight into the comprehensive and deep nature of the educational and societal context. Further reading will help build a deeper knowledge base. As was noted in Chapter 1's guidelines for processing information in this book, educators should focus on the information that they find most useful to them and, of course, believe that transformation is possible.

Conclusion

Just in case readers did not get the meaning of the title of this chapter, "Liberty and Justice for All? Breaking the Code", this chapter has explained that oppression has been codified into everyday practices, polices, norms, values, rules, and mores. These codes are not readily apparent to the uncritical eye. Understanding how systemic oppression works will help readers began to see that, although the US espouses the ideals of liberty and justice for all, there are many systems that interfere with this possibility. So, readers now know *some* of the codes and have some of the keys to unlock the codes (decolonize classrooms) and can begin to teach in a more intentional and informed manner on behalf of the children.

   I am aware that parts of this chapter were more complex than some readers may have wished. Returning to the foundation metaphor, many readers only want to see the final product, the finished home. However, skipping this chapter to get to the strategies will make for a weak foundation that will have difficulty sustaining itself and that will be only superficially useful in transforming classrooms and schools for African American students. The goal of this book is to liberate, inspire, mobilize, and educate its readers. The conceptual framework is the foundation that will make this goal possible.

The Bad News

In 1992, in his classic, widely read and cited book, *Faces at the Bottom of the Well*, Derrick Bell proclaimed that racism is permanent. It is important that educators acknowledge that race and racism are endemic and ingrained aspects of the teaching and learning processes and in society. However, there is good news.

The Good News

Most people are good people and fight against racism in order to keep it from being worse (Bell, 1992). The alternative—not doing anything—means that we inadvertently contribute to it. As educators, we are powers of good. As Bell notes, a succession of consistent actions taken against racism is a victory in itself. However, we cannot naively "go to battle" without a game plan and the necessary tools to fight against racism. The remainder of this book provides those tools by making strategies for dismantling structural inequities in schools explicit. Using the tools provided as a starting point, educators from any background can become strong advocates for African American students.

> Our lives begin to end the day we become silent about things that matter.
> (Martin Luther King Jr., 1929–1968)

"Teachers are often simultaneously perpetrators and victims, with little control over planning time, class time, or broader school policies—and much less over the unemployment, hopelessness, and other 'savage inequalities' that help shape our children's lives" (Au, Bigelow, & Karp, 2007, p. x). Yet, there are many aspects of schooling over which teachers *do* have power. Teachers can recognize and question the values and culture being promoted in their classrooms. Otherwise, as this chapter has shown, they will likely socialize their students to accept the power relations of our society that are unevenly distributed along lines of race, class, gender, religion, sexual orientation, ability, age, and other social identities (Au, 2008/2009; Segura-Mora, 2008).

"As people come to a critical level of understanding of the nature of oppression and their roles in this systemic phenomenon, they seek new paths for creating social change and taking themselves toward empowerment or liberation" (Harro, 2000b, p. 463). Hopefully, this chapter will encourage educators to move out of their comfort zones and to be open to the professional knowledge bases on anti-oppressive teaching. These knowledge bases can inform and influence personal experiences and dispositions. Before reading the next chapter, this is a good time to review the guidelines for processing this information to ensure the best possible chance of reflecting deeply on new information. Chapter 3 focuses on critical literacy, and Chapter 4 focuses on AAL. Both of these chapters address generic issues that span all grade levels and subjects. Some readers may want to skip to Chapter 5, which provides examples of CRP in classrooms in different subjects (e.g., language arts, mathematics, science, social studies, and art), in elementary, middle, and high schools. However, the information and strategies presented for critical literacy and AAL are fundamental for teaching content. Educators would be wise to spend time at the beginning of the semester focusing on these two areas. This does not imply that regular curriculum standards would not be taught, as many can be taught while focusing on critical literacy and AAL. However, if K–12 classrooms are to be transformed, there is a need for sustained, critical, and explicit focus on these topics. I refer readers back to the NAEP data in Figures 1.2–1.4, which show academic outcomes over nearly *40 years*(!) using conventional methods. I argue that the standards are apparently not being taught anyway, so, on behalf of the children, I encourage educators to consider the critical literacy and AAL information as foundational for teaching content.

Key Points From the Chapter

1. The conceptual framework helps educators understand the rationale for the four broad strategies and approaches used in this book (critical literacy, counternarratives, CRP, and contrastive analysis).
2. A twofold framework was presented that focused on social identities and structural inequities.
3. Three levels of oppression were presented: individual, institutional, and societal/cultural. Oppression at all three levels can be intentional or unintentional.
4. We are born into a specific set of social identities, and these social identities predispose us to unequal roles in the dynamic system of oppression.
5. There are many models that explain oppression and colonization processes.
6. Paulo Freire's theory of antidialogical action is explained as one example of how colonization develops and how the system maintains itself. Four dimensions of any type of oppression were shared: (1.) conquest, (2.) divide and rule, (3.) manipulation, and (4.) cultural invasion.
7. Decolonizing, critical, and African emancipatory theories will be useful for thinking about responses to oppressive cycles.

Activities

1. Look for examples of the four dimensions of oppression (conquest, divide and rule, manipulation, cultural invasion) in society and schools.
2. What are some examples of American ideals in action in the US to help understand how subtextual messages are always playing and how we come to internalize these without knowing it?
3. View the video clips below to see examples of commentaries on "divide and rule":
   (a) video clip from the movie *Hotel Rwanda* about divisions between two ethnic groups in Rwanda—"Hutu and Tutsi" (length about 1 minute);[3]
   (b) historical video clip of Malcolm X discussing divisions between Africans who were enslaved in the US—"House and Field Negroes" (length: 1 minute, 57 seconds).[4]
4. View the video story about Saartijie Baartmn, who was pejoratively referred to as Hottentot Venus, for an example of manipulation of images (length: 4 minutes, 56 seconds).[5]

5. To learn more about how self-hatred (a form of cultural invasion or internalized oppression) develops among some Blacks, view the video link and listen to Dr. Amos Wilson discussing the phenomenon (length: 49 minutes, 58 seconds).[6] What insights did you glean? What points did you agree or disagree with?

6. View the video of the *Essence Black Women In Hollywood* awards speech from Lupita Nyong'o as best supporting actor in the movie *12 Years a Slave*, to hear the impact of cultural invasion on notions of Black beauty (length: 4 minutes, 54 seconds).[7]

7. Use the four dimensions of oppression (conquest, divide and rule, manipulation, cultural invasion) to reflect on the video "A Girl Like Me" (length: 7 minutes, 15 seconds).[8]

8. For additional information on examples of contemporary legal manipulation affecting African Americans, read Michelle Alexander's book, *The New Jim Crow: Mass Incarceration in the Age of Colorblindness* (2012).

9. Examine school policies to decide if they need to be changed to ensure equity for Black students (e.g., guidelines for access to gifted education (can grades be used in lieu of standardized test scores, for example, as many African American students may not meet the set cut-off score?)).

10. Read Bobbie Harro's chapters on the "Cycle of Socialization" (2000a) and "Cycle of Liberation" (2000b) for additional information on how these cycles teach us how to play our roles in oppression and how to break the cycle, respectively.

11. View the DVD *True Colors* to see examples of discrimination against Blacks in housing, employment, shopping, and everyday experiences. This documentary features Diane Sawyer with *ABC News* and follows two professional male discrimination testers, one Black and one White, in a variety of settings (Lukasiewicz & Harvey, 1991/2005) (18 minutes runtime). Reflect on the following questions:

    (a) Are the types of discrimination shown in the video still prevalent? Provide evidence to support your answer.

    (b) How does the discrimination viewed in the video fit with American ideals (e.g., "liberty and justice for all", equal opportunity employer, *e pluribus unum*)?

    (c) How is discrimination learned? How did the type of discrimination shown in *True Colors* begin?

    (d) How is discrimination unlearned?

    (e) What are the implications for teaching African American students?

12. Thinking about individual versus institutional levels of oppression:

    (a) Is there White racism?

    (b) Is there Black racism?

(c) Make two columns, one labeled "White racism" and the other "Black racism." In each respective column, write examples of how each type of racism adversely impacts the lives of people as an entire group of people (e.g., How does White racism affect the lives (housing, jobs, healthcare) of Black people? How does Black racism affect the lives (housing, jobs, healthcare) of White people?)

Resources

1. Rethinking Schools:[9] Readers can find many teacher-friendly, short articles on social justice issues with classroom examples and ideas.
2. Teaching Tolerance:[10] Teaching Tolerance offers free resources such as DVDs, publications, lesson plans, and activities that will be useful for getting started and sustaining the effort to fight against oppression and to have equitable classrooms for African American and other minoritized students.

Notes

1. Retrieved May 14, 2015 from www.brainyquote.com/quotes/quotes/a/anaisnin120256.html
2. See www.nytimes.com/2009/12/06/weekinreview/06Luo.html; www.cbsnews.com/news/black-names-a-resume-burden/; www.nber.org/digest/sep03/w9873.html
3. See www.starpulse.com/Movies/Hotel_Rwanda/Videos/?vxChannel=&vxClipId=&clip_id=gXmYvVfLEOFVNiVgbRVGWQ&video_title=Hotel+Rwanda+-+Clip+-+Hutu+Or+Tutsi
4. Retrieved 15 May, 2015 from www.youtube.com/watch?v=znQe9nUKzvQ
5. Retrieved 15 May, 2015 from www.youtube.com/watch?v=iQ7mmMe4klQ
6. Retrieved 24 May, 2015 from www.youtube.com/watch?v=z0goH9kqZyQ
7. Retrieved 15 May, 2015 from www.youtube.com/watch?v=ZPCkfARH2eE
8. Retrieved 15 May, 2015 from www.youtube.com/watch?v=z0BxFRu_SOw
9. See www.rethinkingschools.org/index.shtml
10. See www.tolerance.org/

References

Alexander, M. (2012). *The new Jim Crow: Mass incarceration in the age of colorblindness*. New York: The New Press.

Au, W. (2008/2009). Decolonizing the classroom. Lessons in the multicultural education. *Rethinking Schools, 23*(2), 27–30.

Au, W., Bigelow, B., & Karp, S. (2007). Introduction: Creating classrooms for equity and social justice. In W. Au, B. Bigelow, and S. Karp (Eds.), *Rethinking our classrooms: Teaching for equity and justice* (2nd ed., Vol. 1, pp. x–xi). Milwaukee, WI: Rethinking Schools.

Baldwin, J. (1955/1983). *Notes of a native son*. New York: Bantam.

Banks, J. A. (2006). *Race, culture, and education: The selected works of James A. Banks* (pp. 181–190). New York: Routledge.

Bell, D. A. (1992). *Faces at the bottom of the well: The permanence of racism*. New York: Basic Books.

Boutte, G. (1999). *Multicultural education: Raising consciousness.* Atlanta, GA: Wadsworth.

Boutte, G. S. (2002). *Resounding voices: School experiences of people from diverse ethnic backgrounds.* Needham Heights, MA: Allyn & Bacon.

Boutte, G. S., Hopkins, R., & Waklatsi, T. (2008). Perspectives, voices, and worldviews in frequently read children's books. *Early Education and Development, 19*(6), 1–22.

Enriquez, V. (1992). *From colonial to liberatory psychology.* Quezon City, Philippines: University of Philippines Press.

Fanon, F. (1963). *The wretched of the Earth.* New York: Grove.

Featherstone, J. (1995). Letter to young teacher. In W. Ayers (Ed.), *To become a teacher: Making a difference in children's lives* (pp. 11–22). New York: Teachers College.

Fordham, S. (1988). Racelessness as a factor in Black students' school success: Pragmatic strategy or Pyrrhic victory? *Harvard Educational Review, 58*(1), 54–84.

Fordham, S. (1996). *Blacked out: Dilemmas of race, identity, and success at Capital High.* Chicago, IL: The University of Chicago Press.

Freire, P. (1970/1999). *Pedagogy of the oppressed.* New York: Continuum.

Freire, P. (1973/1998). *Education for critical consciousness.* New York: Continuum.

Freire, P. (1985). *The politics of education. Culture, power, and liberation.* Westport, CT: Bergin & Garvey.

Gallard, A. J. (1993). Learning science in multicultural environments. In K. Tobin (Ed.), *The practice of constructivism in science education* (pp. 171–180). Hillsdale, NJ: Lawrence Erlbaum.

Gould, S. J. (1996). *The mismeasure of man.* New York: W. W. Norton.

Greene, M. (1995). *Releasing the imagination. Essays and education, the arts, and social change.* San Francisco, CA: Jossey-Bass.

Halagao, P. E. (2010). Liberating Filipino Americans through decolonizing curriculum. *Race Ethnicity and Education, 13*(4), 495–512.

Hale, J. (2001). *Learning while black. Creating educational excellence for African American children.* Baltimore, MD: Johns Hopkins University Press.

Hardiman, R., Jackson, B., & Griffin, P. (2007). Conceptual foundations for social justice education. In M. Adams, L. A. Bell, & P. Griffin. (Eds.), *Teaching for diversity and social justice* (2nd ed., pp. 35–66). New York: Routledge.

Harro, B. (2000a). The cycle of socialization. In M. Adams, W. J. Blumenfeld, R. Castaneda, H. W. Hackman, M. L. Peters, & X. Zuniga (Eds.), *Readings for diversity and social justice* (pp. 15–21). New York: Routledge.

Harro, B. (2000b). The cycle of liberation. In M. Adams, W. J. Blumenfeld, R. Castaneda, H. W. Hackman, M. L. Peters, & X. Zuniga (Eds.), *Readings for diversity and social justice* (pp. 463–469). New York: Routledge.

Helms, J. E. (2008). *A race is a nice thing to have. A guide to being a White person or understanding the White persons in your life* (2nd ed.). Hanover, MA: Microtraining.

Herrnstein, R. J., & Murray, C. (1994). *The bell curve: Intelligence and class structure in American life.* New York: Free Press.

Howard, G. (2006). *We can't teach what we don't know: White teachers, multiracial schools* (2nd ed.). New York: Teachers College Press.

King, J. E. (2005). *Black Education: A transformative research and action agenda for the 21st century.* Mahwah, NJ: Lawrence Erlbaum.

Koppelman, K. L., & Goodhart, R. L. (2005). *Understanding human differences: Multicultural education for a diverse America.* Boston, MA: Pearson.

Laenui, P. (2000). Process of decolonization. In M. Battiste (Ed.), *Reclaiming indigenous voice and vision* (pp. 150–160). Vancouver, CN: UBC Press.

Lukasiewicz, M. (Producer), & Harvey, E. (Director). (1991/2005). *True colors* [DVD video]. United States: CorVision.

Lynn, M., Jennings, M. E., & Hughes, S. (2013). Critical race pedagogy 2.0: Lessons from Derrick Bell. *Race Ethnicity and Education, 16*(4), 603–628.

Monroe, C. R. (2013). Colorizing educational research: African American life and schooling as an exemplar. *Educational Researcher, 42*(1), 9–19.

Morrison, T. (1997). The official story. Dead man golfing. In T. Morrison & C. Brodsky Lacour (Eds.), *Birth of a nation'hood: Gaze, script, and spectacle in the O. J. Simpson case.* New York: Pantheon.

Perry, T. (2003). Achieving in post-civil rights America: The outline of a theory. In T. Perry, C. Steele, & A. Hilliard III. (Eds.), *Young, gifted, and Black. Promoting high achievement among African-American students* (pp. 87–108). Boston, MA: Beacon Press.

Perry, T., Steele, C., Hilliard, A. III. (2003). *Young, gifted, and Black. Promoting high achievement among African-American students.* Boston, MA: Beacon Press.

Quigley, W. P. (2003). *Ending poverty as we know it: Guaranteeing a right to a job at a living wage.* Philadelphia, PA: Temple University Press.

Salas, K. D., Tenorio, R., Walters, S., & Weiss, D. (2004). *The new teacher book. Finding purpose, balance, and hope during your first years in the classroom.* Milwaukee, WS: Rethinking Schools.

Segura-Mora, A. (2008). What color is beautiful? In A. Pelo (Ed.), *Rethinking early childhood education* (pp. 3–6). Milwaukee, WS: Rethinking Schools.

Shaull, R. (1970/1999). Foreword. In P. Freire, *Pedagogy of the oppressed* (p. 11–16). New York: Continuum.

Strobel, L. M. (2001). *Coming full circle: The process of decolonization among post-1965 Filipino Americans.* Quezon City, Philippines: Giraffe Books.

Watkins, W. H. (2005). Colonial education in Africa: Retrospects and prospects. In J. E. King (Ed.), *Black education. A transformative research and action agenda for the new century* (pp. 117–134). New York: Routledge.

Wolfram, W., & Fasold, F. (1974). *The study of social dialects in American English* (Center for Applied Linguistics). Englewood Cliffs, NJ: Prentice-Hall, Inc.

Woodson, C. G. (1933/1990). *The mis-education of the Negro.* Trenton, NJ: Africa World Press.

3

CRITICAL LITERACY

Providing Mirrors and Windows for African American Students

Proposition 3.1 Not all groups in our society have equal power.

Proposition 3.2 The voices and worldviews of Africans and African Americans need to be substantively included in all types of text.

Proposition 3.3 African American students and their teachers need to be "adept" at "reading" the world and understanding issues of power.

One may be able to read and write and yet may not be critically literate. "To become more fully human is to become ever more critically aware of one's world and in creative control of it" (Hammond, Hoover, & McPhail, 2005, p. 10).

Just as the conceptual framework presented in Chapter 2 is based on the understanding that oppression exists, and, thus, decolonizing and emancipatory pedagogies are needed for the education of African American students, likewise, the strategies used in classrooms must follow this line of reasoning as well. This chapter focuses broadly on critical literacy. Critical literacy is the process of reading texts in an active, reflective manner in order to better understand power, inequality, and injustice in human relationships and contexts. From a critical literacy perspective, texts are defined broadly, including any means through which individuals communicate with one another using the codes and conventions of society, including songs, the Internet, books, magazines, conversations, pictures, movies, television, cartoons, environments, interactions, and other media. Given this definition, educators at all levels and in all content areas use texts and would benefit from developing critical literacy skills. In this chapter, examples and strategies for using critical literacy with books, songs, and videos will be the primary focus. However, a larger focus on *reading the world* and actively studying interactions and subtexts will be important skills for teaching African American and other minoritized students. When African American students are taught to uncritically accept texts and histories that reinforce their marginalized position in society, they easily never learn to question their position (Delpit, 2012).

> Taught the same economics, history, philosophy, literature and religion which have established the present code of morals, the Negro's mind has been brought under the control of his oppressor. The problem of holding the Negro down, therefore, is easily solved. When you control a man's thinking you do not have to worry about his actions.
>
> You do not have to tell him not to stand here or go yonder. He will find his "proper" place and will stay in it. You do not need to send him to the back door. He will go without being told. In fact, if there is no back door, he will cut one for his special benefit. His education makes it necessary.
>
> (Woodson, 1933/1990, p. xiii)

> Critical literacy is not a singular practice that can be implemented according to a set of guidelines. Critical literacy entails a set of beliefs about social justice and ways of reading the world that entail valuing the knowledge that students bring while helping them use literacy to act for change in their communities.
>
> (Compton-Lily, 2004, p. 58)

Therefore, although I provide lots of examples and possibilities, they are not intended to be prescriptive or exhaustive.

Educators who facilitate the development of critical literacy encourage students to interrogate societal issues and institutions in order to critique the structures that serve as norms, as well as to demonstrate how these norms are not experienced by all members of society. Critical literacy refers to a conscious state of mind—of students and educators alike. Readers should keep in mind the key areas of change (knowledge base, dispositions, instruction, and curricular approaches) that were mentioned in Figure 1.1 in Chapter 1. This chapter provides opportunities for readers to reflect on all four areas.

Critical literacy is important for all students; however, for Black students, it takes on a special significance. Because the cultural memories of African Americans have been and are still being obliterated as a part of ongoing cycles of oppression, it is important that the school curriculum be examined, interrogated, and debunked (King, 1992; King & Swartz, 2014). It is, perhaps, surprising to some readers to find out that many myths, inaccuracies, and omissions are included in the curriculum. Reviewing and reflecting on the four dimensions of oppression may help make the manipulations and cultural invasions apparent. Nevertheless, in response to the omnipresent question guiding this book (*And how are the Black children?*), there is a need to begin the healing process necessary for the reinstatement of Black students' humanity and worth through the use of decolonizing, critical, and African American emancipatory pedagogies. To some, it may seem odd to think about teaching as a healing process. However, I ask that readers keep in mind the larger societal and educational landscapes, the ongoing structural inequities, and the devaluation of Black students that were mentioned in Chapters 1 and 2. As noted by Perry, Steele, and Hilliard (2003), schooling for Black children is often a very different cognitive, psychological, and social experience. As we think together about ways to ensure that *the children are well* (and, hence, society is well), the idea of the need for healing as a part of the educational process for Black children makes sense. Healing will begin, not only through telling more complete and truthful stories about history, but also through critically engaging students and educators in the process. In a nutshell, educating African American students is about more than ensuring that they meet the immediate academic requirements for respective grade levels and content areas (though these are certainly short-term goals); it is about sustaining and restoring cultural memories that were omitted or distorted (King, 1992). Critical literacy can be used to ensure that Black students have the tools necessary to be culturally competent in their own culture as well as global cultures. Importantly, it can be used to help interrupt the covert ethnicide that threatens Black children's culture and spirits. Let's start by reflecting on books and literature used in classrooms.

Critical Literacy and Books and Literature

My guess is that most K–12 teachers use books that are recommended in the district or state curricula. These books may not reflect African and African American presence and perspectives. In this chapter on critical literacy, recommendations will be made for substituting, supplanting, and replacing some of the texts that are used in classrooms, as well as providing opportunities for students to research African and African American texts. As part of the ongoing learning

Box 3.1 Pause and Reflect on Books Used in Classroom

Briefly think about the books that you use (including textbooks).

- How, if at all, are African Americans depicted (e.g., positively, negatively, neutrally, infrequently, frequently)?
- To what degree do the books provide opportunities for African American students to learn about their culture in a positive and substantive way?
- To what degree do the books provide opportunities for African American students to learn about other cultural groups in a positive and substantive way?

curves that I hope this book promotes, educators should not worry if their current books do not reflect substantive and informed coverage of African Americans. You are certainly not alone. As Richard Milner reminds educators, start where you are, but don't stay there (Milner, 2010). Remember, we are all teachers and learners. If you happen to be one of those teachers, in the minority, who does have substantive and informed books or textbooks, you are to be commended. Either way, this chapter should provide insights into how critical literacy processes can be used to more effectively teach African American students in all subject areas and grade levels. Remember to extrapolate from the examples provided and tweak for your respective grade levels and topics in a way that makes sense for your respective context.

> Critical literacy is particularly relevant for the members of the teaching profession because curriculum decisions are now being made by politicians, wealthy publishing companies, and others who may have no reputable insights into how children become literate and who have vested interests in the maintenance of existing power arrangements. We of the teaching profession must spot the inaccuracies and distortions that are promoted about the teaching of literacy so that we can work together with parents and children to achieve high levels of literacy necessary for life in this current time.
>
> (Wilson, 2002, p. 143)

The list below describes key assumptions of critical literacy practices for books and textbooks. An important caveat is that books/textbooks alone will not be sufficient for changing the negative social and academic trends faced by Black children in K–12 schools. As will be seen in Chapters 4 and 5, ongoing dialogues with students are also important for interrupting the oppressive cycles that African American students face. However, as reading and story times are highly regarded and pervasive practices in classrooms, homes, and libraries, students of all ages (yes, even young children) can be taught to be critical readers and to identify and clarify ideological perspectives in books.

Assumptions of Critical Literacy

Below are some of the key assumptions of critical literacy:

- Literature is political; it is a vehicle for education and a major means for teaching and indoctrinating youth (Apol, 1998; Boutte, 2002; Boutte, Hopkins, & Waklatsi, 2008). Adults often mediate the meanings of books when reading or introducing them to their students. For example, when teachers like a book, this preference is also conveyed to students in many ways, including enthusiastic readings or discussion. The reverse is also true.

I once heard a ninth-grade English teacher introduce two book choices to her students the following way: "*Of Mice and Men* [Steinbeck, 2009] is a great book. It is also short and easy to read. *The Bluest Eye* [Morrison, 2007] is difficult to read and hard to understand." Given the teacher's commentary, which book do you think most of the ninth-grade students chose? Enough said.

• Issues of voice and power are central to understanding books. Whose voices are heard? Whose are silenced or missing? Whose histories are privileged or disprivileged? The sharing of one's world, experiences, and vision allows people to define themselves.

• Books and textbooks should affirm the culture of all students (Bishop, 2012). That is, they should serve as mirrors in which students can see their lived experiences reflected in a positive way. Books should also serve as windows that allow students to learn about the lives of others. Bishop (2012) also used the metaphor of "sliding glass doors" that allow students to go beyond glimpsing into the lives of others and, indeed, add on new dimensions to their own lives.

• Curriculum standards and skills use books that children can identify with, and these books can be critiqued beyond "the main idea".

• Books should not be presented as neutral and having only one possible reading. Critical literacy allows students and teachers to engage in problem posing—questioning hegemonic assumptions.

• Readers (even children) can become aware of the assumptions of a book. The first step is to identify and clarify the ideological perspectives at work—not to evaluate, discredit, or applaud a writer's ideology, but simply to see what it is (Apol, 1998).

• Books can be read from different positions. Apple (1992) offered four categories:

1. dominant read—accept messages at face value;
2. negotiated read—dispute a particular claim, but accept overall tendencies or interpretations of the text;
3. oppositional read—reject dominant tendencies and interpretations; the reader repositions him- or herself in relation to the text and takes on the position of the oppressed; or
4. a contradiction or combination of the three responses above.

Others note that oppositional reads are particularly important, given the inaccuracies in textbooks and other books (King, 1992; King & Swartz, 2014).

• As published documents, books can be considered by readers as official and legitimate information. "This is the consequence and function of official stories: to impose the will of the dominant culture" (Toni Morrison, as cited in Perry & Delpit, 1998). This implies the need for ongoing stories and books that provide multiple perspectives and counternarratives (intentional, planned, and continuous counters to the dominant narrative).

- Students and teachers can engage in critical literacy practices *and* develop a *love* of reading at the same time. The two goals are not oppositional and can coexist.
- "What makes students powerful is not simply their acquisition of the standard code, but their fluency in content knowledge and their familiarity with many literatures and the language of many different disciplines" (Perry et al., 2003, p. 57).
- "Children have a right to access a wide variety of books and other reading material in classroom, school, and community libraries" (Mason & Schumm, 2003).

Diaspora Literacy

> The education of any people should begin with the people themselves, but Negroes thus trained have been dreaming about the ancients of Europe and about those who have tried to imitate them.
>
> (Woodson, 1933/1990, p. 32)

As noted in the previous section on "Assumptions of Critical Literacy," and as will be noted in Chapter 5 on CRP, the voices and histories of all students should be included in the curriculum. Diaspora literacy is one process for doing so with African American students. Emanating from a Black studies paradigm, diaspora literacy was defined by Dr. Joyce King (1992) as Black people's knowledge of their (collective) story and cultural dispossession. Diaspora literacy relates to people with African origins, wherever they are in the world (e.g., Caribbean, Africa, US, Brazil, Europe). Diaspora literacy assumes that people in the African diaspora have informed and indigenous perspectives that lead to self-recognition, healing, and "re-membering" (King, 1992; King & Swartz, 2014). This process allows Black students to repossess their stories, including cultural identity as "Africa's children" (King, 1992, p. 321). As noted by Wade Nobles (personal communication, October 11, 2013), "The experiences of one generation becomes the history of the next generation, and the history of several generations becomes the traditions of a people."

King (personal communication, September 27, 2014) notes that Blacks should strive for diaspora literacy, "in order to recover our heritage from ideological knowledge, distortion and omission but also so that we can relate to and be useful in the liberation struggle here and on the continent." For example:

> We should not dismiss or over-simplify the ways that Africans participated in slavery, but that is not the beginning of the story and we need a deeper deciphering analysis because this narrative about "Africans selling their own

brothers and sisters" drives a wedge among us and deprives us of a human feeling of connectedness to the Motherland. What it does to white people and others is a whole other issue.

How do we (or might we) recognize the child we are observing as an *African* American, as connected to, and collectively a part of, the circle of African time? How is an entire system of education shaped by the lack of our own memories (or knowledge) of an event:

> like the Middle Passage, one so very traumatic that it forever changed the very time, space, and spirit of humanity in that there would have been no African diaspora, no African Americans without it? . . . But the power and relevance of the memory endures.
>
> (Dilliard, 2012, p. 9)

In K–12 schools, the history of African American students is limited, one-sided, and often inaccurate, and typically begins with slavery. Many African American students experience shame and embarrassment, and many teachers feel discomfort and do not have adequate information for discussing the topic. From a diaspora literacy perspective, it is useful to use a "*Sankofa*" approach (Dilliard, 2012; King, 1992). The word "*Sankofa*," of the Akan people of West Africa, can be translated as "to reach back and get it". *Sankofa* is represented by a mythical bird whose body is facing forward (representing the future) and whose head is looking backward (representing the past; see Figure 3.1). It is a symbol for Africans in the diaspora of keeping a knowledge of history in the forefront of consciousness when teaching current and future generations of African American students. Some may think that a focus on Africa and African history does not address school standards; however, this is not the case. It is included in most school standards; however, many textbooks gloss over the topic, and supplemental information is needed. Additionally, professional development is needed for teachers to build their knowledge bases on the topic as well. The larger lesson to learn is that African Americans are not an ahistorical people; however, the history before enslavement has not been taught in schools.

In 2011, as a part of a Fulbright–Hays Group Projects Abroad program, Dr. Susi Long (University of South Carolina) spent 4 weeks in Sierra Leone, West Africa, on a *Sankofa* project. Sierra Leone was selected because of direct links between Sierra Leonean and Gullah language and culture in the Sea Islands of South Carolina and Georgia (as well as the larger African American community across the US). The knowledge base that connects West African and African American culture, although widely reported in professional literature, is glaringly absent from curricula in schools and preservice teacher education programs. The dimensions of Black culture shown in Box 1.4 in Chapter 1 can also be seen across the African diaspora; however, most African American youth and adults

FIGURE 3.1 *Sankofa* Bird.

have not been taught this. Readers may rightly recognize this as the "divide and conquer," "manipulation," and "cultural invasion" dimensions of oppression discussed in Chapter 2.

The 13 *Sankofa* project participants included 7 K–12 classroom teachers from high need schools, 5 university faculty members who worked in preservice teacher education, and the social studies coordinator from the South Carolina State Department of Education. In Sierra Leone, participants gained firsthand knowledge to support their development of curricula that (a) reflected the rich resources of Sierra Leonean and African American cultural and linguistic heritage, (b) incorporated global and international perspectives, and (c) supported academic achievement for African American students by using the information to teach language arts and social studies standards. There is a website that provides highlights of the trip.[1]

Teaching About Diaspora Literacy in Schools

It should go without saying that information on history should be filtered through critical literacy lenses: not limited to Black History Month, but integrated throughout the year, along with other relevant topics. Africa has contributed as much to humankind as Europe has, and early civilization of the Mediterranean world was influenced by Africa (Woodson, 1933/1990). As a society, we will not be thoroughly educated until we learn as much about Africans as is known about other people. Most African American students go to school to learn about the history of other people, conceivably so that they can go out and imitate them, rather than to provide humanity with a vision of something new (Woodson, 1933/1990). Instead, historical accounts should provide information and critique of various historical areas such as:

1. African history (particularly West African countries where African Americans came from): Teach about the ancient African empires of Mali, Ghana, and Songhay.
2. African science: Teach that the "ancient Africans of the interior knew sufficient science to concoct poisons for arrowheads, to mix durable colors for paintings, to extract metals from nature and refine them for development in the industrial arts. Teach students about the chemistry in the method of Egyptian embalming which was the product of the mixed breeds of Northern Africa, now known in the modern world as 'colored people'" (Woodson, 1933/1990, pp. 18–19).
3. African arts: Show the influence of African art on the history of Greece, Carthage, and Rome (Woodson, 1933/1990).
4. Enslavement (particular attention should be paid to slave narratives and the resistance of African people who were enslaved): African American students can be proud of our legacy of perseverance, agency, and strength. There is no other group in history that has been subjected to such harsh atrocities as slavery for nearly three centuries and yet has excelled in so many areas.
5. Post-enslavement: Teach about Reconstruction and Jim Crow—in the US, Canada, and the Caribbean, as there are many parallels.
6. Desegregation and resegregation in the US and the New Jim Crow.

During every era, it would be interesting to critically examine legal cases and constitutional manipulations and events (e.g., the 13th, 14th, and 15th Amendments to the Constitution; Dred Scott; *Plessey v Ferguson*; *Brown v Board of Topeka*; the three-fifths compromise; the one-drop rule).

A few general tips for teaching about African and African American history are provided below (Boutte & Strickland, 2008).

1. Use primary and secondary documents when possible.
2. Use role-play.
3. Make information relevant to students.
4. Invite resource people (e.g., African griots and historians, grandparents).
5. Use videos and audiotapes when possible.
6. Make connections between African cultures and African American culture.
7. Defy myths and cultural invasion about "sub-Saharan" African by providing accurate information.

8. Let students interact with historical figures through letter writing, drawing, dialogue poems, spoken word, and role-play. However, caution should be exercised in role assignments/selections when dealing with topics such as slavery. Tips for teaching about the enslavement of African people are presented in the next section.

Teaching About the Enslavement of African People

Discussing the enslavement of African people is difficult for many K–12 teachers. Some prefer topics that they perceive as being less sensitive. Nevertheless, from a critical literacy point of view, teachers should not gloss over difficult issues. Issues should be handled sensitively, and there are times when educators will be unsure or uncertain as to what to do. If we accept that we are both teachers and learners, then we can develop comfort around not being perceived as omnipotent. In the meantime, students will appreciate your sincere attempts. Several tips and examples are provided below. As with most lists provided in this book, this one is not intended to be exhaustive, and, congruent with the dynamic nature of knowledge, the recommendations below may be altered over time.

1. It is important to spend a proportionate time on life before slavery, even if the textbook does not. Here, you may want to assign students to research life in Africa before enslavement. They will need specific guidelines directing them to look for examples of language use, cultural values, developments/ technology, economic system, and the like. The point is that you do not want to reify stereotypes about Africa being undeveloped jungle and other negative stereotypes. African literacy began in the Sahara more than 5,000 years ago (e.g., alphabet used by Egyptians, Meroites, Phoenicians, and Ethiopians). Likewise, universities existed in West Africa (e.g., Sankore University in Timbuktu). Writing on paper is only one sign and symbol means of communication in classical African civilization. Other forms of communication in Africa include(d) woven designs, shapes and designs of Ashanti gold weights, hair braids, architecture, and drum sounds. Historians in Africa also memorized the histories of their "nations" and people for future recitation.
2. Often, textbooks are incomplete and may require supplemental readings. A sample of books is listed below.

   Books for younger students (preschool—fifth grades) include:

   – Ellis, V. F. (1989). *Afro-bets First Book About Africa*. Orange, NJ: Just Us Books.
   As with all books, this invites critiques. More will be said about this later. There is one part of the book that talks about Africans selling slaves, which will need to be closely critiqued, and teachers will need to research this in order to tell the story from African perspectives (King, 1992).

Books for older students (middle/high school):

- Achebe, C. (1994). *Things Fall Apart*. New York: Anchor Books.
- McKissack, P., & McKissack, F. (1994). *The Royal Kingdoms of Ghana, Mali, and Songhay. Life in Medieval Africa*. New York: Henry Holt.

Books that can be used across age groups:

- Haskins, J., & Benson, K. (1998). *African Beginnings*. New York: Lothrop, Lee & Shepard.
- Thompson, C. (1998). *African Civilizations. The Asante Kingdom*. New York: Franklin Watts.

3. An important part of discussing slavery is to *name* the oppression and the oppressors. Hence, the terminology used is key. Instead of using the term, "slave," the term "enslaved Africans" or "enslaved people" should be used. "Slave" connotes objectification and does not capture the humanity of the person. Likewise, instead of the term "Trans-Atlantic slave trade," it should be referred to as the "European enslavement of Africans." Focusing on the ocean (traveling across the Atlantic) does not name the perpetrators.

4. "If history is to have value beyond a literary form of collecting antiques, it must provide a guide to action. For those struggling against oppression and for justice, history must appraise the past to suggest political, social, and economic strategies for the present and future. Like schooling, history, too, is inescapably political" (Butchart, 1988, p. 333). Hence, discussion of enslavement should include a critical discussion and can even be connected to various types of slavery in the world today and what can be done. Delpit (2012) reports visiting a 10th-grade classroom and a discussion that included house slavery, skilled slavery, urban slavery, and mental slavery.

5. This topic presents a chance to let the students research some of the slave castles on the west coast of Africa. In conjunction with this assignment, students can research the culture of the people from those areas prior to Europeans' enslavement of the people.

6. Include a discussion on the impact of African culture on the development of America. "The United States of America would not exist were it not for the labor of enslaved Africans" (Delpit, 2012, p. 187). Much of American food, music, literature, art, inventions, and agriculture has been influenced by Africans (Delpit, 2012).

7. Consider the impact of African culture on African American culture. There is a need to unite, particularly as systemic efforts have served to divide the two groups.

8. Discuss enslavement of other groups as well, but be sure to point out differences. For example, the cruel and sustained form of chattel slavery encountered by Africans is unparalleled in the world.

9. Carefully research the topic—you should do this for all topics.

10. African American history should not center on slavery, but should focus on other issues as well.

11. Slavery can be discussed within the context of other migration patterns; however, distinctions should be made between voluntary and involuntary/ forceful entries into the US. This also lends itself to discussions regarding the oppressive treatment of other people of color, such as Native and Mexican Americans.

12. Neither Whites nor Blacks should be portrayed as being monolithic.

13. Slavery discussions need to include a deconstruction of typical historical accounts and also address the moral/immoral issues of slavery.

14. Attention should be given to agency among slaves, such as in uprisings, revolts, and insurrections (e.g., Denmark Vesey, Nat Turner). Organizational skills used by people in the Underground Railroad should also be highlighted (e.g., Harriet Tubman successfully leading 300 slaves to freedom; spirituals,[2] quilts, other symbols, and strategic tactics used such as following the North Star and the Big Dipper/Drinking Gourd). A discussion of abolitionists (White, e.g., John Brown, and Black) is important.

15. Capture the humanity of Africans who were enslaved. For example, Nathaniel Smith (2009), an English teacher who taught 10th–12th graders in a high school in Pennsylvania, used photos from 1863 taken around the time of emancipation that Frederick Douglas hoped to use as part of an anti-slavery effort to educate people against slavery. Nathaniel Smith, the teacher, is a White man, who taught in a majority White school (98 percent White; 98 percent middle or upper socioeconomic status) (adapted from Smith, 2014). His justification for studying slavery and issues of race was that it was necessary to understand the context of the literature that they would read (a unit on slave narratives and another on the Harlem Renaissance). Students watched videos such as a PBS film: *Race, The Power of an Illusion*.[3] His curricular premise was that people can discover and address their own racism more effectively when they understand that all racial categories are political and socially constructed lines. Using a collection of photographs of newly emancipated Black people that Frederick Douglass wanted to use for his anti-slavery slogan,[4] Mr. Smith gave each student a photograph and gave them 3 minutes to write a description of their photo and to describe how it may have been used in the anti-slavery campaign. Students were to come up with a slogan for their photos. Mr. Smith did not mention the race of the people in the photos and cut off the captions, except for the people's names. Interesting and generative dialogue occurred, as Mr. Smith's students, who had professed to being colorblind, readily described the photos in racial terms. Such activities can lead to rich discussions of the humanity of people who were enslaved.

16. Include the voices of enslaved people through the use of slave narratives,[5] documents, and literature (King, 1992). Two sample books are listed below:

- Hurmence, B. (1984). *My Folks Don't Want Me to Talk About Slavery.* Winston-Salem, NC: John F. Blair (contains 21 oral histories of former North Carolina people who were enslaved).
- Hurmence, B. (1989). *Before Freedom. When I Just Can Remember.* Winston-Salem, NC: John F. Blair (contains 27 oral histories of former South Carolina people who were enslaved).

17. Always consult parents and administrators regarding what you are teaching. This will head off any controversies, as discussed later in this chapter.
18. Consider using a collection of texts that approach the issues from several perspectives. The importance of multiple perspectives will be discussed later. A list of books that make up a text set on representing different perspectives on enslavement is below. These books can be used for elementary-, middle-, and high-school students. Some discretion is advised in terms of how material is presented, and none of the books should be presented in isolation from other activities listed above. Many will need to be revisited several times.

- Chbosky, S. (1988). *Who Owns the Sun?* Kansas City, MS: Landmark Editions. This was written by a 14-year-old White female to point out the inhumanity of slavery. A Black son seeking insight from his father poses the question, "Who owns the sun?" (He also inquires about who owns the sky, flowers, etc., to which the father explains that the world is full of beautiful things that cannot be owned, but loved and appreciated by everyone. This prompts the son to ask how his father (and he—both enslaved people) can be owned. This story is a strong commentary on the immorality of slavery. That it was written by a White youth makes the point that the horrors of slavery affect the humanity of all of us.
- Erickson, P. (1977). *Daily Life on a Southern Plantation 1853.* New York: Lodestar Books. A detailed portrait of a cotton plantation in the South before the Civil War, it is based on a real plantation home in Louisiana and contains more than 130 original color photographs of artifacts and interiors from the "Big House" and slave quarters. It presents the daily life of the plantation owners and their enslaved Africans. It also has a timeline, glossary, and list of places to visit. The White author wrote the book to present a "factual" account of life on a plantation. Using critical skills presented below, readers will see that the book presents a sanitized version of events. For example, a comparison of the slave auction in this book with the one in the Lester text will show major differences. The Erickson text shows an orderly auction that depicts Black people (light-skinned, for the most part), fully dressed (shoes too), standing together with their families. The Lester book shows enslaved Africans half-dressed, dark-skinned, and in manacles. Likewise, the Erickson book shows the manacles in a picture by themselves; the Lester book shows

them on people—quite different effects. As noted by Apol (1998), both stories are needed to tell a comprehensive story from multiple perspectives.

- Lester, J. (1998). *From Slave Ship to Freedom Road*. New York: Dial Books. This uses interactive text and beautiful illustrations to point out both the horrors and triumphs of enslaved people. It is written by the acclaimed African American author Julius Lester, who intentionally seeks to involves readers emotionally in the book.
- Ringgold, F. (1991). *The Invisible Princess*. New York: Dragonfly Books. This is a fairy tale, written by a Black, female author, that expresses the enslaved Africans' desires for peace, freedom, and love.
- Thomas, V. M. (2001). *No Man Can Hinder Me. The Journey From Slavery to Emancipation Through Song*. New York: Crown. This contains an audio CD that includes 18 spirituals, including songs from Africa and the Middle Passage.

Biographies may also be used (and video documentaries). Sample biographies include:

- Douglass, F. (1995). *The Life of Frederick Douglass*. Mineola, NY: Dover.
- Krass, P. (1988). *Sojourner Truth. Antislavery Activist*. New York: Chelsea House.
- McGovern, A. (1965). *Runaway Slave. The Story of Harriet Tubman*. New York: Scholastic.

Civil War and Reconstruction Era

Readers may be surprised to know the lengths that Whites went through to disable Black communities. Most people are familiar with the lynching, but may not know about the systematic burning down of Black schoolhouses and direct violations of constitutional rights (Butchart, 1988, 2010). Yet, through it all, Blacks persevered, hoped, and thrived. As Anderson (2007) notes, Black have overcome larger "gaps" than the current "achievement gap," from dramatically increased literacy rates to high-school graduation rates, and these stories need to be told. Readers who desire additional information should see Anderson (2007) and Butchart (1988, 2010).

The Black National anthem, "Lift Every Voice and Sing," was written during this period. It is also called "The Negro National Hymn," "The Negro National Anthem," "The Black National Anthem," and "The African-American National Anthem." It was written as a poem by James Weldon Johnson (1871–1938) and then set to music by his brother, John Rosamond Johnson (1873–1954), in 1900. It is an uplifting and hopeful anthem.[6]

Civil Rights Era

When capturing the essence of the Civil Rights era, it is important to show grassroots efforts and organization within Black communities, churches, universities, and social groups. Typically, many of the stories told focus on one or two people (e.g., Dr. Martin Luther King and Mrs. Rosa Parks). Focusing on individuals undermines the collective struggles that occurred. Youth were very active and should be studied. Readers should take caution not to glorify Dr. King while vilifying activist groups such as the Black Panthers or people such as Malcolm X and Angela Davis. In-depth study will reveal that most leaders had a common goal of Black liberation. Additionally, when Dr. King is studied, popularly used, sanitized versions of King's work undermine his critical messages for liberation. One such message is King's famous, "Birth of a New Nation Speech."[7]

Many teachers find it useful to use video series such as *The Eyes on the Prize*. Numerous biographies that show children on the frontline of struggling for civil rights and equal schooling exist (e.g., Ruby Bridges). The liberation songs used during the Civil Rights Movement capture the spirit of determination and hope and should be studied.

- Carson, C., Garrow, D. J., Gill, G., Harding, V., & Hine, D. C. (1991). *Eyes on the Prize. Civil Rights Reader. Documents, Speeches, and Firsthand Accounts From the Black Freedom Struggle. 1954–1990*. New York: Penguin Books.
- Coleman, E. (1996). *White Socks Only*. Morton Grove, IL: Albert Whitman.
- Coles, R. (2010). *The Story of Ruby Bridges*. New York: Scholastic.
- Ringgold, F. (1999). *If a Bus Could Talk. The Story of Rosa Parks*. New York: Aladdin.
- Welch, C. A. (2001). *Children of the Civil Rights Era. 1950s to 1960s*. Minneapolis, MN: Carolrhoda.

Contemporary Life in the US and in the African Diaspora

To round out discussions on African and African American history, it is important to spend time discussing contemporary issues as well, so that achievements can be illuminated. An example will be presented later of a teacher, Jennifer Strickland, who has conversations with her students about current events in Black communities. Efforts to show counternarratives are important. For example, when studying countries in Africa, a balance of focus should be placed on the urban and rural (village) areas. This holds true for the US and elsewhere in the diaspora. Three classroom examples of teachers engaging in diaspora literacy are provided below. All three teachers took my course on "Educating African American Students" (in different classes over the years). Much of the course's content is included in this book. At the same time, each of them came with a sincere desire (disposition) to effectively teach African American students, and they were all open to learning.

Classroom Examples

Before sharing the examples, let me make a few comments about teaching diaspora literacy in racially integrated school contexts. Although the focus of this book is on Black students, as humans, we are all interconnected. So, although diaspora literacy is especially important and takes on special significance for African American students, White students benefit from a truthful curriculum as well. Just as African American students need mirrors and windows, so too do White students and other CLD students. Also of concern is how these topics are handled in majority White settings in which there are African American students and when misconceptions and inaccurate information is being taught about Black history— or when Black history is not taught at all. Although I note the race of each teacher in this and other chapters, it is important to remember that one of the guidelines for processing information in this book is to focus on what is useful to you. Knowing the danger of colorblindness and its role in oppressive cycles (that's another conversation, for another time), I name the races of the teachers. However, as will be discussed in Chapter 5, the salient features to observe are the teachers' actions, thoughts, and the strategies that they are using.

Classroom Example: Teaching About Africa and the Enslavement of African People

Jennifer Strickland, a White kindergarten teacher,[8] has taught about African history and kings and queens to her students (Boutte & Strickland, 2008).[9] Conventional *wisdom* regarding what young children are capable of processing makes many early childhood teachers understandably leery about venturing into historical topics. Most teachers of young children in U.S. schools believe in focusing on the *here and now*. Ironically, most early childhood teachers feel comfortable with children routinely acting out historical themes in fantasy play (e.g., Cinderella) or children's endless fascination with dinosaurs, but have difficulty conceptualizing that children can do the same with real events.

Notwithstanding the controversial nature of teaching historical information to young children, Mrs. Strickland felt compelled to introduce the topic and follow up on themes that interested the children. As she explained to a White father who complained about her teaching African and Africa American history, "most African American children will probably never learn anything about their history in school." So, for Mrs. Strickland, finding a way to teach about African and African American history became a compelling ethical quest.

Mrs. Strickland realized that her challenges would be making the topic relevant to the children and explaining what she was doing to the other kindergarten teachers. To present information to the children, Mrs. Strickland built upon the African American oral tradition of storytelling (Boykin, 1994; Hilliard, 2005) to relay stories about kings and queens in Africa and to teach about slavery. She also integrated dramatic play, concrete artifacts, and books. A professor who had been to Africa several times also visited the class as a resource person and provided artifacts that were used to set up a classroom African museum (see Figure 3.2).

Mrs. Strickland spent several weeks teaching students about aspects of Africa in an effort to deconstruct some of the common misconceptions and to provide children with information about a continent that is seldom examined beyond the surface level in most schools. This task becomes more difficult when one is trying to teach kindergartners in particular about worlds that are geographically and historically beyond their own. To make the lessons more concrete, Mrs. Strickland presented the class with a large map of Africa and created a song to teach them the names of African countries (see Figure 3.3). Her kindergartners quickly and eagerly learned the song and later presented it at an assembly. She introduced several picture books to demonstrate and discuss historical and contemporary points. After reading a book about real African princesses, the children could readily name the princesses. Following one child's suggestion, Mrs. Strickland copied pictures of the princesses and posted them on the large map of Africa, so that children could remember where each was from. African princes were also discussed, and children enjoyed role-play. In discussions with Mrs. Strickland about

FIGURE 3.2 African Artifacts.

FIGURE 3.3   Maps of Africa.

her activities, she said that she wanted "our children" (as she frequently refers to African American children)[10] to know that their history did not begin with slavery and provided a counternarrative to the prevailing images of only White kings and queens. Below is a list of books that she read on princesses.

- Hansen, J. (2004). *The Amazing Lives of Africa's Royal Women*. New York: Jump at the Sun.
- Myers, W. D. (1999). *At Her Majesty's Request: An African Princess in Victorian England*. New York: Scholastic.
- Price, L., & Dillion, D. (1990). *Aida*. New York: Gulliver.
- Steptoe, J. (1987). *Mufaro's Beautiful Daughters. An African Tale*. New York: Lothrop, Lee & Shepard.

The students became quite involved with the idea of being kings and queens. Mrs. Strickland provided different styles of Kente cloth for the students to use during dramatic play. Learning that African kings and queens had great rule over their land stimulated children to act out their interpretations of what life was like in ancient Africa.

Overall, an important goal for Mrs. Strickland was to present powerful counternarratives to pervasive messages that do not value and build on the wisdom and values found in Black communities. *Counternarratives* are continuous and planned actions to counter the dominant ideology regarding the capacities of Africans (Perry et al., 2003). As published works are considered to be "legitimate and official knowledge" in society (Apple, 1992), Mrs. Strickland's literature selections served as a formal way of validating aspects of Black culture. The typical invisibility of Black perspectives and storylines in school literature collections undermines the importance and centrality of Black worldviews (Boutte, 2002; Boutte & Hill, 2006). Counternarratives are crucial because of the prevailing ideologies and negative stereotypes about African Americans, in society, in general, in the media, and in the curriculum.

Although the school in which Mrs. Strickland teaches is 96 percent African American, midway through the unit, a parent of the only European American child in her classroom expressed concern about what he considered to be an overemphasis on Black history. He wanted to know when Mrs. Strickland would teach about *White* history. Diplomatically noting that the core of the elementary-, middle-, and high-school curriculum was White culture, Mrs. Strickland explained that his daughter and the other students were learning information that would likely not be taught for the rest of their school careers. She pointed out that his daughter was very interested in the topic and had been the one who recommended that they add pictures of the princesses to the map, next to the countries of origin. Elaborating further, Mrs. Strickland added that his daughter and the rest of the students were learning about cultures beyond their own (e.g., African cultures). She invited the parent to visit the class at any time (which he did), and, in the end, Mrs. Strickland formed an ally instead of an opponent. Although Mrs. Strickland admitted to being a bit nervous about the conversation, her conviction that she should extend the current curriculum beyond the mere illusion of inclusion of African peoples and perspectives outweighed her anxiety.

As part of the study of African kings and queens, the children brought up the fact that Blacks had been enslaved. Following, their lead, Mrs. Strickland ventured into the study of slavery, a complex and provocative topic. Notifying parents and administrators of her intent, Mrs. Strickland wanted children to leave with a balanced view of the topic. While conceptualizing her unit on slavery, Mrs. Strickland consulted guidelines for teaching about slavery and historical events from a lecture in the "Educating African American Students" course that I taught.

Sometimes, physical or tangible illustrations are more meaningful to children; hence, they role-played the journey across the Atlantic during the Middle Passage and were given the opportunity to have string wrapped around them so that they could barely move. The most astounding aspect of the unit was that the students did not want the study to end, although it had gone on for several weeks. Learning about Africa and African history had impacted their lives to the point that they were willing and able to teach others (including their parents) about kings and queens who were not in the bedtime stories but in history books. When Mrs. Strickland asked the students to tell her one new fact that they had learned about Africa that they thought was important for others to know, a Hispanic male stated, "I learned that Europeans brought Africans to America," and an African American female said, "I learned that African women sometimes cut their hair to keep bugs out." Their words are infectious, but their illustrations are resonating. To see 5-year-olds drawing pictures of Africans chained together on a ship headed for America is breathtaking, but to know that it was tempered with knowledge of African kingdoms before and accomplishments of African Americans after-wards was satisfying. As the comparison and contrast of slavery times and today in Figure 3.4 illustrates, children developed a rudimentary understanding of injustices perpetrated during slavery. Overall, Mrs. Strickland felt that she was successful in reinforcing understanding of, and pride in, African and American cultures. We can only hope that her responsive teaching will help to buffer the children throughout their school experiences, as that of other early childhood teachers has done (Paley, 2000; Pedersen, Faucher, & Eaton, 1978).

Mrs. Strickland and the children frequently, almost daily, looked at the world map or globe and reviewed the information that they had already covered, but then went on to explore new aspects of African culture and the cultures that surrounded them (Figure 3.3). Although early childhood educators typically think of maps as too abstract for young children, and we generally agree if they are used in isolation, the context and relevance of the surrounding activities make all the difference.

Finally, for standards-conscious educators, the curriculum standards that were addressed during the activities are listed below. The fact that the standards were

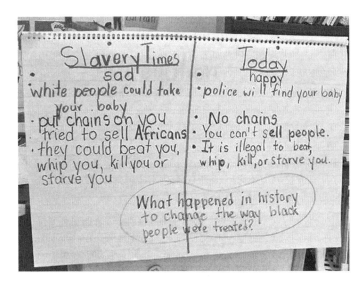

FIGURE 3.4 Kindergartners' Comparison of Slavery.

more or less post hoc versus narrowly leading our work reiterates the notion that teachers who teach broadly and with depth will cover the standards and more. Importantly, children will learn and be critically engaged.[11]

- Social studies:
    - The student will compare the daily lives of children and their families in the US in the past and today.
    - The student will demonstrate an understanding of key American figures and symbols.
    - The student will demonstrate an understanding of his/her surroundings.
    - The student will demonstrate an understanding of different businesses in the community and the idea of work.
- Science:
    - The student will address all of the inquiry process skills required of kindergarten students. Those skills are the following: (1.) observation, (2.) classification, (3.) measurement, and (4.) communication.
- Language arts:
    - Every reading goal: The student will draw upon a variety of strategies to comprehend, interpret, analyze, and evaluate what he or she reads.
    - Every writing goal: The student will write for different audiences and purposes.

- Every communication goal: The student will recognize, demonstrate, and analyze the qualities of effective communication.
- Every research goal: The student will access and use information from a variety of appropriately selected sources to extend his or her knowledge.

Below is a classroom example that reflects a White, high-school teacher's concern with some of the curriculum materials on the Civil War.

Classroom Example: Interrupting Negative and Incomplete Curricular Stereotypes of Black People

Jeffrey Eargle, a White male teacher, taught in a small (727 students), rural high school in South Carolina. Of the students, 66 percent were White, 28 percent were African American, and 6 percent were Hispanic. Additionally, 42 percent of the students were eligible for free or reduced-price lunch. Teaching 11th-grade U.S. history in South Carolina, Mr. Eargle began a unit on the Civil War in late November, using his district's pacing guide based on the chronology of the state standards. To introduce the unit, students had an assignment to complete a graphic organizer of the major themes of the war, as found in the Civil War episode of *America: The Story of Us*, the History Channel's 10-part series on U.S. history. Though not a perfect instructional tool, the series served well as an introduction to a unit, had quality special effects and visuals that grasped students' attention, and was generally aligned with the South Carolina state standards. The 45-minute episode opened with a segment on the horrors of combat resulting from technological advances such as the Minié ball, proceeded to a segment on Lincoln's election, leadership, and use of the telegraph to conduct the war, and then came to a segment on battlefield medicine.

One day, as the film played, Mr. Eargle was sitting in the back of the classroom next to Ben, an African American male student. About 25 minutes into the episode, Ben leaned over and whispered, "Mr. Eargle, this is about the Civil War, right?" "Yes, Ben," responded Mr. Eargle.

Ben, looking at him with an expression that conveyed amusement and confusion, asked, "Then where are the Black people?" Mr. Eargle gave Ben an approving nod and a smile, conveying pleasure in Ben's critique of the episode. Knowing that the episode ended with a segment on the Emancipation Proclamation and all-Black army regiments, Mr. Eargle looked a Ben and said, "Wait about five minutes and they'll show up." Ben, detecting that Mr. Eargle understood the absurdity of excluding African Americans for such an extended length of time in a Civil War documentary, responded with a smile.

Ben was a typical teenager. He worked hard when he found relevance in the material, content, and skills being learned. He did not work hard when he did not see relevance. He was deemed a "tough one to teach" by some in the school, although Mr. Eargle never had a problem with him. In fact, Ben and Mr. Eargle would often chat in the hall before class, when typically Ben would question Mr. Eargle regarding whether he had seen this movie or watched that game. Ben, like all children, wanted to know that his teachers cared about him, and he desired to see himself in the subjects he studied.

As a social studies teacher, Mr. Eargle is concerned about how African Americans are portrayed in the South Carolina social studies standards. This is especially a concern considering that South Carolina's U.S. history standards are held in high esteem nationally for their substance and rigor (Stern & Stern, 2011), and yet the African American pass rates on the U.S. history end-of-course exam are nearly half those of White students.

This experience led Mr. Eargle to investigate how state standards included master narratives of slavery and African Americans prior to the Civil War. Using a critical textbook analysis approach, he examined the 2011 South Carolina social studies academic standards support document for the 11th-grade "United States History and the Constitution" course (South Carolina Department of Education, 2012). The findings indicated that the support document did not offer a complete narrative of slavery and African Americans, perpetuated a negative image of African Americans, excluded themes of African American heroism, and maintained myths related to slavery.

Classroom Example: Teaching About Contemporary Issues in Africa

Kayla Hostetler teaches high-school English in a small, rural town in the South. The school comprises students from several small towns and has approximately 250 students (about 53 percent African American; 39 percent White; 7 percent Hispanic; and less than 1 percent other ethnicities). Most of the students (77 percent) receive free or reduced-price lunch.

Moving from a small, northern town of about 800 people to a smaller southern town with fewer than 250 people was a culture shock for Mrs. Hostetler, a White woman from Pennsylvania. Quickly, she developed a relationship with her students by engaging in dialogue with them and positioning herself as a learner. She consulted the academic literature to figure out ways to make her teaching and curriculum more relevant. For example, standards required her to teach poetry; therefore, she incorporated a Slam Poetry/Poetry Out Loud unit. Importantly, while adding additional speaking opportunities and building on orality, which is a part of Black culture, she did not lessen the writing requirements for her students and held high expectations of them. She surveyed the students to find out what type of music they liked and then used the songs within her curriculum. She also spent time attending sporting events, churches, and other social gatherings that her students frequented, so that they would know that she supported them outside the classroom, and that they were a part of her community/family. She helped students learn to code-switch between AAL and Standard English (SE) using contrastive analysis (more on this in Chapter 4). She also developed a wonderful relationship with the students' parents. She integrated African American and African literature into the classroom. One of the books that she used was *A Long Way Gone*, which chronicles the experiences of a child soldier in Sierra Leone.

Before reading this novel, students studied human rights and the Universal Declaration of Human Rights. They read several poems by African authors. Mrs. Hostetler noted that it was very difficult to find short stories that had a positive outlook. She used African myths and folktales. When they read the novel, *A Long Way Gone*, she took time to focus on positive details in the book, not just the negatives. For example, they studied the stories Ishmael shares from his culture (Bro Spider, Pig story, etc.), the importance of his family, his name-giving ceremony, and other cultural examples. The class also discussed the hope and determination that the main character still held, despite his experiences as a child soldier. The students' reactions to the novel varied, but many students shared that they could connect to Ishmael. They also expressed that, if Ishmael could come back from being a soldier and be successful, then they too could get out of some difficult situations and be successful.

Seeking firsthand accounts of African experiences, Mrs. Hostetler also invited a speaker from Rwanda, who spoke about her childhood before and after the war. One of the teachers at Mrs. Hostetler's school was born in Sierra Leone and visited her class to share pictures and stories of her childhood and trips back to Sierra Leone. Her love for her country was obvious to the students. The teacher from Sierra Leone provided examples of traditions as well as contemporary connections.

Summary Comments About Diaspora Literacy

I spent half of my 1st- through 12th-grade school career in segregated schools. Each week, we were shown films on Black heroes and heroines. At the time, I did not realize the value of this education or that this was a part of diaspora literacy. It instilled in me a sense of love of Black people and gave me much to be proud of. This is sorely missing in schools today.

Liberation Literature

> For the slaves, literacy was more than a symbol of freedom, it was freedom.
> (Perry et al., 2003, p. 13)

> Liberation is accomplished, in part, by overcoming the shackles of illiteracy.
> (O'Neil, as cited in Hammond et al., 2005, p. 10)

Building on diaspora literacy approaches and consideration, literature used in the classroom should be liberatory. Many of the books that Mrs. Strickland used can be classified as liberation literature. Liberation literature includes books that portray various aspects of Black culture allowing African American students to have a mirror of, and window into, social, cultural, and historical awareness, with their culture at the center, not as an additive or referent, but as worthy of serving as curriculum in its own right, qualifies as liberation literature.

1. It celebrates the strengths of the Black family as a cultural institution and vehicle for survival.
2. It bears witness to Black people's determined struggle for freedom, equality, and dignity.
3. It nurtures the souls of Black students by reflecting back to them, both visually and verbally, the beauty and competencies that we, as adults, see in them.
4. It situates itself, through its language and its content, within African American literary and cultural contexts.
5. It honors the tradition of story as a way of teaching and as a way of knowing (Bishop, 2007, p. 273).

A sampling of liberation literature from the Children's Defense Fund Freedom Schools Curriculum is presented below.[12]

Elementary Level

*   *Grandpa, Is Everything Black Bad?* by Sandy Lynne Holman (The Culture CO-OP, 1998–2000);
*   *Cornrows*, by Camille Yarbrough (Coward, McCann & Geoghegan, 1979);
*   *Cracking the Wall: The Struggle of the Little Rock Nine*, by Eileen Yarbrough (Lerner Publishing Group, 1997);
*   *Dizzy*, by Jonah Winter (Arthur A. Levine Books, 2006);
*   *Everybody Cooks Rice*, by Norah Dooley (Carolrhoda Books, 1991);
*   *Follow the Drinking Gourd*, by Jeannette Winter (Knopf, 1988);
*   *Happy Birthday, Jamela!* by Niki Daly (Frances Lincoln, 2006);
*   *Imani's Music*, by Sheron Williams (Atheneum Books for Young Readers, 2002);
*   *Jamaica Louise James*, by Amy Hest (Sagebrush Education Resources, 1997);
*   *Kid Caramel Private Investigator: Case of the Missing Ankh*, by Dwayne J. Ferguson (Just Us Books, 1997);
*   *Ebony Sea*, by Irene Smalls (Longmeadow Press, 1996);
*   *Kenya's Word*, by Linda Trice (Charlesbridge, 2006);
*   *Ma Dear's Aprons*, by Patricia C. McKissack (Atheneum Books for Young Readers, 1997);
*   *Read For Me, Mama*, by Vashanti Rahaman (Boyds Mills Press, 1997);
*   *Sienna's Scrapbook: Our African American Heritage Trip*, by Toni Trent Parker (Chronicle Books, 2005);

- *Alvin Ailey*, by Andrea Davis Pinkney (Hyperion Paperbacks for Children, 1995);
- *The Bus Ride*, by William Miller (Lee & Low Books, 1998);
- *Destiny's Gift*, by Natasha Anastasia Tarpley (Lee & Low Books, 2004);
- *Gettin' Through Thursday*, by Melrose Cooper (Lee & Low Books, 2000);
- *Goodnight, Daddy*, by Angela Seward (Morning Glory Press, 2000);
- *Jazzy Miz Mozetta*, by Brenda C. Roberts (Farrar Straus Giroux, 2004);
- *Sélavi, That is Life: A Haitian Story of Hope*, by Youme (Cinco Puntos Press, 2004);
- *The Spider Weaver: A Legend of Kente Cloth*, by Margaret Musgrove (Scholastic, 2001);
- *Freedom School, Yes!* by Amy Littlesugar (Philomel Books, 2001).

Middle-/High-School Level

- *We Beat the Street: How a Friendship Pact Led to Success*, by Drs. Sampson Davis, George Jenkins, and Rameck Hunt, with Sharon M. Draper (Dutton Children's Books, 2005);
- *A Raisin in the Sun*, by Lorraine Hansberry (Holt, Rinehart, & Winston, 2000);
- *The Skin I'm In*, by Sharon Flake (Jump at the Sun/Hyperion Paperbacks for Children, 1998);
- *Slam!* by Walter Dean Myers (Scholastic, 1998);
- *The Way a Door Closes*, by Hope Anita Smith (Macmillan, 2003);
- *Copper Sun*, by Sharon M. Draper (Simon and Schuster, 2006);
- *The Diary of LaToya Hunter: My First Year in Junior High*, by LaToya Hunter (Vintage Books, 1993);
- *Think Big*, by Ben Carson (Zondervan, 2005);
- *I Thought My Soul Would Rise and Fly*, by Joyce Hansen (Scholastic, 2003);
- *Miracle's Boys*, by Jacqueline Woodson (Penguin, 2000);
- *Bud, Not Buddy*, by Christopher Paul Curtis (Delacorte Press, 1999);
- *Double Dutch*, by Sharon M. Draper (Atheneum Books for Young Readers, 2002);
- *Getting Away with Murder: The True Story of the Emmett Till Case*, by Chris Crowe (Phyllis Fogelman Books, 2003).

(Jackson & Boutte, 2009, p. 113)

Biographies and literature representing different areas of students' interests (e.g., engineering, art) can be used as liberation literature. Both contemporary and historical figures and both genders should be considered. Students can and should have opportunities to tell their own stories and those of their families and communities as well. These stories can be told using a variety of genres and styles, in a way that makes sense to the students. Next, I discuss considerations for including multicultural literature in classrooms as a way to open windows to worlds beyond the students' own.

Multicultural Book Collections—Windows Into The World

In terms of thinking about books used in K–12 classrooms and book collections, I suggest possible categories to consider in order to develop comprehensive and deep coverage of many possibilities of being human. First, I present suggested categories of books for elementary grades. Second, I present considerations for middle- and high-school book collections. Rather than view these recommendations as exhaustive checklists, they should be used as ideas for reflecting on whose voices are being heard in classrooms and whose are missing.

Multicultural Collections for Elementary Grades

Books should be included as part of regular routines and content and read more than once, when time allows. The following categories of book are suggested (Boutte, 1999; Boutte, 2002; Boutte et al., 2008):

1. books representing various ethnic groups (e.g., African, Asian, biracial, European, Latino, and Native Americans);
2. books representing different religious groups;
3. books representing both genders;
4. books representing various socioeconomic statuses;
5. books representing people with disabilities;
6. books representing different age groups;
7. books representing lifestyles (e.g., single parents', grandparents');
8. books representing people who are lesbian, bisexual, gay, transsexual, queer, etc.;
9. books representing international perspectives;
10. books that present both *historical* (e.g., folktales, biographies) and *contemporary* depictions of people from a particular ethnic group;
11. books representing holidays in many different cultural traditions (e.g., Passover, Easter, Three Kings Day, Hanukkah, Kwanzaa)—if holidays are addressed in the classroom at all;
12. fairytales, folktales, and fables from different cultural groups (e.g., African, Asian, Latino); there are hundreds of versions of Cinderella available, so be sure to read ones from other cultural groups; many African fables and folktales can be used to teach lessons about life;
13. books depicting males and females in nontraditional roles;
14. books that show people from different cultures working together;

15. books that emphasize both similarities *and* differences among people—there are several book series that do so (e.g., Ann Morris and Ken Heyman have several books that focus on different themes (e.g., hats, families, homes, tools, bread, weddings, play) with real photos of people around the world); other books such as *What the World Eats* (D'Aluisio & Menzel 2008);

16. multicultural books from various disciplines (e.g., art, music, science, math, social studies);

17. books written in different dialects and languages—many of these can be found in audio form so that students can hear authentic pronunciations; alternatively, parents or community members can record themselves reading the books.

For each category of social identity, it is a good idea to consult book reviews and to share the books with others from the same social group to find out what issues may arise. For example, I once shared the book *Tikki Tikki Tembo* (Mosel, 1968) with two of my doctoral students—one was Chinese and the other was Taiwanese. I was aware of some of the stereotyping of Chinese names that was in the book; however, I wanted to get a sense of what they thought. Both of them brought up issues that I would not have thought about. The Chinese student said that she knew of no practice in China in which first-born sons were given long names. The Taiwanese student said that, though the characters were not pictures of real people, the illustrations looked more *Japanese* than Chinese—a distinction that most Americans have not learned to make (and one area in which many stereotypes exist). They both also shared examples of Chinese children's books that they liked. Later, I will discuss the idea of pairing two books together

FIGURE 3.5 Sample of a Multicultural Book Collection—Elementary School

to present multiple perspectives. A sample of a balanced multicultural book collection for elementary school is shown in Figure 3.6.

Middle and High School

High-school lists around the country tend to include a limited set of book choices. *Time Magazine's* (2010) list of the top 10 books on high-school reading lists includes the usual suspects listed below. The guidelines that follow the list suggest ways to move beyond the monopoly of "classics" so that other books can also be added (Boutte, 1999; Stotsky, 1994).

- *To Kill a Mockingbird*
- *Of Mice and Men*
- *A Separate Peace*
- *The Catcher in the Rye*
- *Animal Farm*
- *Lord of the Flies*
- *The Great Gatsby*
- *A Farewell to Arms*
- *The Scarlet Letter*
- *Macbeth*

Recommendation for Middle-/High-School Book Lists

1. Introduce literature by and about members of all ethnic and socially defined groups in this country over the course of students' school years—these would include numbers 1.–9. in the elementary list above.
2. Offer some literature each year about a few different cultural and ethnic groups—including religious groups such as Amish, Shakers, Chasidim, Hindus, Muslims, Buddhists, etc. Cover a range of groups, some religious, some secular, some based on gender, and so forth.
3. Show how indigenous cultures differ now and historically. Avoid romanticizing.
4. Include literary works about the immigrant experience in this country that, across works, show a variety of responses to their experiences.
5. Feature literary works with male or female characters (regardless of race and ethnicity) who demonstrate a variety of positive and negative qualities. Neither gender has a corner on virtue or vice.
6. Include literary works that feature, across works, both negative and positive characters who are members of particular ethnic, racial, or religious groups, rather than just one type of character.
7. Include literary works in which White America is portrayed as containing decent, civic-minded people, as well as prejudiced or mean-spirited

individuals. An overdose of "White guilt" literature may cause students to associate multicultural literature with "White guilt" literature. In short, Whites should not be viewed as acultural.

8. Include literary works about members of ethnic or social groups that feature a range of themes, not just those focusing chiefly on contemporary political and social issues.

9. Include books that show members of ethnic groups coping with the kinds of situation or problem that may arise in the lives of many human beings and have little to do with their ethnicity.

10. Eliminate some books to make room for newer works from time to time. Replace more contemporary works (published since 2000) with older works, as there seem to be fewer pre-20th-century works than 21st-century works. A reasonable balance of the two is necessary for encouraging interdisciplinary curricula with history departments, for familiarizing students with our literary past, and for helping them understand the evolution of contemporary literature.

11. Reduce the number of works about those groups that may be overrepresented in the curriculum to reflect a broader range of groups.

Examining Biases and Ideologies in Texts

An important part of critical literacy is to examine books beyond a dominant or surface read. Here, readers are encouraged to teach students to examine the ideologies and subtexts of books by asking questions such as:

> What does this book ask about you as a reader? How does it position you? What does it assume about your beliefs, values, experiences? Are you willing to go along with those assumptions? Are there aspects of the text you wish or feel compelled to resist or refuse?
>
> (Apol, 1998, p. 38)

The goal is not to censor or discard books, but rather to critically read them and to ascertain the surface ideology or "lesson" to be learned, as well as the unspoken, underlying message or passive ideology of the author or the times (Apol, 1998). "What are the assumptions upon which the text depends? Are the text's 'official' ideas contradicted by unconscious assumptions? If they are, what might it mean?" (Apol, 1998, p. 38). Apol encourages readers to:

> Think not only about what the text says, but about what it does not say as well. Who are the people who "do not exist" in the story? Whose voices are given prominence? Whose voices are not heard? What might the silent or the silenced voices say? What parts of the story seem absolutely "obvious" or "natural" to you—so much a part of "the way things are" that you may

have difficulty identifying them at all? Since all literature constructs a *version* of reality, why do you think these ideas seem so convincingly realistic? Which of your own experiences, assumptions, or beliefs do you feel most strongly when you interact with this literature? How can an awareness of your own cultural background impact the way you read the text?

(p. 38)

In general, critically literate readers interrogate assumptions that are being made about the universal applicability of frequently used (and beloved) books. For example, when I visited my son's fourth-grade class in 2005, there was bulletin board with the caption, "Fall Into a Good Book," listing the following set of books[6] that students were going to read in this class—and in the district (read "official curriculum"):

- *The Mystery of the Pirate's Treasure* (1984)
- *The Great Brain* (1967)
- *The Castle in the Attic* (1985)
- *The Sign of the Beaver* (1983)
- *The Secret Garden* (1911)
- *The Indian in the Cupboard* (1980)
- *My Side of the Mountain* (1959)

My reflection on the list is, first, that none of the books was published in the 21st century. Second, I noticed that most the books featured White, male characters. I found that the two books that intended to include storylines of American Indians were problematic. In both books, there were negative stereotypes about Native Americans. For example, in the book *The Sign of the Beaver* (Speare, 1984), the Indians speak in short, choppy English, and the White male is positioned as having superior knowledge, even though he would not have survived without the help of the Indian people. I also found the daily accounting of events to be unengaging. However, my son loved the book! This is a nice segue to one of the subsequent sections that points out the importance of presenting multiple perspectives and listening to multiple interpretations of texts.

As noted by Scholes (as cited in Sheridan, 2010), one of the goals of critical literacy is to move beyond "teaching literature" and begin "studying texts" (p. 2). In addition to examining the ideologies of texts, readers can also examine texts for different types of bias. As is the case with trying to discern the ideologies in a book, the goal is not to censor books for the purpose of eliminating them from educators' collections. The purpose is to figure how to view books comprehensively and teach students to do so. It is possible that books may have biases in them and still be enjoyed and critiqued. Below are a few types of bias that readers may look for in books and textbooks (Sadker, Sadker, & Long, 1993).

1. *Linguistic bias*: Examine books for culturally loaded terms such as "black sheep" or "jew down." Also, look for sexist language such as fireman and dissemination.
2. *Stereotyping*: Examine storylines and illustrations for stereotypes (negative and positive) that are based on ethnicity, gender, socioeconomic status, religion, and other social identities.
3. *Invisibility*: Examine your overall book collections and textbooks for systematic exclusion of races, socioeconomic statuses, etc. The underlying question is who is missing?
4. *Imbalance*: Examine your overall book collections and textbooks for imbalance in terms of the proportion of groups presented. Actively seek to include more than one group of people.
5. *Unreality*: Be sure not to gloss over controversial issues or provide an unrealistic portrayal of difficult issues (e.g., slavery, discrimination, prejudice, homelessness). Figure out how to discuss these in age- and culturally appropriate ways.
6. *Fragmentation*: Be sure not to fragment information by presenting books or information on groups that are marginalized as unique occurrences rather than integrated in the text. Examples of fragmentation in textbooks include using books that are mainly focused on Whites or men and presenting an occasional story on people of color (Martin Luther King in a social studies textbook) or women (Marie Curie in a science textbook).

Providing Multiple Perspectives

From a critical literacy perspective, texts (books and other texts) should not be presented as if they represent the only perspective on a topic. Indeed, on most issues, there are multiple coexisting (sometimes conflicting) stories. In history, stories are often told from the perspective of Whites, and the voices of African Americans and other marginalized people are omitted or told in incomplete, inaccurate, or distorted ways. Look at the video link of Nigerian–American author, Chimamanda Adichie, delivering her widely viewed Ted talk, "The Danger of a Single Story."[14] In her talk, Adichie acknowledges that our lives and cultures are composed of many overlapping stories. She warns that, if we listen or hear only a single story, we run the risk of making critical misunderstandings.

In classrooms, teachers can engage students in writing dialogue poems that share two sides of the same issue or event. An example is the dialogue poem "Two Women",[15] which also has an explanation of how to write poems. Another example, "Honeybees," can be found in Peterson (2007). Dialogue poems can also be used to assess students' understandings of multiple perspectives.

Another Ted talk, by Lisa Bu, encourages people to read books in pairs.[16]

Classroom examples of teachers engaging multiple perspectives exist. For example, Mary Cowhey (2006), an elementary-school teacher in Massachusetts, engaged students in seeing historical figures from a perspective different than the ones presented in history books. Students also learned about Christopher Columbus, George Washington, and Thomas Jefferson as well-known owners of enslaved people. After discussing the Declaration of Independence, one of her second-grade students penned a note to Thomas Jefferson that read, "Dear Thomas Jeffrson [*sic*]. I like the Declaration of independence but wait you own slaves it is like your [*sic*] braking you own law. Love Beth" (p. 130). Clearly, this student gets the idea that humans are not one-dimensional people.

After recognizing that her students had different perspectives than those typically presented about the police in texts, Compton-Lily (2004), a first-grade teacher in a mid-size urban district, engaged her students in an inquiry unit that investigated the perspectives held by people in the community.

Other ideas for helping students view multiple perspectives include comparing and contrasting various versions of the same story (e.g., *Little Red Riding Hood*, *Cinderella*). Students will have opportunities to begin to understand that stories are socially constructed and influenced by the persons telling them. This is not a difficult understanding for most children, as they do a great job of reading other aspects of their world. For example, they readily know that one parent may say yes to something, whereas another parent will say no. Likewise, they know which teachers will accept late work and which will not. Hence, they strategically figure out whom to ask what.

Using books, such as those by Howard Zinn (his website will be presented later as a resource), that provide historical accounts told from the perspectives of the people who are oppressed (e.g., Arawak indigenous people versus the typical story about Columbus) is important for interruptions to the distortions in history. Likewise, Rethinking Schools (also referenced in the list of resources in Chapter 2) provides materials that help contribute to multiple perspectives on topics.

Cartoons, Music, Television, Movies, Internet, and Other Media

Critical literacy skills can be used for any type of text. A few examples are provided below.

Cartoons

- "Racial Stereotypes in Children's Entertainment" (7 minutes, 19 seconds).[17]
- "Disney's Peter Pan—What Makes the Red Man Red? (2 minutes, 31 seconds).[18]
- "Mickey Mouse Monopoly: Disney, Childhood & Corporate Power" (5 minutes, 45 seconds).[19]

Television Shows

- "What Would You Do? Man Racially Profiled While Shopping in N.Y. Store" (8 minutes, 57 seconds).[20]

Engaging Black students in reading the world will help develop critical consciousness, which will be discussed in Chapter 5 as an important dimension of CRP. Homework assignments can be given to example popular song lyrics, Internet sites, and the like.

Handling Challenges to Books

By now, many readers are thinking, "I can't do that in my classroom. Parents will protest." I end the discussion of critical literacy by discussing some of the politics of using critical literacy and multicultural texts. In Chapter 2, it was pointed out that schools are not neutral places. This must be remembered as educators seek to navigate the land mines involved when using transformative educational approaches that are designed to question and change the status quo. It is helpful to recall *why* this work is important and what it means to continue to teach in conventional ways. More than four decades of academic literature, educational reforms, testing trends, and the like have demonstrated what happens to Black children under conventional conditions and using conventional strategies. Hence, if we as educators want *the children to be well*, we must figure out thoughtful ways of using what is known in the knowledge base for our respective educational spaces. Consider the short case study below.

Case Study

A group of White parents of a majority White high school (20 percent African American students) object to their children being required to read four books by African American authors. They complain that the curriculum is being watered down.

1. As a teacher in the school, how would you handle this situation? (Be specific regarding what you would do, and why).
2. Support your comments with theories, research, or other scholarly literature.

Steps to Take When Faced With a Book Challenge

To head off controversy:

- Anticipate possible challenges.
- Ask parents to contribute to developing school reading programs (Durbin, 2005).

- Be prepared to defend your choices by referencing the standards that will be taught.
- Negotiate academic freedom clauses in collective-bargaining contracts (Durbin, 2005).
- Discuss book choices with members of the administration (e.g., principal, curriculum specialist).
- Collaborate with other teachers, if possible and feasible, when selecting book choices.

When conflict flares anyway:

- Meet with the complaining parent(s) and attempt to hear their points and share yours.
- Share the standards that you are using.
- Invite the parent to visit the class and to read the book.
- Provide a copy of the district's formal curriculum materials review policy (Durbin, 2005).
- While the complaint is being reviewed, keep the material available to other students.
- Seek support from the administration, other teachers, and parents.

Many readers are familiar with the story of a third-grade, White teacher's experience with reading the children's book *Nappy Hair* (Herron, 1997) to her students in Harlem.[21] I hasten to add that there are many more stories about teachers successfully using multicultural literature in K–12 classrooms, so this story is not really a cautionary tale as much as it is one that synthesizes key points of this book. The teacher, though well intentioned, did not realize that schools are highly political spaces. It is important to know enough about the students and their communities (e.g., understand the politics of Black hair), develop a relationship with the parents, communicate with administrators and others in the school about book choices that may get pushed back, and critically evaluate books. It may be helpful to read book reviews (when available) or talk to persons representing the ethnicity in the book to get an idea of issues that you may not see or think about. That is, teachers would be wise to anticipate multiple reads on the book.

Although I was very aware of the issues surrounding Black hair, I had an experience with the same book that reminded me that different people read and interpret the same book differently. While sharing a text set to affirm Black hair (which included *Nappy Hair*), several of my mostly 20-something White preservice teachers exclaimed, "Dr. Johnson hates that book!" "Are you sure?" I queried. I knew Dr. Johnson very well as a friend and colleague and was aware that she was an author of African American children's books. "Did she say *hate*?" I wanted to know.

I could barely wait to get home to email Dianne (Dr. Johnson) and tell her that the preservice teachers had mistakenly thought that she hated *Nappy Hair*. Dianne confirmed that the students were correct. She said that she would tell me why later. When we talked a few days later, Dianne explained why she hated the book, adding that she hated it more, each time she read it.

I knew that Dianne, as a children's book author, takes the written word seriously and filters all of it through her desire to have positive images of Black children. Although I have always stressed critical literacy, examination of unspoken ideologies, and multiple perspectives, I had difficulty reconciling that there was something substantive that escaped my self-alleged sharp lenses. This troubled me greatly, and I still loved the book.

A few weeks later, I came across an article on the book *Nappy Hair* that was published by another one of my colleagues (Jeffries, 2002). The three of us sat down for lunch and discussed the book and our perspectives, reexamining several themes. The beauty of this situation is that here we were, three African American women—each with different viewpoints—seeing the book through our eyes and worldviews. Dr. Rhonda Jeffries focused on the rhetorical aspects of the book and the beauty of AAL. I loved the AAL features (e.g., call and response) and the counternarrative about Black intelligence and Black hair. Dianne said that a Black author should take care to mention Africa at least once. I pointed out that Herron had done so twice. Dianne conceded this point and decided that she still did not like the book. Looking closer than before, I now admitted that the illustration of the main character on the front of a book looked somewhat like a caricature. I still love the book—which proves the point that a book can be critiqued for stereotypes and the like and also be loved. By the way, the author of the book explained that the book was meant to be a positive counternarrative on Black female's hair (Jeffries, 2002). I later found yet another article by one of my African American colleagues and friends, Dr. Michelle Martin, on the book (1999). She focused on the beauty of Black hair. When I share the book in my courses, I share all of these perspectives.

Like most things in life, there are no unilateral perspectives, which is the beauty of critical literacy. Our multiple perspectives do not have to be resolved; they can and do coexist. Likewise, African American students will have different reads on text—which will encourage rich dialogue. Such conversations are a welcome relief from asking students to do dominant reads on the book and to give *the main idea*—as if there is only one.

Key Points From the Chapter

1. Critical literacy skills are key for all levels of education and content areas.
2. Diaspora literacy helps African American students learn about and reclaim their heritage. It begins with Africa instead of with enslavement, as is often done in schools. It makes linkages between the past, present, and the future.

3. Several considerations and tips are provided for teaching about the enslavement of African people.
4. Three classroom examples have been shared.
5. A discussion of liberation literature has been included.
6. Guidelines have been provided for assembling multicultural book collections for elementary- and for middle-/high-school levels.
7. Suggestions have been made for examining ideologies and biases in books.
8. Steps should be taken to prevent parental challenges to books; however, if challenges do occur, certain actions are recommended.

Conclusion

The critical literacy components discussed in this chapter are some of many possibilities that exist. Reading the world includes reading all aspects—including looking at symbolism in language (e.g. using "black" to convey bad (Boutte, 2002; King, 1992). Teaching requires courage (Delpit, 2012). In closing and reflecting on what needs to be done in classrooms, I offer the advice of an elder and scholar/activist extraordinaire, Dr. Adelaide Sanford (personal communication, October 4, 2012). We need to learn how to "be courageous without being suicidal." That means: We need to become politically astute about how schools and other systems work. We are best equipped to transform the system when we are informed and take reflective actions, in conjunction with others. Remember to relate what you are doing to the school curriculum. I cannot understate the important of ongoing dialogue with administrators, parents, and communities to get buy-in.

Activities

1. Briefly think about the books that you use (including textbooks) to determine *if* and *how* people of color are depicted. Are most of the books mirrors and windows for children of color? How is discrimination (gender, ethnic, social class, language, religion, etc.) produced and reproduced in the context of schools and schooling? Why do you choose the books that you use in your classroom?
2. Put together a counternarrative text set for your grade level and subject that will allow for sustained focus on a concept. For example, the text set or group of readings could convey the message that African Americans are intelligent or beautiful. The discussion of African American contributions to science would be an example for middle- or high-school students (see commentary in Chapter 5 with Charlease Kelley-Jackson). Alternatively, you can assign this task to students and let them research several readings on one topic. Below is an example of a text set for elementary school that focuses on females. This can be shared and discussed regarding the values that are being put forth

(e.g., communalism, family, self-love). Many African American books will capture dimensions of Black culture.

- Wyeth, S. D. (1998). *Something Beautiful*. New York: Doubleday Books for Young Readers. A young African American girl in an urban city initially sees only ugliness in her neighborhood. After looking for something beautiful in her neighborhood and talking with neighbors and her mother, she is able to see beauty in places that she had not noticed initially—including herself. This experience provides her with the agency to put forth her own efforts to beautify the neighborhood.
- Barnwell, Y. M. (2005). *No Mirrors in My Nana's House*. Orlando, FL: First Voyager Books (comes with a CD by Sweet Honey in the Rock). This book affirms the beauty of a girl whose view of life is influenced by her grandmother, who loves her and sees her beauty and the beauty of her neighborhood. The child, therefore, is buffered from the outside world's narrative about her skin color, other physical features, and her neighborhood.
- Kissinger, K. (1994). *All the Colors We Are* (written in Spanish and English). St. Paul, MN: Redleaf Press. This book uses real photos of children with a variety of skin colors from different ethnicities. It provides a simple explanation for how we get our skin color. Discussing melanin and how it works in our skin interrupts stereotypes and misconceptions about skin color.
- Steptoe, J. (1987). *Mufaro's Beautiful Daughters. An African Tale*. New York: Lothrop, Lee & Shepard. This is an African version of the Cinderella story. Unlike the popularly told Cinderella story, the book shows the value of caring for one's community and environment. In Chapter 5, an example is provided of a teacher, Mrs. Strickland, using this book. Mrs. Strickland, the kindergarten teacher mentioned in the classroom example, used this book as one in a text set on African princesses. Figure 3.6 illustrates that children viewed beauty beyond physical characteristics.
- Machado, A. M. (1994). *Nina Bonita*. Brooklyn, NY: Kane/Miller. I became familiar with this book after reading Alexandro Segura-Mora's (2008) article, "What Color is Beautiful," which was published in *Rethinking Schools*. Segura-Mora had read the book to her kindergarten students after overhearing one of her students convey that he did not like his skin color and would take pills to change his color to White. The book features a very dark Black girl, Nina Bonita, and a white rabbit, who loves the girl's color. In the story, the rabbit learns from Nina Bonita's mother that children get their color from their parents. This book is great for opening discussions about Black skin color.

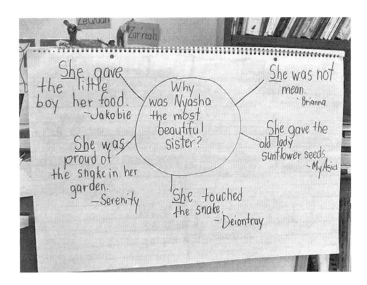

FIGURE 3.6 Kindergartners' Reflections on Beauty.

Commentary on the text set: Collectively, the books will provide an avenue for engaging in dialogue about conceptions of beauty to determine where misconceptions exist and to reflect on ways to counter them. It might be useful to add a contemporary book showing African beauty, as the only book in the set about Africa is a historical tale and set in a village. One possible book that may complement this group is *A Triangle for Adaora. An African Book of Shapes* (Onyefulu, 2001). I love the depiction of a beautiful female with short, natural hair. Her sense of self-possession is evident throughout the story, and her family and community value and care for her. Yet, it would be nice to add an African urban context as a parallel to the other African American books in the text set. Nevertheless, even the best text set will not be able to address everything, which is why the process of having dialogue about these topics is important.

3. Consider counternnarrative music, such as "Video" by India Arie.[22] Let students discuss the messages there and find other examples.

4. Examine book adoption policies and processes. Who sits on the selection committee? Can Black parents and community members be a part of the process? How are the perspectives of Blacks presented in textbooks? Are there better choices available?

5. An example of connections between West African and African American culture can be seen in the video clip of the movie *Rize*, which features a dance style called crumping, which is a sort of "play fighting."[23] View the clip and notice the similarities in the dances. How might you teach about

this in classrooms, as African American students are often not aware of these "*Sankofa*" connections?

6. Help students create strong textual lineages—books that they read that will change their lives in significant ways. Books should be enabling in that they prompt students to be, do, and think differently (Tatum, 2009).

Resources

1. The Zinn Education Project promotes and supports the use of Howard Zinn's best-selling book, *A People's History of the United States*, and other materials for teaching a people's history in middle- and high-school classrooms across the country. Zinn's history books (including the ones for children) tell historical events from the perspective of the oppressed. The website offers more than 100 free, downloadable lessons and articles, organized by theme, time period, and reading level. Its goal is to introduce students to a more accurate, complex, and engaging understanding of United States history than is found in traditional textbooks and curricula.[24]
2. The National Underground Railroad Freedom Center, Cincinnati, Ohio, contains a number of exhibits regarding freedom, historical and current.[25]
3. The Penn Center is located on St. Helena Island, one of South Carolina Sea Islands, and at the heart of Gullah culture. Penn Center is the site of the former Penn School, one of the country's first schools for freed slaves.[26]
4. Igbo Landing, St. Simon's Island, Georgia. In May, 1803, a group of 75 Nigerian Igbo people, chained together and destined for a life of enslavement, chose to drown themselves at this historical site.
5. *Hidden Colors* is a documentary about the untold history of people of color around the globe. The trailer can be found on imdb.com.[27]
6. The Children's Defense Fund is a nonprofit child advocacy organization that works to ensure a level playing field for all children. Of particular interest may be the Freedom Schools, which use liberation literature and the Cradle to Prison Pipeline campaign.[28]
7. Perry, T., Moses, R. P., & Wynne, J.T., Cortes, Jr., E., & Delpit, L. (2010). *Quality Education as a Constitutional Right. Creating a Grassroots Movement to Transform Public Schools.* Boston, MA: Beacon Press.
8. Sertima, I. V. (1976). *They Came Before Columbus. The African Presence in Ancient America.* New York: Random House.
9. Diouf, S. A. (2000). *Kings and Queens of West Africa.* New York: Scholastic.
10. Degruy, J. A. (2005). *Post Traumatic Slave Syndrome. America's Legacy of Enduring Injury and Healing.* Milwaukie, OR: Uptone Press.
11. Segura-Mora, A. (2008). What Color Is beautiful? In A. Pelo (Ed.), *Rethinking Early Childhood Education* (pp. 3–6). Milwaukee, WS: Rethinking Schools.
12. Tenorio, R. (2009). Brown Kids Can't Be in Our Club. In W. Au (Ed.), *Rethinking Multicultural Education. Teaching for Racial and Cultural Justice.* Milwaukee, WS: Rethinking Schools.

Notes

1. See www.ed.sc.edu/ite/faculty_research_projects/sankofa.asp (accessed May 19, 2015).
2. A sampling of a spiritual can be found on this link: www.youtube.com/watch?v=RRpzEnq14Hs (accessed May 19, 2015).
3. See www.pbs.org/race/000_General/000_00-Home.htm (accessed May 19, 2015).
4. See www.common-place.org/vol-02/no-02/fried/fried-2.shtml (accessed May 19, 2015).
5. The following links provide examples of slave narratives:

    • http://memory.loc.gov/ammem/collections/voices/ (accessed May 19, 2015);
    • http://rememberingslavery.soundprint.org/audio.html (accessed May 19, 2015);
    • www.lib.unc.edu/stone/webguide/index.html?display=print_items&item_id=80TT (accessed May 19, 2015).

6. See www.youtube.com/watch?v=MyS3HPInHtI (accessed May 19, 2015).
7. www.dailykos.com/story/2008/12/22/676149/-MLK-Jr-and-The-Birth-of-a-New-Nation (accessed May 19, 2015).
8. Demographics in Mrs. Strickland's classroom included 30 children—26 African American, 2 Mexican American, 1 biracial American (AA/MA), and 1 European American.
9. Portions of the description of Mrs. Strickland's classroom and teaching were included in the following article, which is used here with permission: Boutte, G. S., & Strickland, J. (2008). Making African American Culture and History Central to Teaching and Learning of Young Children. *Journal of Negro Education*, 77(2), 131–142.
10. As pointed out by the title of Lisa Delpit's book, too many teachers view Black students as *other people's children*: Delpit, L. (1995). *Other People's Children. Cultural Conflicts in the Classroom*. New York: The New Press.
11. Mrs. Strickland is now teaching at a historically Black college and working on her doctoral degree in early childhood education.
12. Jackson, T., & Boutte, G. (2009). Liberation Literature: Positive Cultural Messages in Children's and Adolescent Literature at Freedom Schools. *Language Arts*, 87(2), 108–116. Copyright 2009 by the National Council of Teachers of English. Reprinted with permission.
13. The dates of the books were not posted on the board. I list them here for the readers.
14. See www.ted.com/talks/chimamanda_adichie_the_danger_of_a_single_story.html (accessed May 19, 2015).
15. See www.carla.umn.edu/articulation/polia/pdf_files/dialoguepoems.pdf (accessed May 24, 2015).
16. See www.ted.com/talks/lisa_bu_how_books_can_open_your_mind.html?utm_source=newsletter_weekly_2013-06-01&utm_campaign=newsletter_weekly&utm_medium=email&utm_content=talk_of_the_week_swipe (accessed May 19, 2015).
17. See www.youtube.com/watch?v=fS3e-n8Mj7I (accessed May 19, 2015).
18. See www.youtube.com/watch?v=Y_at9dOElQk (accessed May 19, 2015).
19. See www.youtube.com/watch?v=byaMd_PNyIY&feature=related (accessed May 19, 2015).
20. See www.youtube.com/watch?v=YDanZpek5iM (accessed May 19, 2015).
21. See www.adversity.net/special/nappy_hair.htm (accessed May 19, 2015).
22. See www.youtube.com/watch?v=Mq86e4Fhja0 (accessed May 19, 2015).
23. See www.youtube.com/watch?v=RlsDhcVj5bE (accessed May 19, 2015).
24. See https://zinnedproject.org/ (accessed May 19, 2015).
25. See www.freedomcenter.org/ (accessed May 19, 2015).
26. See http://penncenter.com/ (accessed May 19, 2015).
27. See www.imdb.com/title/tt1857724/ (accessed May 19, 2015).
28. See www.childrensdefense.org/ (accessed May 19, 2015).

References

Anderson, J. (2007). The historical context for understanding the test score gap. *National Journal of Urban Education and Practice, 1,* 1–21.

Apol, L. (1998). But what does this have to do with kids? Literary theory and children's literature in the teacher education classroom. *Journal of Children's Literature, 24*(2), 32–46.

Apple, M. W. (1992). The text and cultural politics. *Educational Researcher, 21*(7), 4–11.

Bishop, R. S. (2007). *Free within ourselves: The development of African American children's literature.* Portsmouth, NH: Heinemann.

Bishop, R. S. (2012). Reflections on the development of African American children's literature. *Journal of Children's Literature, 38*(2), 5–13.

Boutte, G. (1999). *Multicultural education: Raising consciousness.* Atlanta, GA: Wadsworth.

Boutte, G. S. (2002). The critical literacy process guidelines for examining books. *Childhood Education, 78*(3), 147–152.

Boutte, G. S., & Hill, E. (2006). African American communities: Implications for Educators. *New Educator, 2,* 1–19.

Boutte, G. S., Hopkins, R., & Waklatsi, T. (2008). Perspectives, voices, and worldviews in frequently read children's books. *Early Education and Development, 19*(6), 1–22.

Boutte, G. S., & Strickland, J. (2008). Making African American culture and history central to teaching and learning of young children. *Journal of Negro Education, 77*(2), 131–142.

Boykin, A. W. (1994). Afrocultural expression and its implications for schooling. In E. Hollins, J. King, & W. Hayman (Eds.), *Teaching diverse populations: Formulating a knowledge base* (pp. 243–273). Albany, NY: State University of New York Press.

Butchart, R. E. (1988). "Outthinking and outflanking the owners of the world": A historiography of the African American struggle for education. *History of Education Quarterly, 28*(3), 333–366.

Butchart, R. E. (2010). Black hopes, White power: Emancipation, reconstruction, and the legacy of unequal schooling in the U.S. South, 1861–1880. *Paedagogica Historica, 46,* 33–50.

Compton-Lily, C. (2004). *Confronting racism, poverty, and power: Classroom strategies to change the world.* Portsmouth, NH: Heinemann.

Cowhey, M. (2006). *Black ants and Buddhists: Thinking critically and teaching differently in the primary grades.* Portland, MN: Sternhouse.

D'Aluisio, F., & Menzel, P. (2008). *What the world eats.* New York: Random House.

Delpit, L. (2012). *"Multiplication is for White people." Raising expectations for other people's children.* New York: The New Press.

Dilliard, C. B. (2012). *Learning to (re)member the things we've learned to forget. Endarkened feminisms, spirituality, & the sacred nature of research & teaching.* New York: Peter Lang.

Durbin, K. (2005). Books under fire. *Teaching Tolerance,* 47–51.

Hammond, B., Hoover, M. E. R., & McPhail, I. P. (Eds.). (2005). *Teaching African American learners to read: Perspectives and practices.* Washington, DC: International Reading Association.

Herron, C. (1997). *Nappy hair.* New York: Dragonfly Books.

Hilliard, A. G. (2005). Pedagogy in ancient Kemet. In B. Hammond, M. E. R. Hoover, & I. P. McPhail (Eds.), *Teaching African American learners to read. Perspectives and practices* (pp. 24–42). Washington, DC: International Reading Association.

Jackson, T., & Boutte, G. (2009). Liberation literature: Positive cultural messages in children's and adolescent literature at freedom schools. *Language Arts, 87*(2), 108–116.

Jeffries, R. (2002). An analysis of the impact of Carolivia Herron's *Nappy Hair* on literacy and literature. *Journal of Curriculum Theorizing, 18*(2), 65–76.

King, J. E. (1992). Diaspora literacy and consciousness in the struggle against miseducation in the Black community. *Journal of Negro Education, 61*(3), 317–340.

King, J. E., & Swartz, E. E. (2014). *"Re-membering" history in student and teacher learning. An Afrocentric culturally informed praxis.* New York: Routledge.

Martin, M. H. (1999). Never too nappy. *Horn Book Magazine, 75,* 283–288.

Mason, P. A., & Schumm, J. S. (2003). *Promising practices for urban reading instruction.* Newark, DE: International Reading Association.

Milner IV, H. R. (2010). *Start where you are, but don't stay there: Understanding diversity, opportunity gaps, and teaching in today's classrooms.* Cambridge, MA: Harvard Education Press.

Morrison, T. (2007). *The bluest eye.* New York: Random House.

Mosel, A. (1968). *Tikki Tikki Tembo.* New York: Henry Holt.

Onyefulu, I. (2001). *A triangle for Adaora. An African book of shapes.* London: Frances Lincoln.

Paley, V. G. (2000). *White teacher.* Cambridge, MA: Harvard University Press.

Pedersen, E., Faucher, T. A., & Eaton, W. W. (1978). A new perspective on the effects of first-grade teachers on children's subsequent adult status. *Harvard Educational Review, 48*(1), 1–31.

Perry, T., & Delpit, L. (1998). *The real Ebonics debate: Power, language, and the education of African-American children.* Boston, MA: Beacon Press.

Perry, T., Steele, C., Hilliard, A. III. (2003). *Young, gifted, and Black. Promoting high achievement among African-American students.* Boston, MA: Beacon Press.

Peterson, B. (2007). Teaching for social justice. One teacher's journey. In W. Au, B. Bigelow, & S. Karp (Eds.), *Rethinking our classrooms: Teaching for equity and justice* (2nd ed., Vol. 1, pp. 28–34). Milwaukee, WI: Rethinking Schools.

Sadker, M., Sadker, D., & Long, L. (1993). Gender and educational equality. In J. A. Banks (Ed.), *Multicultural education: Issues and perspectives* (pp. 111–128). Boston, MA: Allyn & Bacon.

Segura-Mora, A. (2008). What color is beautiful? In A. Pelo (Ed.), *Rethinking early childhood education* (pp. 3–6). Milwaukee, WS: Rethinking Schools.

Sheridan, D. M. (2010). Fabricating consent: Three-dimensional objects as rhetorical compositions. *Computers and Composition, 27*(4), 249–265.

Smith, N. (2014). Reconstructing race. In W. Au (Ed.), *Rethinking multicultural education: Teaching for racial and cultural justice* (2nd ed., pp. 315–322). Milwaukee, WI: Rethinking Schools.

South Carolina Department of Education. (2012) *United States history and Constitution support document.* Columbia, SC: South Carolina Department of Education.

Speare, E. G. (1984). *The sign of the beaver.* New York: Yearling.

Steinbeck, J. (2009). *Of mice and men.* New York: Penguin.

Stern, S. M., & Stern, J. A. (2011). *The state of state U.S. history standards 2011.* Washington, DC: The Thomas B. Fordham Institute.

Stotsky, S. (1994). Academic guidelines for selecting multiethnic and multicultural literature. *English Journal, 83*(2), 27–33.

Tatum, A. (2009). *Reading for their life: (Re)Building the textual lineages of African American adolescent males.* Portsmouth, NH: Heinemann.

Time Magazine (2010). Top 10 books you were forced to read in school. Retrieved on September 30, 2010 from www.time.com/time/specials/packages/completelist/0,29569,2

Wilson, L. (2002). *Reading to live: How to teach reading for today's world.* Westport, CT: Heinemann.

Woodson, C. G. (1933/1990). *The mis-education of the Negro.* Trenton, NJ: Africa World Press.

4

LOVING THE LANGUAGE (AFRICAN AMERICAN LANGUAGE)

Proposition 4.1 No language is better or worse than another.

Proposition 4.2 African American Language is a legitimate, rule-based, systemic language and is the primary language of many African American students.

Proposition 4.3 The goal is to maintain African American Language and to add Mainstream American English.[1]

> Every conversation about black speech is a conversation about black intelligence and ultimately black humanity.
>
> (Michael Eric Dyson, as cited in Alim & Smitherman, 2012, inside cover page, no pagination)

> If an African American child is seen as language deficient, we can show that the behavior of the teacher actually changes toward that child as compared to "normal" children. He or she will engage the child in communication less and pay less attention to the child . . . It is this teaching behavior and not the language of the child, no matter how different, that creates the problems for learners.
>
> (Hilliard, 2002, p. 101)

> When beginning teachers come into minority communities, many are unable to understand the students' home language, social interaction patterns, histories, and cultures. Thus they cannot truly educate the students. Their perceptions of deficiency and competence are socially and culturally constructed. Without greater exposure to the students' culture teachers lack the tools with which to make sense of much that transpires in the classroom.
>
> (Ladson-Billings, 1994, p. 134)

And how is the children's language? It is strong and one of the most complex English dialects in the US (Alim & Smitherman, 2012; Rickford & Rickford, 2000). It possesses five present verb tenses and other complex linguistic features that other U.S. dialects can only dream about. The language practices of AAL speakers "reflect a generational continuity that has stood the test of time and they continue to demonstrate the uniqueness of Black folks' journey in this land" (Smitherman, 2006, p. 64). Yet, AAL speakers are faced with ongoing, systemic linguicism. In general, many AAL speakers and their teachers do not know the value and complexity of the language. In fact, it is subjected to mass attempts at linguicide, as many people try to extinguish it. The continuous linguistic profiling caused by linguistic imperialism will need to be interrupted in order for *the children to be well.*

Let me pause and ask readers to monitor their reactions to the strong opening statements. Misinterpreted, some readers may think that I am vilifying teachers (and perhaps students). The use of a strong terms such as attempted "linguicide" (the killing of one's language), linguistic profiling, and linguistic imperialism may sound a bit dramatic to readers; however, most educators do not realize that AAL is a legitimate, rule-governed language system (Alim & Smitherman, 2012; Boutte & Johnson, 2012, 2013) and, thus, try to eradicate it. Many teachers and students (including AAL speakers themselves) view AAL as slang, incorrect English, or broken English (Boutte, 2007). If readers are beginning to feel some discomfort, do review the guidelines for processing this information that were presented in Chapter 1 and recognize this as a learning opportunity. Also, it may be helpful to quickly peruse the concepts about individual and institutional levels of oppression presented in Chapter 2, to realize that "good" people can and do contribute to oppression (including linguistic oppression—linguicism). Developing a critical knowledge base and accompanying dispositions that value AAL will go a long way to help educators (who are well intentioned) understand why eradicating AAL is not the goal.

The title of the chapter is "Loving the Language," drawing from Toni Morrison's comments that many Black people are in love with "the saying of words, holding them on the tongue, experimenting with them, playing with them" (Alim & Smitherman, 2012, p. 175).

> The language, only the language . . . It's a love, a passion. Its function is like a preacher's: to make you stand up out of your seat, make you lose yourself and hear yourself. The worst of all possible things that could happen would be to lose that language . . . It's terrible to think that a child with five different present tenses comes to school to be faced with books that are less than his own language. And then to be told things about his language, which is him, that are sometimes permanently damaging . . . This is a really cruel fallout of racism.
>
> (Toni Morrison, as cited in Alim & Smitherman, 2012, p. 167)

Consider the two examples below of AAL speakers who are in love with their language. The first example is from an account by my husband and me about our twin granddaughters, when they were between the ages of 4 and 6 and had a strong preference for speaking AAL (Boutte & Johnson, 2013). The second is from dialogue between Samy Alim and a high-school AAL speaker (Alim & Smitherman, 2012).

Example 1: Loving the Language

Contrary to pervasive deficit perspectives and narratives about AAL and ongoing microaggressions (daily cultural assaults) against it in school, our 2-year study of our granddaughters' (Janiyah and Jaliyah) language revealed that the girls sometimes viewed MAE/SE as bothersome and tedious; hence, there were times when they actively resisted it. At other times, they embraced it, when they determined that using SE instead of AAL made sense (Boutte & Johnson, 2013).

We captured aspects of their emergent biliteracy and bilingualism (literacy in, and speaking of, two language systems—AAL and SE) as they navigated between the two literacies and languages. We demonstrated their transliterate and translingual confidence and proficiency. Both girls used AAL almost exclusively at home. Everyone else in their immediate home spaces (mother, grandparents, and one of their uncles) is bidialectal. Another uncle speaks AAL primarily. The girls reveled in their AAL and developed a tacit, rudimentary awareness of some aspects of it. "Once I overhead Janiyah singing, 'She hit the flo'. She laughed conspiratorially with her sister and asked her, 'Did you hear me? I said 'flo'!" (Boutte & Johnson, 2013, p. 307). This liberatory celebration of intentional use of AAL both surprised and pleases us.

Sometimes, the girls had the presence of mind and audacity to make fun of others speaking SE:

> On another occasion, for instance, Jaliyah excitedly told me, "Nina said that she have balloons on her house." "Has," I "modeled," to which Jaliyah replied, "She *has* balloons on her house, *okay* Dear?" Another time at the dinner table, I reminded Janiyah, "Remember we say *they*, not them" to which, Janiyah replied matter-of-factly, "I don't really care what *we* say!" and continued with *her* story told in *her* way.
>
> (Boutte & Johnson, 2013, p. 307)

One day, as we were riding in my SUV, and the girls were talking to each other as if I were not there, I overheard Janiyah say a few words in AAL and laugh. She confided in her sister, "Sometimes I just like talking country" (her name for AAL).

Second Example: Loving the Language

In the example below, Latasha is a high-school African American Language speaker, and Samy Alim (linguistic expert) is interviewing her (Alim & Smitherman, 2012, p. 176):

> *Latasha:*   Yeah, like the way I talk to my teacher ain't the same way I talk with the 3L click.
>
> *Alim:*   3L Click? What's that?
>
> *L:*   All of our names begin with "L," so we named our click aft that, the 3L Click. It's me, LaToya, and Lamar.
>
> *A:*   And how is the way y'all talk different from the way you talk to the teacher?
>
> *L:*   Well, it's like, you know the rapper, Nelly?
>
> *A:*   Yeah, yeah.
>
> *L:*   How he say everything like "urrr," like for "here" he'll be like "hurrr"?
>
> *A:*   Yeah! [Laughing] "I ain't from round hurrr!"
>
> *L:*   [Laughing] That's how we try to talk!
>
> *A:*   Why, though?!
>
> *L:*   Cuz we like it!

As noted in both examples, Black youth are often more interested in exploiting differences between SE and AAL, as well as interregional differences in AAL styles, than they are "with simply mimicking White ways of speaking" (Alim & Smitherman, 2012, p. 307). Indeed, youth already know, in a tacit way, that the "worst of all possible things that could happen would be to lose that language" (Toni Morrison, as cited in Alim & Smitherman, 2012, p. 167).

Before reading further, you should pause for a minute to reflect on what you know about AAL (sometimes referred to as Ebonics). Write down examples of words, phases, and other aspects of the language system that you may have heard.

Assumptions for This Chapter

1. The discussion of language diversity falls under the larger umbrella of appreciation of students' cultures and diversity. The goal is to help students understand that no language is better or worse than another. Educators may start by reading a book written in any U.S. dialect and noting differences. Additional recommendations for getting started will be provided later.

2. What we think of AAL as a language has more to do with what we think of the people speaking the language. Pejorative perceptions of AAL, or any language for that matter, often have more to do with larger sociopolitical beliefs about the *group of people* who speak the language, rather than the

structure and validity of the actual language itself (Boutte, 2007; Woodson, 1933/1990). As a group, African Americans continue to be marginalized economically, educationally, politically, and socially in the US, and so it is not surprising that AAL, a language system used by a large number of African Americans, has not been and is not currently respected. For example, contrast how French people and culture are thought of with how Black people and culture are thought of. People think of French people as having "high culture," excellent cuisine, fashion, etc. Readers may reflect back on the activity in Chapter 1 in Box 1.2. In a racially stratified society such as the US, Black people are not highly valued as a group. Hence, many people hold Black culture and language in low esteem. A critical approach helps educators and teachers think about complex issues of language and power.

3. Since no language is better or worse that the other, AAL should be thought of as a co-parallel language to MAE.

4. Every dialect, every language, is a way of thinking. "To speak means being able to use a certain syntax and possessing the morphology of such a language, but it means above all assuming a culture and bearing the weight of a civilization" (Fanon, 1952/2008, pp. 1–2).

5. Even after 12 years of conventional language arts and English instruction, the majority of AAL speakers will exit school without SE proficiency. Linguistically informed strategies such as contrastive analysis and code-switching have been shown to be more effective (Craig, Zhang, Hensel, & Quinn, 2009; Lemoine, 1999; Wheeler & Swords, 2006).

6. Ongoing contrastive analysis is useful for helping AAL speakers develop metalinguistic awareness and add MAE to their linguistic repertoires. However, both code-switching and code meshing should be the goal (both of these will be discussed in the next section).

7. Because language pervades every subject and grade level, it is important for teachers to have some familiarity with AAL in order to figure out strategies for helping students add MAE/SE to their language repertoires.

African American Language—What it Is

AAL refers to "the language system characteristically spoken in the African American community" (Nieto, 1996, p. 389). AAL is referred to by a number of names, such as: African American English, African American Vernacular English, Black English, and Ebonics—to name a few. The term "African American Language" acknowledges the relationship to West African languages (Nieto, 1996; Smith, 1998). AAL follows a set of linguistic rules for sounds, grammar, meanings, and social use (Alim & Smitherman, 2012; Boutte, 2007; Baugh, 1999; Kinloch, 2010; Linguistic Society of America, 1997; Rickford, 1999; Smitherman, 1977/1985, 2006).

Many AAL speakers and their teachers do not know that AAL is not "broken English." Misconceptions about AAL are pervasive and longstanding (Baugh, 1999;

Boutte, 2007; Boutte & Johnson, 2012, 2013). For example, some features of AAL are mistakenly thought to be slang and/or grammatical errors (Boutte, 2007).

In 1972, J. L. Dillard estimated that 80 percent of African Americans spoke only AAE, another 10–14 percent were bidialectal, and the remainder spoke only SE. Recent estimates show that these percentages have changed little since then. AAL is the primary language used by 80–90 percent of African American children in their homes and communities (Banks & Banks, 1997; Baugh, 1999; Hoover, 1998; LeMoine, 1999; Smitherman, 1997).

African American Language is a Parallel Language System to Standard English

Because AAL has linguistic structures and rules, it should be thought of as a parallel language to SE, instead of as being lower on the hierarchy of language systems (Smitherman, 2006). Viewing AAL as a parallel language means that both languages are valid in their own right. Importantly, our goal as educators is to respect and extend whatever language(s) children speak. We should seek to help children add SE to their language repertories, without denigrating their home language.

There is debate in the linguistic community regarding whether AAL is a distinct language or whether it is a dialect. There is no consensus among linguists (Rickford, 1999), but I agree with Smitherman (2006) that dialects are often viewed as corruptions of a given language. Therefore, I prefer the term African American Language versus African American English, African American Vernacular English, Ebonics, or other terminology. Viewing AAL as a co-parallel language to SE (instead of referring to it as a dialect) allows me to elevate my emphasis on the linguistic capabilities of AAL speakers (Smitherman, 2006). Most linguists concede that, even if AAL is considered a dialect, it is among the most distinctive of all English dialects and it differs substantively from SE (Rickford, 1999). Acknowledging that decisions about whether AAL is considered a dialect or a language are based more on sociopolitical rather than linguistic reasoning, we echo Baldwin's question: "If Ebonics isn't a language, then tell me, what is?" (as cited in O'Neil, 1998, p. 38). Regardless of the terminology used, there is consensus that AAL is rule-governed and systematic. It is also important to recognize that a person's language not only reflects his or her culture, but it is also a way of thinking (Fanon, 1952/2008; Smitherman, 2006). Following this line of logic, attempts to eradicate a person's language can potentially be socially, emotionally, psychologically, and cognitively damaging.

Linguicism

"Linguicism can be defined as discrimination and oppression based on one's language" (Schniedewind & Davidson, 1998). Like other forms of oppression, it can occur on an individual level, where a person holds and acts on beliefs and attitudes that support or perpetuate language discrimination and oppression. Often, it is not intentional and can occur at both unconscious and conscious levels, and it may be active or passive. Examples include making fun of people who have an "accent" or referring to AAL as "broken English," "bad English," and the like. Such individual linguistic acts intimate that certain language systems or ways of speaking are inherently superior to others.

Linguicism can also occur on institutional and cultural/societal levels and, like individual linguicism, can be intentional or unintentional. At the institutional level, a network of institutional structures, policies, and practices creates advantages and benefits for people who speak the language of power—SE (Delpit, 1995)—and disadvantages people who do not—for instance, the U.S. declaration that English is the "official" language, or states that mandate instruction in English only. At the societal/cultural level, social norms, roles, rituals, language, and music also reinforce the belief that one language is superior to another.

> AAL has been subjected to continuous, multi-generational linguicism, which for the most part, has not escaped the consciousness or psyche of many AAL speakers (Boutte, 2007). . . . To fully comprehend why AAL is often viewed negatively requires at least a rudimentary understanding of how oppression occurs and maintains itself. In addition to the structural inequities in school and societal practices and policies, linguistic oppression also frequently occurs via microaggressions, which take the form of subtle, automatic, verbal and nonverbal exchanges that denigrate people of color. For example, when AAL speakers speak in classrooms and their teachers either verbally or nonverbally convey the message that the students' language is incomprehensible, or when SE speakers laugh at AAL speakers' language and this ridicule is not interrupted by the teachers.
>
> (Boutte & Johnson, 2013, pp. 303–304)

Examples of Linguicism

Consider the four comments about AAL from two White females, one African American male, and a Filipino female. The common themes of disrespect for AAL should be evident.

Example 1: Personal Conversation With an African American Professor

> Whenever Black athletes spoke in African American Language during television interviews before or after games, I would cringe. They were an embarrassment and represented what I thought to be an unacceptable level of ignorance. For my part, I spoke hyper-"correct" Standard English as a

stark contrast and testimony to the world that there are intelligent Black men. Thanks to Gloria, I have engaged in and revisited an Africancentric and critical knowledge base which reawakened my deep appreciation for African American Language and culture.

(G. J., personal communication, February 2, 2007)

This professor admits to "drinking the kook-aid" (internalizing pervasive negative narratives about AAL). Initially, he viewed AAL as an embarrassment and responded to AAL speakers negatively.

Example 2: Personal Communication During a Seminar on African American Language

A White, female literacy coach laughingly conveyed her experience teaching in a majority African American town in South Carolina. Desiring to reward her children for good behavior, she asked them what they would like. They all agreed that they wanted *annihilators* (at least, this is what she thought they said). Thinking that this was the latest trend in toys and confident that she could find them, she ventured to store after store, with no success. Finally, she had to return to the children to ask them again what they wanted and discovered that they were asking for *Now and Laters* (a kind of taffy candy sold in packs)—one child showed her the candy, as he had brought one to school (personal communication, January 21, 2009).

This example may seem like a harmless misunderstanding, but daily instances of being sent the message that one's language is incomprehensible (when the speaker thinks they are speaking the same language) convey that there is something wrong with the language.

Example 3: Written Journal Reflection by a White Female Teacher

Isn't it amazing that four or more years of teacher training hardly prepares us for the realities we face in the classroom? My first year of teaching was also a daily nightmare of finding myself woefully unprepared. I taught first grade and was doing a getting to know you activity with the children early in my first year. One question I asked each child was "what is your favorite food?" One black girl said something I could not understand at all after many uncomfortable repetitions, so I had to take her to a neighboring teacher who also was black to translate for me! I was a city girl from Minnesota who knew nothing about African American culture, much less southern culture. I felt like a CLD [Culturally and Linguistically Diverse] student!

(White female teacher, personal communication,
October 23, 2009; used with permission)

We do have to question how it is that Blacks and Whites can coexist, and, yet, many Whites are unable to understand AAL. Interestingly, SE and AAL share about 80 percent of the same vocabulary, though the syntactic structure and phonology are different.

Example 4: Comment by a Filipino Professor in a Seminar About Writing

A Filipino professor at a historically Black university explained her puzzlement with African American students who do not speak SE. They say, "How is you?" She conveyed that she did not know what they were saying at times and was surprised that they lived in the US and did not speak English (personal Communication, July 8, 2010).

This example represents a typical reaction to AAL speakers. It is not clear to me how non-AAL speakers cannot figure out what their students are saying, based on the context. There is nothing incomprehensible about "How is you?" When I asked the professor about dialects in her native home, she explained that there were many. Interestingly, she did not view AAL as an English variation or dialect, but, rather, "incorrect English." Unfortunately, the students' overtures to connect with the professor and inquire about her welfare ("How is you?") were regarded with disdain and confusion.

None of these examples is uncommon. All four are examples of individual levels of linguicism. With the exception of the comments by the African American professor, the other three also influence instructional practices, which moves them to the institutional level of linguicism. As we examine the structure and rules of AAL, it becomes clear that it is based on a set of rules that make sense—and can be understood by others. The next section examines typical responses to linguicism.

A Classroom Example of Linguicism

> If school considers someone's language inadequate, they'll probably fail.
> (Stubbs, as cited in Delpit and Dowdy, 2002, p. xvii)

Consider the following typical classroom scenario in which an African American child is reading the text, with the teacher's assistance.

Text:	Yesterday I washed my brother's clothes.
S:	Yesterday I wash my bruver's clothes.
T:	Wait, let's go back. What's that word again? [Points at washed]
S:	Wash.

T:	No. Look at it again. What letters do you see at the end? You see "e-d." Do you remember what we say when we see those letters on the end of the word?
S:	ed.
T:	OK, but in this case we say washed. Can you say that?
S:	Washed.
T:	Good. Now read it again.
S:	Yesterday I washed my bruver . . .
T:	Wait a minute, what's that word again? [Points to brother]
S:	Bruver.
T:	No. Look at these letters in the middle. [Points to brother] Remember to read what you see. Do you remember how we say that sound? Put your tongue between your teeth and say/th/.

The lesson continues in this way. What is happening here? The teacher "corrects" the student's AAL-influenced pronunciations and grammar, while ignoring the fact that the student had to have comprehended the sentence in order to translate it into AAL. It is important for teachers not to confuse a new language system with reading comprehension. Children become better readers by having opportunities to read. Overcorrection will cause the child to be less likely to become a fluent reader (Delpit, 1998). Later, strategies will be presented that can help teachers better achieve their goal of teaching reading, while not assaulting the child's language. Typically, writing activities lend themselves to rewriting and, thus, provide better opportunities to teach children to translate from one language system to the next. It is important to note that the term "translate" is used, instead of "correct." "Translate" connotes that the child has a complete language system intact and is following the rules of that system. If the child pronounces "brother" as "bruver," the child is actually *correctly using* AAL's phonological system, as will be explained. The child, then, needs to learn how to translate the word into SE. More details will follow as examples of the rules and structure of AAL are discussed. However, a discussion of how AAL speakers respond to linguicism will be presented first.

Responses to Linguicism

Borrowing from one of King's (2005) 10 key principles of Black education:

African Americans are likely to use one of three modes of responses to racism and accompanying linguicism: (1) Adaptation; adopting what is deemed useful; (2) Improvisation; substituting or improvising alternatives that are more sensitive to African American culture; and (3) Resistance; resisting that which is destructive and not in the best interests of African Americans. Thus, AAL speakers who respond using the first mode (Adaptation) are likely to learn to code switch and alternate between using SE and AAL, depending on the context and benefits).

(Boutte & Johnson, 2013, p. 304)

These speakers are likely to use AAL in informal settings and SE in formal settings. AAL speakers who improvise find ways of making AAL work for them (e.g., blending the two languages in their speech and writing). These types of improvisation are referred to as "code meshing" or "code mixing" (Canagarajah, 2006; Kirkland & Jackson, 2009; Young, 2009). Finally, AAL speakers may figure out (consciously or not) that the best way of maintaining their psychological and social center is to resist using SE altogether; thus, they opt not to code-switch and to flourish primarily in their AAL proficiency. Acknowledging that neither AAL nor SE is really "pure" or uninfluenced by others, speakers who opt for this response intentionally choose AAL as their predominant language. Speakers who chose to speak AAL as their primary language may be likely to consciously gravitate toward opportunities and activities that lend themselves to appreciation of AAL strengths (e.g., church, hip-hop, spoken word). I readily note that any of these three adaptive responses makes sense, depending on a variety of factors, such as familial, educational, and social influences, and scaffolding opportunities. Speakers may also alternate between the responses.

African American Language

> In the study of language in school, pupils were made to scoff at the Negro dialect as some peculiar possession of the Negro which they should despise, rather than directed to study the background of this language as a broken-down African tongue—in short to understand their own linguistic history, which is certainly more important for them than the study of French Phonetics or Historical Spanish Grammar.
>
> (Carter Godwin Woodson, 1933/1990, p. 19)

As prophetically noted by Woodson more than eight decades ago, many African Americans and AAL speakers are not aware of the linguistic history and rules of AAL. Indeed, the language is one of many examples of the strong legacy of African culture. Despite attempts to eradicate it, it has remained—defiant, beautiful, and whole.

Features of African American Language[2]

Although different variations of AAL exist (e.g., Creole, Gullah), there are common underlying rules and patterns across geographic regions in the US. Additionally, linguistic patterns among some people in the African diaspora who speak English are similar to those of AAL speakers in the US (Bailey, 1965; Baugh,

1980; Holm, 1984; Smitherman, 1977/1985, 1999/2001; Turner, 1949). In the mid 1990s, when a delegation from Sierra Leone visited St. Helena, South Carolina, where Gullah (an AAL variety) is spoken, speech patterns were indistinguishable between the two groups (Boutte, 2007). The existence of common patterns among AAL speakers in various regions of the US and in the African diaspora counters assertions that features of AAL are simple SE errors. A parallel can be made to Jean Piaget's theory of cognitive development. Piaget's theory was developed based on his observations that children at various stages made the same types of "errors" (e.g., 4-year-olds consistently made errors in conservation tasks). Piaget concluded that the "errors" were indeed developmental patterns governed by underlying cognitive structures. Likewise, AAL is a well-ordered, complete system, with rules for forming sounds, words, sentences, and nonverbal elements. Common examples of phonology, syntax, semantics, and pragmatics are presented in the subsequent section. The samples are not intended to be exhaustive. Additionally, readers should consult referenced literature in order to understand the complexity and scope of AAL.

Phonology

Phonology refers to the sound system of a language. Like other languages, AAL has common sound patterns. Many of the phonological rules are derived from West African languages (Smitherman, 1977/1985, 1999/2001; LeMoine, 1999). A few sample features are listed in Table 4.1 on page 116) (Smitherman, 1977/ 1985; Wolfram & Fasold, 1974). AAL examples are presented first and then contrasted with SE.

Syntax

Syntax refers to the rules for combining words into acceptable phrases, clauses, and sentences. Examples are provided in Table 4.1 (Smitherman, 1977/1985, 1998; Wolfram & Fasold, 1974). As noted on Table 4.1, AAL's linguistic rules allow double or multiple negation, do not require linking verbs, and keep the verb the same for present, past, and future tenses.

Semantics

Semantics refers to the meaning of words and word relationships in messages. Because of the rules guiding the semantic feature of AAL, new words are continuously generated (Smitherman, 1994). The generative semantic feature of AAL is probably the source of the misconception that AAL is slang. Although slang exists in any language system, underlying rules for AAL include continuous suspension of literal definitions and using cultural inversion. Historically, it has been necessary for African Americans to speak in codes that others could not understand. For example, many spirituals, folktales, and quilts contained symbolism and messages that were purposely disguised, so that White slave owners could not detect them. bell hooks (1994) comments on this "protective" semantic phenomenon (linguistic guerilla warfare):

> To heal the splitting of mind and body, we marginalized and oppressed people attempt to recover ourselves and our experiences in language. We seek to make a place for intimacy. Unable to find such a place in standard English . . . When I need to say words that do more than simply mirror or address the dominant reality, I speak black vernacular. There, in that location, we make English do what we want it to do. We take the oppressor's language and turn it against itself. We make our words a counter-hegemonic speech, liberating ourselves in language.
>
> (p. 175)

Because of the semantic rules that guide AAL, new words are continuously generated (Smitherman, 1994). Generational differences can be seen in the use of new terminology in AAL, and older generations are unable to decipher the meanings used by youth. Hence, the intent to cloak the meaning of the word is achieved. Again, this serves a purpose. Semantic examples are presented below (Smitherman, 1977/1985, 1994, 1998; Wolfram & Fasold, 1974):

- frequent use of metaphors: lyrics, poems, folktales, ministers, orators; consider Martin Luther King's "I Have a Dream" speech or Maya Angelou's "Still I Rise" poem;
- cultural inversion: the meanings of words that may have been intended to be inflammatory are reversed to remove the impact (e.g., dog/dawg; nigger/nigga); while the word "nigga" is used as a term of endearment among some (e.g., contemporary song lyrics) and viewed as obscene and offensive to others, it illustrates the concept of cultural inversion;
- tonal semantics: changing the meaning of a word by varying the tone (adding more or less emphasis), rhythm, and vocal inflection—"Girl, you *wearing* that hat" (meaning the hat looks extremely good on her).

Pragmatics

Pragmatics has to do with the function of language in social contexts—the styles of speaking. Social constraints govern one's use of language in specific contexts (e.g., knowing what can be said, how and when it can be said, and to whom it can be said). The appropriate use of language in different contexts is a part of pragmatics. For example, whenever I travel to another country, I research what is considered to be appropriate, inappropriate, rude, courteous, etc. Not only do I research the pragmatic aspects before traveling, but I also study conversations and actions. For example, when in Ghana, West Africa, for the first time, I quickly

TABLE 4.1 Features of African American Language

Features/rules	AAL	SE
Phonological features of AAL and SE		
Substitution of the "th" phoneme	dem	them
	wif, wit, or wid	with
Different stress patterns	po'lice	po lice'
No distinction between words that sound alike	fine/find = fine	fine/find
	cold/coal = coal	cold/coal
	mask/mass = mass	mask/mass
Consonant blends are often substituted or deleted	axe	ask
Examples of AAL syntax		
Make it simple—e.g., delete linking verbs	You a pretty girl	You are a pretty girl
Two or more negatives are allowed	You don't have no shoes	You don't have any shoes
Use of the habitual "be" to connote perpetual emphasis	He be hittin' me	He is always hitting me (note there is no direct literal SE interpretation for the habitual "be")
Regularize when possible—maintain same form	I is, you is, he, she, or it is, we is, you is, they is (note the verb remains the same throughout (regularization)	I am, you are, he, she, or it is, we are, you are, they are (note the verb changes—is irregular)
Regularize when possible—maintain same form; third person singular remains the same	I swim, you swim, he, she, or it swim, we swim, you swim, they swim	I swim, you swim, he, she, or it swims, we swim, you swim, they swim (note the verb change in 3rd person singular)
Regularize when possible—maintain same form; reflective pronouns do not change form	His/hisself, their/theirselves	His/himself, their/themselves
Plurals	Five cent (note the plural marker is the number itself (more than one = plural))	Five cents (note there are two plural markers: the number "five" and the "s" on "cents")

Possessive	John chair (note that the possessor (John) serves to indicate possession)	John's chair (note two possessive markers: name of possessor—John and apostrophe "s")
Past tense	I look out the window (note: typically will not hear or see the "ed" in writing or orally. However, sometimes the "ed" is overemphasized (hypercorretion) and the oral pronunciation becomes "look-D" (Smitherman, 1977/1985))	I looked out the window
Topicalization	That teacher she mean (two topics/subjects—"teacher" and "she"	The teacher is mean

Examples of semantics

Keep the language generative; improvise; be creative	"Shawty" (shorty)—a female, someone that a person likes; "swag"—style	Slang is used, but not typically generated; often co-opted from AAL; does not change as rapidly as AAL
Use cultural inversion—reverse the meaning and function of words	"Dawg" (dog)—term of endearment; "nigga"—term of endearment	Not typically done
Speak in codes	Symbolism—metaphors, coded language in songs, quilts, folktales, etc.	Symbolism exists, but is often used formally in books, speeches, music—not necessarily in everyday speech

Pragmatics

Communicate impressively	Signifying; playing with the language	
Speak with soul, personal style, and verve	Circular and energetic conversations are okay; dramatic repetition is used; episodic stories	Mundane/lackluster—even-toned, occasional changes in tone; topic-centered stories
More than one person can speak at a time	Overlapping and co-narration are permitted	Sequential; turn-taking
Speak directly; be efficient	Direct commands	Indirect commands
Use nonverbal language		
Involve your audience	Call and response	Okay to talk to a group without involving the audience

Source: Boutte, 2007

noticed that it is considered rude not to ask about people's families (e.g., "How is your mother?"), and it is a good idea to mention God a few times during the conversation.

AAL has two dimensions: language and style (Smitherman, 1977/1985, 1998). Pragmatics refers to the rules for using the language in social contexts. Many describe it as the soul, style, or spirit of the language (Rickford & Rickford, 2000). Asa Hilliard (2002) summarizes by saying that the basic rule is to "communicate impressively" (p. 95). Anyone who has communicated cross-culturally understands that how something is said is as important as what is being said. The stylistic beauty of AAL is best appreciated by those who are linguistically informed (Smitherman, 1977/1985). In general, the rules reflect characteristics of Black culture (Hale-Benson, 1986; Hilliard, 1992): involve the audience or listener, be engaging and animated, and use nonverbals. As with other cultural communication styles, certain ways of communicating are discourteous. In the case of AAL, it is discourteous for the listener not to give a response or feedback to the speaker (Smitherman, 1977/1985). In the following there are a few pragmatic examples, which are also briefly summarized in Table 4.1:

- Signification/Joanin'/The Dozens refers to the stunning and clever verbal art of insult in which a speaker humorously puts down and talks about the listener (Smitherman, 1977/1985). The ultimate insult is to talk about the listener's "mama." To be proficient, quick wittedness is required. Signification is used by all age groups and both genders. According to Smitherman (1977/1985), it contains all of the following characteristics:

    - indirection, circumlocution;
    - metaphorical images (images rooted in the everyday world);
    - humor, irony;
    - rhythmic fluency;
    - teachy, but not preachy;
    - directed at person(s) present in the speech situation (signifiers do not talk behind your back);
    - punning, play on words;
    - introduction of the semantically or logically unexpected.

An excellent example of signification can be seen in the movie *Roll, Bounce* (Scene 5 on the DVD). An example in Zora Neale Hurston's (1937/1965) book, *Their Eyes Were Watching God*, can be found on pages 78–79.

- Co-narration and overlapping are allowed in conversations. That is, more than one speaker can speak at a time. (In schools, AAL speakers are often disciplined for this stylistic form of discourse.)
- There are different ways of questioning and telling a story. Stories tend to be episodic (focusing on episodes), rather than topic-centered (Delpit, 1998).

In her study, Heath (1982/1992) observed that AAL speakers asked more open-ended versus closed-ended, school-type questions (e.g., "What is that like?" vs. "What color is the sky?").

- Direct (efficient) rather than indirect commands are used (e.g., "Sit down now!" vs. "Can you sit down now?") (Delpit, 1995).
- Conversations are circular rather than linear, interrelating several points.
- Nonverbals are used (e.g., giving "five," sucking teeth, rolling eyes, hands on hips, stomping). Remember, historically and currently, it is adaptive for Black people to read their contexts and to communicate with each other inconspicuously.
- Call and response are used—involving the audience is an African tradition.
- Dramatic repetition is employed.
- Metaphors and proverbs are frequently used.
- Cultural familiarity is found (e.g., "dawg, brotha, sista").
- Tonal semantics are used to engage the listener.

Look for pattern activities at the end of this chapter.

Linguistic Parallels Between AAL and Other Languages

Examining parallels between AAL and other languages further illustrates the point that AAL is based on a linguistic rule system (see Table 4.2). It is curious that AAL tends to be regarded as substandard, whereas other languages applying the same linguistic rules are not. For example, see how a French-speaking person would pronounce the "th" sound (Table 4.2). In sum, in order to effectively teach speakers of AAL, both educators and speakers will first need to understand the legitimacy and history of AAL. The next section addresses educational implications.

Educational Implications

Although recognizing that a "standard" (mainstream) form of English exists as the language of power in schools and much of society (Delpit, 1995; Delpit & Dowdy, 2002), the world is richer than it is possible to express in any single language or dialect. The goal of school, then, should not be to eradicate the child's first language, but to add other language systems to his or her linguistic repertoires.

Viewing SE as the prototype and AAL as on the opposite end of the continuum is culturally invasive. AAL is a co-equal language system and it also influences what is thought of as MAE (Alim & Smitherman, 2002). Teachers and students from all ethnic groups would benefit from ongoing counternarratives that reject dominant notions about AAL as inferior and ahistorical (Perry & Delpit, 1998; Perry, Steele, & Hilliard, 2003; Smitherman, 1977/1985). In schools, AAL should be recognized as a legitimate, rule-governed system, embraced in classrooms, and used as a bridge for SE proficiency.

TABLE 4.2 Linguistic Parallels Between AAL and Other Languages

Linguistic feature	SE example	AAL example	Other languages
Syntax: double negation	"I don't have a hat" (two negatives are not permitted)	"I *don't* have *no* hat" (two or more negatives are permitted)	French: "Je *n'*ai *pas* un chapeau" (two negatives are required)
Syntax: using an "s" to designate plural regular nouns	"That costs *five* dollars" (two plural markers)	"That costs *five* dollar"★ (one plural marker; the number serves to indicate plurality)	Chinese (speaking English): "That costs *five* dollar" (one plural marker; the number serves to indicate plurality)
Phonology	"This is my hat"	"Dis is my hat." "I am going wif you" (substitution of "th" phoneme with "d"	French-speaking: "Zis is my hat." "I am going wiz you" (substitution of "th" phoneme with "z"; another common substitution can be seen in many East Indian speakers who substitute the "w" sound with "v"; example: "vife" for "wife"

Note: Negatives are in italics. ★ Another variation that would typically be noted in AAL would be subject–verb regularization (e.g., "That *cost* five dollar"). For the purpose of example, only one feature is highlighted

Source: Boutte, 2007

A misconception commonly held by many educators is that many speakers of AAL could speak "properly," if only they put forth sufficient effort (Baugh, 1999). Because classroom instructional practices are not always linguistically informed, language can become a primary source of inequality surrounding the lives of students who come to school labeled with a speech variety that is stigmatized in society (Banks & Banks, 1997; Boutte & Johnson, 2013). The goal of education, however, should be to add to the language repertoire(s) that is/are already present in the lives of students. As cognitive repertoires are built on prior knowledge, educators must validate and affirm the students' home language if proficiency in SE is to be obtained (LeMoine, 1999). Indeed, educators should help AAL speakers learn to negotiate both AAL and SE, thus gaining access to wider opportunities, while honoring the history and traditions of their families and communities.

Educators wishing to help AAL speakers develop SE proficiency will need to enhance their linguistic knowledge and understanding of AAL. In addition to reading selections from the reference list, the video *American Tongues* (Alvarez & Kolker, 1988), which examines language varieties in the US and their social implications, is recommended. Educators should also inquire into their own language histories to illuminate their beliefs about different language varieties. Additionally, the affective aspect of language must be acknowledged. Like any new concept, students will not likely learn SE if they are not motivated or if they feel anxious (LeMoine, 1999). Therefore, strategies recommended in the next section (e.g., contrastive analysis and code-switching) will be important for helping to start with the students' language.

Presenting SE and AAL as co-equal language systems will require relevant student engagement with both AAL and SE. Reframing AAL as a legitimate language system implies that the goal is not to "correct" AAL speakers, as speakers are following the correct rules for AAL (see Table 4.1 for sample AAL rules). Rather than thinking of "correcting" AAL, one can actually think in terms of a *translation* from one language system (e.g., SE) to another (e.g., AAL). In other words, students' linguistic repertoires are being expanded so that they have more than one way to communicate and so that they can learn SE, the "language of power" (Delpit, 1995).

Getting Started

One way to open the conversation about language variations might be to read aloud from a book that contains AAL[3] and invite children to notice the examples. Kayla Hostetler, the high-school English teacher mentioned in Chapter 3, shared:

> In order to learn more about AAL, I listened to what students said and took notes. I kept a teaching notebook, where I excitedly scribbled down sentences that caught my attention when students were having conversations or reading aloud. These notes were usually starting points for mini lessons on contrastive analysis. Contrastive analysis is the comparing and contrasting of two language systems. I also used students' writing as data and looked for patterns to guide lessons on contrastive analysis.
>
> (Personal communication, June 2014)

Contrastive Analysis

A key strategy recommended for helping students add SE to their existing language repertoires is contrastive analysis. Contrastive analysis is a method used to contrast the grammar of home languages (e.g., AAL) with SE. It involves comparing and contrasting the linguistic structures of two languages or language systems. It allows AAL speakers to engage in metalinguistic analysis of their own language and can be done orally and in writing. One research study of African American university students demonstrated that contrastive analysis resulted in 59.3 percent fewer AAL features in writing, as opposed to 8.5 percent fewer AAL features when traditional methods were used (Taylor, 1991; Lindblom, 2005). Other studies with elementary students have also demonstrated that contrastive analysis is effective for teaching AAL speakers to add on SE, as well as improving reading and writing outcomes for the students (Fogel & Ehri, 2000; Wheeler & Swords, 2006).

Other benefits of contrastive analysis include:

- increased ability to recognize differences between AAL and SE;
- more proficient student editing of their own work for differences, vocabulary, and syntax;
- greater facility in the use of SE structure, in both oral and written forms;
- enhanced appreciation and acceptance of their home language (LeMoine, 1999; Wheeler & Swords, 2006).

Contrastive analysis strategies for teaching AAL speakers SE proficiency should focus on both oral and written language. Young children may spend more time with oral activities (such as role-playing different scenarios). A large collection of literature written in AAL and SE is important to share with students. Lyrics (appropriate ones) from songs can also be used to translate AAL to SE, or vice versa. Activities should be bidirectional (translation of AAL to SE and SE to AAL).

Although I am not promoting a specific program, *English for Your Success* (LeMoine, 1999) is a straightforward guide and resource that contains strategies and activities that can be used in pre-kindergarten through to eighth-grade classes. It contains curriculum guides for each grade level and videos of actual classrooms. It is not a tightly scripted program and offers general tenets that can be adapted for a variety of settings.[4] In order to help AAL speakers learn to translate SE, numerous and ongoing written and oral activities are used (LeMoine, 1999). A few examples are listed below.

Written Activities/Assignments That Can Be Used

Written assignments can be written in AAL first and translated to SE, or vice versa:

- report writing
- logs
- journal writing
- creative writing
- personal biographies
- letter writing
- research reports.

Oral Activities That Can Be Used

- Class discussions
- formal speeches
- dramatizing
- oral reports
- role-play
- interviewing
- musical interpretations
- dialogues
- oral readings
- debating
- sharing opinions
- story/event retell
- audiovisual presentations
- class and individual projects.

It is important to note that AAL has primarily operated as an oral language. Readers who are unfamiliar with AAL may initially find some words difficult to pronounce, and written words may not be readily recognizable. As many books, songs, and other information that are currently written in AAL also come with

FIGURE 4.1 My Queens and Kings Be the Best! An Example From Nichole Folsom.

audio recordings, these may be useful. Alternatively, parents, community members, or students may read the books and record them for later use.

A well-known saying in African American culture is, "If you don't know, you betta ask somebody." In the case of AAL, good resources for the language are the students themselves. For example, teachers may find it useful to collect language samples from the students and use these as a point of instruction (or have students bring in language samples from television, music, home, etc.).

Nichole Folsom, a teacher with the Center of Excellence for the Education and Equity of African American Students (CEEEAAS), whose teaching will be further featured in Chapter 5, used morning messages such as the one seen in Figure 4.1 as opportunities for students to engage in contrastive analysis (as well as to teach other conventional skills). Ms. Folsom uses the "habitual be" ("My

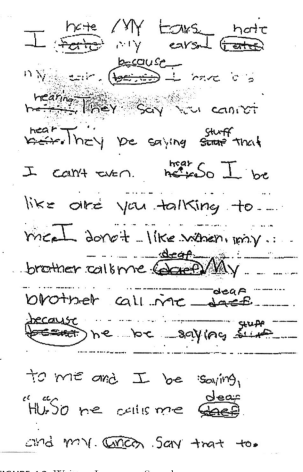

FIGURE 4.2 Written Language Sample.

queens and kings be the best!"), and students orally translate this to SE ("My queens and kings are the best!")—not necessarily a literal translation, as there is no equivalent translation for the "habitual be."

Likewise, Ms. Folsom used students' journals as opportunities to code switch. Figure 4.2 shows an excerpt from a journal. Writing activities lend themselves to rewriting, so students can write their first drafts or informal drafts and later rewrite them. In the case of journals, Ms. Folsom did not have students edit them, as they contained students' feelings and were written as informal pieces. For example, the journal entry in Figure 4.2 was written by a child with a hearing disability, who was very frustrated by it. The journal allowed him an opportunity to express this. Ms. Folsom used the journal entries as a source for finding out more about the students' language and to detect language patterns and AAL features that she could later focus on in a mini lesson. Readers should not focus on other nonconventional spelling, punctuation, and grammatical errors. The purpose of this language sample is to note AAL features used that can inform future instruction (e.g., AAL syntactical features such as "habitual be" and subject–verb agreement).

An example of a language sample that I collected from Ms. Folsom's third grade class can be seen in Table 4.3. These words, phases, and sentences were collected during a regular lesson in which Ms. Folsom was reading a book to the students. It represents comments made by the students during the lesson that contain AAL features. In Table 4.3, I have also listed the SE translation and the AAL rules for the benefit of readers.

In general, I suggest starting contrastive analysis by focusing on one prominent AAL feature that teachers have observed their students using. As students start to pay attention to the differences between the rules of the two systems, their metalinguistic awareness will increase, and they are likely to code-switch more often over time—if they choose to do so. Wheeler and Swords (2006) provide logs and checklists that teachers can use to help students monitor their use of AAL over time. One last point about contrastive analysis: It is not necessary that students learn the name of the AAL features per se (though it is okay if they do); however, teachers and students do need to pay attention to the AAL language patterns that they are using.

Many teachers also use books and excerpts from books for contrastive analysis. A list of books written in AAL can be found on Noma LeMoine's website.[5] It is important to note that books and other texts should be translated from SE to AAL, as well as from AAL to SE. A key point is that contrastive analysis should be ongoing, rather than used once or twice.

Code-Switching

Code-switching is often referred to as "dialect shifting," or "style shifting." It is a technique used to help speakers learn how to modify their language style based

TABLE 4.3 Example of Linguistic Contrastive Analysis Using Language Samples From Elementary Students

Students' language sample	SE translation*	Rules
Dey friends	They are friends	– Th phoneme was substituted with "d" (phonology) – Deletion of linking verb (are) (syntax)
How you know?	How do you know?	Deletion of linking verb (syntax)
'Cause dey always . . .	Because they always . . .	Th phoneme substitution (phonology)
What month come after December?	What month comes after December?	Subject–verb agreement (syntax)
August got three and July has three	August has three and July has three, or August has three and so does July	(This is not necessarily AAL, but it is not "standard"). It is colloquial. Replace "got" with "has"
She don't look mean (referring to Bertha character in the book being read)	She does not (doesn't) look mean	Subject–verb agreement (syntax) (Note: I discourage contractions in formal writing, although they are not grammatically incorrect)
Where she at?	Where is she?	– Deletion of linking verb – Word order in the question (syntax)
Dat dog big now	That dog is big now	– Th phoneme substitution (phonology) – Deletion of linking verb

Note: * Translations are noted for the purpose of illustration only. The second and third columns would be left blank, so that students can complete them. Teachers may group items by AAL feature (e.g., phonology) and give students one or two to translate and to discuss the linguistic rules for both AAL and SE

on the setting. For example, on school tests, SE is typically used; at home, speakers' natural vernaculars are normally used. This logic, although seemingly simplistic and straightforward (and supported by research), is not typically applied in classrooms (Boutte, 2007; Wheeler & Swords, 2006). Using contrastive analysis is helpful to assist students in code-switching. According to Wheeler and Swords (2010), and corroborated by a number of studies presented later, code-switching helps to build flexibility, a skill that plays a significant role in successful literacy learning. Additionally, both code-switching and contrastive analysis have been effectively used with AAL speakers (Wheeler & Swords, 2006, 2010).

Research has shown that there is a relationship between code-switching and students' reading and writing outcomes. Craig et al.'s (2009) investigation of the effect of AAL speakers' code-switching on reading outcomes found that first-through fifth-grade AAL speakers who code-switched had higher reading achievement outcomes. Of the 165 participants in this study, 85 percent code-switched. Wheeler and Swords (2006) also found that direct teaching of code-switching positively impacted the reading achievement of AAE speakers in elementary school.

After observing patterns of students' language, teachers can begin to teach children how to code-switch. One idea is to build on what children already know by discussing how they use language during formal and informal activities (Wheeler & Swords, 2006).[6] Even young children are typically involved in a spectrum of activities that go from informal to highly formal (e.g., sporting activities, church, dining out). Focusing on formal versus informal language should not privilege SE over AAL. Teachers can lead students in discussions, role-plays, storytelling, and other activities to help them differentiate between formal and informal clothing, speech, and behavior. Students can practice speaking for different settings during daily classroom activities. Just as some clothing may be inappropriate for certain settings, language can be effective or ineffective, appropriate or inappropriate, depending on the setting. For example, in an informal setting, a person may use the word "ain't," which may be inappropriate if giving a formal speech. For older children, certain time periods may be dedicated to either formal or informal speaking and writing activities. Once children get the idea of different registers (formal/informal), they (children) can become language detectives and collect language samples to be used for contrastive analysis activities.

Below are examples of role-play activities, which I devised and have used in my courses, that can be done in classrooms to help students use both code-switching and contrastive analysis. The idea is that students will work together in pairs or small groups. In each pair/group, students can plan a 1–3-minute presentation illustrating one of the scenarios below. Students are instructed to use AAL in one of the presentations and SE in the other. They are asked to pay attention to verbal and nonverbal aspects of language (e.g., eye contact, posture, hand gestures, intonation, verve, use of notes, use of metaphors) to be sure that their role-play is congruent with the language style being used. For example, verve is expected when they use AAL. When students are done performing their respective choices (from the list below), classmates discuss whether or not they achieved their goal of demonstrating the language style. We also discuss examples of each style that was used. For K–12 classroom purposes, this idea can be used and tailored to whatever is being taught (e.g., rain forests—students may create a PSA using two different language styles to appeal to different audiences). I note that neither AAL nor SE is "pure," and both contain aspects of the other. The purpose of the exercise, though, is to compare and contrast the features used in both styles.

1. Do a commercial selling a product of your choice. Demonstrate how the commercial might look if it is aired during a Black television show and aimed

at getting the attention of African American youth. Demonstrate how the commercial might look if it airs during the national news on a major, mainstream network.

2. Report a sports event in AAL and again in SE.
3. Serve as a witness to a fight on the playground using AAL and again using SE.
4. Discuss relationship issues (overview of a problem you are having with your significant other) on the *Oprah* show and again on a talk show such as *Jerry Springer.*
5. Give a speech to persuade a group of African American youth from an urban area to vote for a political candidate. Give a speech convincing a group of African American professionals to vote for a political candidate.
6. Summarize the preamble of the U.S. Constitution for two audiences: (1.) urban youth, (2.) African American professionals.

> We the people of the United States, in order to form a more perfect union, establish justice, insure domestic tranquility, provide for the common defense, promote the general welfare, and secure the blessings of liberty to ourselves and our posterity, do ordain and establish this Constitution for the United States of America.

7. Respond to the query "What is a rainforest?" to two different audiences: (1.) a 5-year-old AA speaker, and (2.) a 5-year-old SE speaker. Rainforests are forests characterized by high rainfall. More than half of the world's species of plants and animals are found in the rainforest. At least 3,000 fruits are found in the rainforests; of these, only 200 are now in use in the Western world. The Indians of the rainforest use more than 2,000.
8. Do an analysis of a movie or song (of your choice), first, in SE, and, second, in AAL.
9. Use SE and then AAL to tell a little about yourself.
10. Describe a zoo animal using AAL and SE. Give details about the animal's appearance, the sounds it makes, etc.
11. Give directions of how you can get from the hotel to the convention center in AAL and SE.
12. Create an oral contrastive analysis of your choice.

Moving Beyond Assimilation: Code Meshing

In schools and in academic circles, code-switching has been a strategy of choice, because it honors AAL speakers' vernacular while helping them add on SE. As code-switching has been defined several ways in the extant literature, I clarify that the brand of code-switching that I am advocating is one in which AAL and SE are viewed as co-parallel languages (Boutte & Johnson, 2013; Canagarajah, 2006; Kirkland & Jackson, 2009; Young, 2009). That is, I believe that both AAL and SE speakers benefit from code-switching and mutual exchanges in their language usage. I reject assimilationist, unidimensional, and hierarchical versions of code-switching that support AAL to SE translation/usage, but not SE to AAL. Importantly, I assume that discussions and applications of code-switching (and contrastive analysis alike) must necessarily include discussions of power and hegemony (Kirkland & Jackson, 2009; Young, 2009).

Several scholars have made a strong case for code meshing as the goal (Alim & Smitherman, 2012; Young, 2009). Rather than taking uncritical, conformist, and assimilationist perspectives about language use, they rightly note that there is much to be learned from models of language education in multilingual democracies around the world (Alim & Smitherman, 2012; Dyson & Smitherman, 2009). Research in places such as Sweden, Norway, and other countries has shown that recognizing the legitimacy of other varieties of a language improves standard language learning (Alim & Smitherman, 2012). Recently, a report that appeared in *Education Week* corroborated this finding in a dual-language K–8 Magnet school in Charlotte, North Carolina.[7] It found that African American students actually benefited more than any other group from the bilingual focus in Spanish and, indeed, outscored their non-dual-language peers in reading in all tested grades. The pattern was the same for mathematics. For some of the African American students who speak AAL at home, learning Spanish made them more meta-linguistically aware, which teachers say develops their literacy skills. Teachers in this school also reported that African American students were so highly engaged, it was as if they were in a gifted program, and they were able to make leaps in learning and to get to more interesting topics.

Alim and Smitherman (2012) also noted that South Africa now has 11 official languages included in its constitution, thus elevating African languages to the status of English and Afrikaans. Other countries, such as Peru, have passed innovative multilingual laws that call for the preservation and use of their indigenous languages.

> As educators, it is helpful for us to raise the question, "How are we all involved in perpetuating the myth of a 'standard' and that it is somehow better, more intelligent, more appropriate, more important, and so on than other varieties?" Why do we elevate one particular variety over all others, even when all of our linguistic knowledge tells us that "all languages are equal in linguistic terms"? Why does the "standard" continue to be imposed despite the fact that what we have for a "standard English" in the United States is nothing short of the imposition of White, middle-class language norms? How and why do we continue to measure the worth of People of Color largely by their level of assimilation into dominant White culture?
> (Alim & Smitherman, 2012, p. 191)

Alim and Smitherman (2012) encourage educators to stop apologizing to AAL speakers by saying that that's just the way it is (SE is privileged in jobs, in school, etc.). Instead, they suggest that we begin helping our students imagine the way things can be. Arguments for code meshing resonate with me on many levels, thus presenting a paradox regarding how best to help AAL speaker add on SE (which we, as scholars, speak and benefit from the related privileges), while also transforming our limited conceptions of language.

Finally, it is important to view African American students who speak both AAL and SE as bilingual/bidialectal (Boutte & Johnson, 2012, 2013). If we understand that AAL is rule-governed, then we have to acknowledge that AAL speakers who are learning SE are adding on another language system. Because AAL and SE share common vocabulary, many people fail to recognize the different linguistic rules of AAL. Readers should see Boutte and Johnson (2012) for examples of our twin granddaughters' bilingualism and biliteracy between the ages of 4 and 6—as well as classroom activities that can be used. The poem below, which is written by Dr. Candace Thompson,[8] is an excellent recap of key points in this chapter. She wrote the poem, "as an echo to her middle school students' too often silenced voices" (personal communication, December 17, 2014). The poem was penned in the hopes that her students may be heard as the powerful, intelligent beings that they are.

Who You Be?
By Candace Thompson

Who you be?
You be me?
If you is, then you be free

Free to think
in spaces small
real big thoughts
to scale your wall

You be open?
You be wild?
You think me some stupid chile?

I be more
than your eyes see
I be smart
I be free

Who you be?
And what you bring?
You the kind don't let birds sing?

Ain't your passion on your sleeve?
Can't stand the heat?
Get up and leave

Who you be?
Live it loud
You the teacher
You be proud

Conclusion

Ideally, the discussion of AAL should fall under the broader framework of respect for cultural and linguistic diversity and teaching for liberation. Although this chapter has provided an overview of AAL, readers who seriously want to address instructional issues surrounding AAL need to engage in further study. Collaboration with other interested colleagues will provide support for educators attempting to address the issue. In pre-K–12 schools, administrative and parental support and orientations will also facilitate the goal of validating AAL. Using AAL as a basis for developing SE proficiency will require ongoing and systematic instructional and curricular changes.

As many aspects of African American culture are currently and have historically been viewed in a marginalized fashion, it is difficult for many educators to recognize the validity of AAL as a distinct, rule-governed language system. Because of emotionally intense, often negative, reactions to AAL, it is sometimes difficult to engage in academic discussions about the language system.

Finding strategies for effectively teaching African American English speakers remains a challenge for many educators. Yet, as pervasive evidence indicates, conventional methods are generally ineffective. Two strategies have been recommended in this book that may be useful (contrastive analysis and code-switching). A third strategy, personal thesauruses, is described in the activities below.

Finally, educators will have to acknowledge that we all bring our own language varieties into our classes. Typically, we favor those that are similar to our own. Therefore, the challenge for educators is to find ways, not only to broaden the repertoires of our students, but our own as well. As literacy issues are important in all content areas, the information presented in this chapter should not be considered to only be relevant for language arts or English classes.

Key Points From the Chapter

1. African American Language is referred to by a number of names, such as: African American English, African American Vernacular English, Black English, and Ebonics. AAL follows a set of rules for sounds, grammar, and social use (Alim & Smitherman, 2012; Linguistic Society of America, 1997; Rickford, 1999; Smitherman, 1977/1985; Smitherman, 2006).
2. African American Language speakers experience ongoing linguicism in school.

3. African American Language follows a set of phonological, syntactical, morphological, semantic, and pragmatic rules.
4. Linguistic parallels can be made between AAL and other languages.
5. Two strategies were discussed: (1.) contrastive analysis and (2.) code-switching.

Activities

1. After students have learned about the systematic nature of spoken speech, engage them in an ethnographic project (Language in My Life) that investigates their own language (Alim & Smitherman, 2012). Here, they are asked to collect samples of their own language use outside the classroom over time. Equipped with a notebook (and perhaps categories, including things such as informal and formal language, use of slang), students can collect and analyze examples of their language use in different settings (e.g., with friends at recess, during extracurricular activities, at church, at a concert). As noted by Alim and Smitherman, a project like this one immediately validates the language practices used outside the classroom—for example, in rapping or signifying. It allows them to see their speech behavior as a subject of analysis, thus increasing their metalinguistic analysis. In Alim and Smitherman's work with youth, students began to speak of themselves as style shifters, possessing multiple languages and a range of speech styles.
2. Another project (adapted from Alim and Smitherman's description of Geneva Smitherman's methods used to collect data for her book, *Black Talk: Words and Phrases From the Hood to the Amen Corner* (1994), which give students an opportunity to study AAL patterns, presentation, and style in various contexts) would be to allow them to collect data from several sources:

   – Songs and hit recordings: Students can spend 30 minutes a day listening to CDs or downloads of music and writing down examples of AAL.
   – Radio: Students can listen to a Black radio show of their choice for 30 minutes a day. They are likely to hear "tons of slang words and phrases" (Alim & Smitherman, 2012, p. 183).
   – Movies and television: Students can spend 30 minutes per day watching television shows (e.g., on BET) or Black movies.
   – Community flyers, bulletins, magazines, announcements, or other written materials: These sources can be examined for language usage.
   – Face-to-face interviews: Students can ask people they know for examples of AAL.
   – Participant observation: This would include events in which the students are not only observing, but participating as well.

   Data from this project can be discussed in class regarding insights gleaned about AAL.

3.   Reflect on the following case study: Mr. Johnson, a third-grade teacher in St. Helena, South Carolina, has 21 African American students in his class who speak Gullah—a form of "Black English" or "Ebonics." Mr. Johnson will not let the children in his classroom speak in their natural vernacular (Gullah). He tells them that they need to speak SE in order to do well in society.

   –   Do you support Mr. Johnson's decision? Why or why not?
   –   What are some educational issues that should be considered?
   –   Support your comments with theories, research, or other scholarly literature.

4.   Building on the generative nature of the semantic feature of AAL, teachers can help students develop personal thesauruses (LeMoine, 1999). Each student should create a notebook with 26 pages—one page for each letter of the alphabet. As students use "slang" words (e.g., "swag") or overuse any words (e.g., "good"—"I had a good day." "I feel good"), have them write the word down, along with five synonyms and one antonym. In future writing and speaking instances, students can substitute one of the synonyms from their personal thesauruses in the place of the slang or overused word.[9]

5.   Listen to Jamila Lyiscott'S talk, "What Does It Mean to Be 'Articulate'?" (4 minutes, 29 seconds).[10] Reflect on her commentary on trilingualism.

Resources

1.   Dr. Noma Lemoine's website includes booklists and other resources for AAL and other SE language learners.
2.   Boutte, G. S., & Johnson, G. (2012). Do Educators See and Honor Biliteracy and Bidialectalism in African American Language Speakers? Apprehensions and Reflections of Two Grandparents/Professional Educators. *Early Childhood Education Journal, 41*(2), 133–141.
3.   The Center for Culturally Responsive Teaching has DVDs, apps, and other resources for teachers.
4.   Wheeler, R. S., & Swords, R. (2006). *Code-Switching. Teaching Standard English in Urban CLassrooms.* Urbana, IL: National Council of Teachers of English.

Notes

1. I will use the terms Standard English and Mainstream American English interchangeably, though I am not satisfied with either for reasons beyond the scope of this book. However, most people are familiar with the term "Standard English." Other terms have also been used by others (e.g., "Language of Wider Communication").
2. Portions of this section are drawn from a previously published chapter. Boutte, G. S. (2007). Teaching African American English speakers: Expanding educators and student

repertoires. In M. E. Brisk (Ed.). *Language, culture, and community in teacher education* (pp. 47–70). London: Routledge. Used with permission.

3. An excellent resource that offers a list of books written in AAL by grade level is Dr. Noma Lemoine's website. See www.lemoineandassociates.com/drLeMoine.html (accessed May 20, 2015).

4. Ordering information for this series can be found at www.lemoineandassociates.com/drLeMoine.html (accessed May 20, 2015).

5. See www.lemoineandassociates.com/drLeMoine.html (accessed May 20, 2015).

6. I am not suggesting that AAL be labeled as informal and SE be labeled as formal. However, until students learn the AAL patterns/features, most will understand that we speak differently in different settings (e.g., formal versus informal settings). I will point out later that AAL should not be relegated to informal settings only.

7. Retrieved May 20, 2015 from www.edweek.org/ew/articles/2014/10/15/08dual.h34.html

8. Used with permission. Copyright by Candace Thompson.

9. A download can be purchased from this website: http://culturallyresponsive.org/index.php/dr-hollie/about-dr-hollie (accessed May 20, 2015).

10. Retrieved May 20, 2015 from www.npr.org/2014/11/14/362372282/what-does-it-mean-to-be-articulate

11. See www.lemoineandassociates.com/drLeMoine.html (accessed May 20, 2015).

References

Alim, H. S., & Smitherman, G. (2012). *Articulate while black (Barack Obama, language, and race in the U.S.)*. Oxford, UK: Oxford University Press.

Alvarez, L., & Kolker, A. (Co-Producers). 1988. *American Tongues* [DVD]. Available from CNAM Film Library, 22-D, Hollywood Avenue, Hohokus, NJ, 07423 (40 minutes runtime).

Bailey, B. (1965). Toward a new perspective in Negro English dialectology. *American Speech*, *40*, 171–177.

Banks, J. A., & Banks, C. A. M. (1997). *Multicultural education/Issues and perspectives* (3rd ed.). Boston, MA: Allyn & Bacon.

Baugh, J. (1980). A reexamination of the Black English copula. In W. Labov (Ed.), *Locating language in space and time* (pp. 83–106). Orlando, FL: Academic Press.

Baugh, J. (1999). *Out of the mouths of slaves/African American language and educational malpractice*. Austin, TX: University of Texas Press.

Boutte, G. S. (2007). Teaching African American English speakers: Expanding educators and student repertoires. In M. E. Brisk (Ed.). *Language, culture, and community in teacher education* (pp. 47–70). London: Routledge.

Boutte, G. S., & Johnson, G. (2012). Do educators see and honor biliteracy and bidialectalism in African American Language speakers? Apprehensions and reflections of two grandparents/professional educators. *Early Childhood Education Journal*, *41*(2), 133–141.

Boutte, G. S., & Johnson, G. L., Jr. (2013). *Funga Alafia*. Toward welcoming, understanding and respecting African American Speakers' bilingualism and biliteracy. *Equity and Excellence in Education. Special Issue on Social Justice Approaches to African American Language and Literacies*, *46*(3), 300–314.

Canagarajah, A. (2006). The place of World Englishes in composition: Pluralization continued. *College Composition and Communication*, *57*(4), 586–619.

Craig, H. K., Zhang, L., Hensel, S. L., & Quinn, E. J. (2009). African American English speaking students: An examination of the relationship between dialect shifting and reading outcomes. *Journal of Speech, Language, and Hearing Research, 52*, 839–855.

Delpit, L. (1995). *Other people's children. Cultural conflicts in the classroom*. New York: The New Press.

Delpit, L. (1998). What should teachers do? Ebonics and culturally responsive instruction. In T. Perry & L. Delpit (Eds.), *The real Ebonics debate: Power, language, and the education of African-American children* (pp. 17–26). Boston, MA: Beacon.

Delpit, L. & Dowdy, J. K. (2002). *The skin that we speak: Thoughts on language and culture in the classroom*. New York: The New Press.

Dillard, J. L. (1972). *Black English*. New York: Random House.

Dyson, A. H., & Smitherman, G. (2009). The right (write) start: African American language and the discourse of sounding right. *The Teachers College Record, 111*(4), 973–998.

Fanon, F. (1952/2008). *Black skin, White masks*. New York: Grove Press.

Fogel, H., & Ehri, L. (2000). Teaching elementary students who speak Black English vernacular to write in Standard English: Effects of dialect transformation practice. *Contemporary Educational Psychology, 25*(2), 212–235.

Hale-Benson, J. E. (1986). *Black children: Their roots, culture, and learning styles* (Rev. ed.). Baltimore, MD: Johns Hopkins University Press.

Heath, S. B. (1982/1992). *Ways with words: Language, life, and work in communities and classrooms*. New York: Cambridge University Press.

Hilliard, A. G. (1992). Behavioral style, culture, and teaching, and learning. *Journal of Negro Education, 61*(3), 370–377.

Hilliard III, A. G. (2002). Language, culture, and the assessment of African American children. In L. Delpit & J. K. Dowdy (Eds.), *The skin that we speak: Thoughts on language and culture in the classroom* (pp. 87–105). New York: The New Press.

Holm, J. (1984). Variability of the copula in Black English and its Creole kin. *American Speech, 59*, 291–209.

hooks, b. (1994). *Teaching to transgress. Education as the practice of freedom*. New York: Routledge.

Hoover, M. R. (1998). Ebonics: Myths and realities. In T. Perry & L. Delpit (Eds.), *The real Ebonics debate: Power, language, and the education of African-American children* (pp. 71–76). New York: Teachers College Press.

Hurston, Z. N. (1937/1965). *Their eyes were watching God*. New York: HarperCollins.

King, J. E. (2005). *Black Education: A transformative research and action agenda for the 21st century*. Mahwah, NJ: Lawrence Erlbaum.

Kinloch, V. (2010). "To not be a traitor of Black English": Youth perceptions of language rights in an urban context. *Teachers College Record, 112*(1), 103–141.

Kirkland, D. E. & Jackson, A. (2009). Beyond the silence: Instructional approaches and students' attitudes. In J. C. Scott, D. Y. Straker, & L. Katz (Eds.), *Affirming students' right to their own language. Bridging language policies and pedagogical practices* (pp. 132–150). New York: Routledge.

Ladson-Billings, G. (1994). *The dreamkeepers. Successful teachers of African American children*. San Francisco, CA: Jossey-Bass.

LeMoine, N. (1999). *English for your success*. Maywood, NJ: Peoples Publishing.

Lindblom, K. (2005). Teaching English in the world. *English Journal, 94*(3), 81.

Linguistic Society of America. (1997). *LSA resolution on the Oakland "Ebonics" issue*. Retrieved February 28, 2005 from www.lsadc.org

Nieto, S. (1996). *Affirming diversity: The sociopolitical context of multicultural education* (2nd ed.). White Plains, NY: Longman.

O'Neil, W. (1998). If Ebonics isn't a language, then tell me, what is? In T. Perry & L. Delpit (Eds.), *The real Ebonics debate: Power, language, and the education of African-American children* (pp. 38–48). Boston, MA: Beacon Press.

Perry, T., & Delpit, L. (Eds.). (1998). *The real Ebonics debate: Power, language, and the education of African-American children*. Boston, MA: Beacon.

Perry, T., Steele, C., Hilliard, A. III. (2003). *Young, gifted, and Black. Promoting high achievement among African-American students*. Boston, MA: Beacon Press.

Rickford, J. R. (1999). *African American vernacular English*. Malden, MA: Blackwell.

Rickford, J. R. & Rickford, R. J. (2000). *Spoken soul*. New York: John Wiley.

Schniedewind, N., & Davidson, E. (1998). *Open minds to equality: A sourcebook of learning activities to affirm diversity and promote equity* (2nd ed.). Boston, MA: Allyn & Bacon.

Smith, B. J. (1998). Black English: Steppin up? Look back. In T. Perry & L. Delpit (Eds.), *The real Ebonics debate: Power, language, and the education of African-American children* (pp. 71–76). Boston, MA: Beacon Press.

Smitherman, G. (1977/1985). *Talkin and testifyin: The language of Black America*. Boston, MA: Houghton Mifflin.

Smitherman, G. (1994). *Black talk. Words and phrases from the hood to the amen corner*. Boston, MA: Houghton Mifflin.

Smitherman, G. (1997). Black language and the education of black children. One mo once. *Black Scholar, 27*(1), 28–36.

Smitherman, G. (1998). Black English/Ebonics: What it be like? In T. Perry & L. Delpit (Eds.), *The real Ebonics debate: Power, language, and the education of African-American children* (pp. 29–37). Boston, MA: Beacon Press.

Smitherman, G. (1999/2001). *Talkin that talk. Language, culture and education in African America*. London: Routledge.

Smitherman, G. (2006). *Word from the mother: Language and African Americans*. New York: Routledge.

Taylor, H. U. (1991). *Standard English, Black English, and bidialectalism: A controversy*. New York: Peter Lang.

Turner, L. D. (1949). *Africanisms in the Gullah dialect*. Chicago, IL: University of Chicago Press.

Young, V. A. (2009). "Nah we straight": An argument against code switching. *JAC: A Journal of Rhetoric, Culture, and Politics, 29*(1–2), 49–76.

Wheeler, R., & Swords, R. (2010). *Code-switching lessons: Grammar strategies for linguistically diverse writers: A firsthand curriculum*. Portsmouth, NH: Heinemann.

Wheeler, R. S., & Swords, R. (2006). *Code-switching. Teaching Standard English in urban classrooms*. Urbana, IL: National Council of Teachers of English.

Wolfram, W., & Fasold, F. (1974). *The study of social dialects in American English*. Center for Applied Linguistics. Englewood Cliffs, NJ: Prentice-Hall.

Woodson, C. G. (1933/1990). *The mis-education of the Negro*. Trenton, NJ: Africa World Press.

5

CULTURALLY RELEVANT TEACHING

Views from Classrooms

Proposition 5.1 Culturally relevant teaching focuses on three dimensions of
students' development: academic achievement, cultural competence, and
sociopolitical consciousness.

And how are the children? Conventional educational practices have been generally
ineffective for many African American students, so the children are in dire need
of relevant curriculum, instruction, and assessment. But there is much hope,
because many teachers, despite the most difficult circumstances, do teach African
American students effectively. Some of these examples will be shared in this
chapter.

Many of the examples presented in this chapter are from classrooms of teachers
involved with the CEEEAAS. Others are from teachers cited in the academic
literature or teachers whom I have worked with in other capacities. This chapter
provides opportunities for readers to continue to build the four key areas of change
presented in Figure 1.1 in Chapter 1 (knowledge base, dispositions, instruction,
and curricular approaches). Before sharing examples of culturally relevant teaching,
I will briefly provide an overview of CEEEAAS.[1]

Defying the prevailing negative perceptions about Black children's achievement
and school performance, CEEEAAS put forth its belief "*in the possibility of the
Black child*," as is captured on its logo, shown in Figure 5.1. The figure shows an
adult firmly holding onto two children (who can be symbolically thought of as
male and female). Readers will note that the adult's heart is in the shape of Africa,
connoting that African and African American perspectives should inform
educational practices for Black children. Likewise, the pyramid is intended to
suggest that the history of African American people does not begin with enslavement or in America. It should be noted that the children's bodies extend outside

the pyramid which signifies the dynamic nature of culture which both capture origins and other iterations and transformations over time. The statement, "We believe in the possibility of the Black child," asserts the insistence on focusing on what is *possible*, rather than what is not possible, or cannot be, or has not been done (e.g., as is often put forth in the pervasive and persistent discourse about African American children). The word "children" was purposely selected instead of "students." It is used broadly to cover from pre-birth to age 18. Importantly, it is used to connote the vulnerability of Black youth, as well as the idea that too often Black youth are not seen as children who should be protected and cared for as other children. Instead, they are often marginalized, mislabeled, and even criminalized by the time that they are in third or fourth grade—especially Black males (Buendia, 2011; Kunjufu, 2010; Ladson-Billings, 2011; Lewis, James, Hancock, & Hill-Jackson, 2008). That is, teachers tend to handle other ethnic or social groups as if they are "developing individuals," whereas African American students are often treated as if they are pathological and problematic pre-criminals, who are destined to be relegated to lower-status social and academic positions, and these positions are normal, stable, fixed, and unchangeable (Buendia, 2011; Ladson-Billings, 2011; Milner, 2010; Noguera, 2001).

In 2002, living in a state where 42 percent of the school enrollment comprised African American students—most of whom were not faring well—I founded a statewide center (The Center of Excellence for the Education and Equity of African American Students—CEEEAAS), which focused on effective education of African American students. Focusing on the role that teacher education programs and schools played in the achievement of Black students, CEEEAAS operated from 2002 to 2007 and was guided by the mission to ensure that African American children achieved, educationally and socially, to their fullest potential.

FIGURE 5.1 Logo of the Center of Excellence for the Education and Equity of African American Students.

A basic premise was that educators needed sufficient in-depth understanding of African American students' cultural backgrounds in order to make learning meaningful and transformative, as mainstream methods of acquiring school competencies do not offer universally applicable models of development (Boutte, 2002; King, 1994; Perry, Steele, & Hilliard, 2003). Additionally, CEEEAAS worked with teachers and teacher educators who wanted to *normalize* high achievement for K–12 African American students.

CEEEAAS's mission was multifaceted and included: (a) providing and distributing educational information and resources to PreK–12 educators and community members via workshops, seminars, courses, and annual national conferences; (b) researching and demonstrating effective educational practices and strategies for African American children; (c) decreasing and eliminating the achievement gap; (d) advocating for African American students; and (e) informing and impacting educational policies. CEEEAAS worked with teachers and teacher educators and offered seven services aimed at reducing the "achievement gap" and facilitating the effective education of African American students:

1. undergraduate and graduate courses on "Educating African American Students";
2. demonstration classrooms modeling culturally relevant instruction;
3. article and book studies;
4. an annual conference;
5. an interactive website;
6. a clearinghouse of resources (articles, books, videos); and
7. workshops for educators.

CEEEAAS's Model Teachers

Fourteen model teachers participated with CEEEAAS (see list below). Asterisks indicate the teachers who will be focused on in this chapter on the companion website.[2] Photos of the featured teachers (from CEEEAAS and otherwise) are shown in Figure 5.2. Although the teachers were at varying levels of development in their practice and held a wide range of ideological beliefs, the common denominator among them was that they all enjoyed teaching Black children and were determined to be effective with them and their families. Teachers voluntarily signed up to be model teachers and participated in CEEEAAS's roundtable discussions of articles, book studies, and professional development sessions (e.g., on AAL and CRP).

Elementary School

1. Shawnta Davis, African American female, fourth grade;
2. *Kitty Faden, African American female, curriculum resource teacher;

Nathaniel Bonaparte   William Boyles   Nichole Folsom (Wright)

Edwina Hicklin   Edward Hill   Charlease Kelly-Jackson

William Lenard   Jennifer Strickland   Cassandra Tyler

FIGURE 5.2 Photos of Teachers Featured in This Chapter.

3. *Nichole Folsom, African American female, second and third grades;
4. *Edward Hill, African American male, third grade—African American males;
5. *Jennifer Strickland-Poole, White female, preschool and kindergarten;
6. Brenda Terry, African American female, parent educator.

Middle School

7. Lemuel Patterson, African American male, science;
8. Barbara Smith, African American female, special education;
9. *Cassandra Tyler, African American female, seventh to ninth grades, art.

High School

10. ★Nathaniel Bonaparte, African American male, ninth grade, English;
11. Jill Dowdy, African American female, eleventh to twelfth grade, academically accelerated English;
12. ★Edwina Hicklin, African American female, ninth grade, social studies;
13. Annika Kutz-Smith, White female, science;
14. ★William Lenard, African American male, ninth grade, math.

The books used for the roundtable discussions across the years are listed alphabetically by author, below. These may serve as good resources for readers who want to build their knowledge base. Although not all CEEEAAS teachers participated in all of the book studies, most of them read the monthly articles and participated in the roundtable discussions. It is important to note that CEEEAAS teachers actively worked to build their knowledge bases, which, in turn, influenced their dispositions, instruction, and curriculum decisions. Teachers from local districts and teacher educators from nearby universities also participated in the monthly book or article roundtable discussions. Each roundtable also focused on praxis (reflective actions) for classrooms.

- Delpit, L., & Dowdy, J. K. (2002). *The Skin That We Speak. Thoughts on Language and Culture in the Classroom.* New York: The New Press.
- Ford, D. Y., & Harris, J. J. (1999). *Multicultural Gifted Education.* New York: Teachers College Press.
- Gay, G. (2000). *Culturally Responsive Teaching: Theory, Research, and Practice.* New York: Teachers College Press.
- Hale, J. (2001). *Learning While Black. Creating Educational Excellence for African American Children.* Baltimore, MD: Johns Hopkins Press.
- Hopkins, R. (1997). *Educating Black Males: Critical Lessons in Schooling, Community, and Power.* New York: SUNY Press.
- King, J. E. (2005). *Black Education. A Transformative Research and Action Agenda for the New Century.* New York: Routledge.
- Kozol, J. (2005). *The Shame of the Nation: The Restoration of Apartheid Schooling in America.* New York: Random House.
- Kunjufu, J. (2006). *An African Centered Response to Ruby Payne's Poverty Theory.* Chicago, IL: African American Images.
- Ladson-Billings, G. (1994). *The Dreamkeepers: Successful Teachers of African American Children.* San Francisco, CA: Jossey-Bass.
- Perry, T., & Delpit, L. (Eds.). (1998). *The Real Ebonics Debate: Power, Language, and the Education of African-American Children.* Boston, MA: Beacon.
- Perry, T. (2004). *Young, Gifted, and Black: Promoting High Achievement Among African-American Students.* Boston, MA: Beacon Press.

- Tatum, B. D. (2007). Can We Talk About Race? And Other Conversations in an Era of School Resegregation. Boston, MA: Beacon Press.

CEEEAAS teachers also presented at local, state, and national conferences and attended professional development sessions at conferences, at the CEEEAAS office, and at other venues. For example, the first cohort (five teachers) visited the Los Angeles Unified School Program to observe culturally relevant pedagogical strategies and AAL contrastive analyses strategies. The seven teachers who are the focus of this book were involved for 3 years or more. Either the project director, Dr. Joann Thompson, or I visited their classrooms regularly over this time period and served in participant and observer roles.

What Do Teachers Need to Effectively Teach African American Students?

Drawing from Martin's (2007) framework, we suggest that, in order to effectively teach African American students, one needs three types of knowledge/ skill: (1.) deep content knowledge, (2.) strong pedagogical content knowledge, and (3.) strong CRP. The first two are frequently discussed and are not the focus of this chapter.

CRP is instruction that uses students' cultures and strengths (cultural capital) as a bridge to success in school achievement (Pritchy Smith, 1998). It is not prescriptive, and there is "not a series of steps that teachers can follow or a recipe for being effective with African American students" (Ladson-Billings, 1994, p. 26) or any other group. Once educators become familiar with cultural knowledge bases, they can then modify their instruction and curriculum (King, 1994). Culturally relevant teaching focuses on: (a) academic excellence that is not based on cultural deficit models of school failure; (b) cultural competence that locates excellence within the context of the students' community and cultural identities; and (c) critical consciousness that challenges inequitable school and societal structures (Ladson-Billings, 2002).

In this chapter, I cautiously share examples from actual classrooms, at the risk of trivializing and essentializing the complexities of culturally relevant teaching. By sharing examples, my intent is not to suggest that culturally relevant teaching can be reduced to "recipes" or activities. Instead, I use the examples to suggest general tenets for the process of changing the structure, assumptions, and nature of K–12 teaching. It is not unusual for practitioners to begin the process by adding multicultural information and contributions of famous people to the existing curriculum; however, this chapter provides insights and guidance for practitioners who wish to deepen their efforts using a CRP framework. Yet, without centering issues of power, equity, and culture, efforts will remain superficial and will not likely address the intended long-term goals of reducing structural inequities in school and society (Boutte, Kelly-Jackson, & Johnson, 2010; Castagno, 2009).

Although significant evidence that African American cultural knowledge can contribute positively to school learning exists, it is glaringly missing from the knowledge base of teacher education and in classroom practices (Boutte & Hill, 2006; Hopkins, 1997; King, 1994; Ladson-Billings, 1994/2009). One of the common comments that I hear from teachers is that there are not enough examples of what culturally relevant teaching looks like in real classrooms. Although there are certainly many good examples (e.g., Irvine & Armento, 2001; Ladson-Billings, 1994/2009, 1995; Matthews, 2003; Milner, 2010, 2011), many scholars worry about making CRP sound prescriptive and technical. Concerned that teachers are already de-skilled by publishers' manuals, pacing guides, scripted curricula, and such, many example of CRP focus on general tenets (Boutte & Hill, 2006; Delpit, 1995; Ladson-Billings, 1994/2009; Milner, 2011; Perry et al., 2003), such as the ones shown below. Although the list is not intended to be exhaustive, readers should take a few minutes to reflect on whether these 15 tenets are present in your instruction and write down examples of each.

1. Learning is made relevant.
2. Students' cultures are affirmed and extended.
3. Skills are taught (not simply covered). Teaching and learning must go together. If students are not learning, then instruction is likely to be ineffective.
4. Explicit instruction is needed on unfamiliar information, attitudes, etc.
5. Students are actively engaged (presentations, etc.).
6. Conventional and nonconventional strategies are used.
7. Ongoing counternarratives are provided.
8. Teacher–student relationships are central.
9. Authentic relationships are developed with students.
10. Students are exposed to global perspectives and knowledge (e.g., readings, videos, resources, speakers, internships, travel).
11. Teachers engage in ongoing discussions with students regarding social and political realities.
12. Teachers provide "tough love" and high expectations. Students are not given permission to fail.
13. Students are encouraged to be critical consumers of the curriculum.
14. Instruction is holistic (e.g., focuses on cognitive, emotional, social, moral, and physical development).
15. Focus is on shared and communal responsibility for learning.

Some teachers are able to draw from the 15 tenets and extrapolate to their respective classrooms. However, other teachers benefit from concrete examples. Culturally relevant pedagogy should be very organic and generative in nature. The examples here cannot be transplanted to other classrooms, although they can certainly be adapted. Each teacher's instruction and approach are different.

For example, one of the CEEEAAS teachers, Mrs. Tyler, speaks very softly, never raising her voice above a whisper, whereas another teacher, Mr. Lenard, is known for speaking with emphasis, running around the room, and even standing on top of the table (as reported to me by his students). Each teacher will bring his or her unique personality. Therefore, the examples provided in this chapter are suggestions. In a nutshell, the teacher and students are the most important ingredients in the equation. Culturally relevant teachers bring aspects of themselves into their classrooms. As readers will note below, Ms. Tyler loves art and dolls; Mr. Boyles loves hip-hop; Mr. Lenard loves baseball; Ms. Folsom loves drumming; and Mr. Hill is a thespian.

Some of these dynamic and grassroots elements of CRP may be lost in the description, as I have tried to make aspects of their teaching explicit. The point is that the examples are provided to stimulate ideas for teachers—not to close down ideas or present the examples as finite possibilities. In fact, I will offer suggestions and ideas for building on the examples presented. Teachers should extrapolate from the examples—even when they teach a different subject or at a different grade level. Additionally, you may think of different ways of teaching the same concepts, depending on your particular context and students. That's what culturally relevant teaching is really about. So, the recommended books, activities, and the like may work well in some settings and not so well in others. The idea of sharing the examples is to make it more concrete, less theoretical, and to stimulate ideas.

Teachers in the examples differ in terms of their ethnicities, gender, grade levels, and subject areas. Readers will note that the three dimensions of CRP (academic achievement, cultural competence, and critical consciousness) and many of the 15 tenets are present in the examples. Additionally, even though only a few examples of instruction are presented per teacher, it is important to note that culturally relevant teaching is sustained over time—it is not a one-time or occasional lesson or unit. A benefit of being one of the CEEEAAS teachers was that they did not work in isolation and were able to engage in dialogue and sharing of resources with other teachers. This is also recommended for educators, as the process of collaboration and discussion often enriches and deepens the instruction and reflections.

An important goal in each classroom was to provide powerful counternarratives to pervasive messages that do not value and build on the wisdom and value found in Black communities. As published works are considered to be "legitimate and official knowledge" in society (Apple, 1992), the literature used by the teachers served as a formal way of validating aspects of Black culture. The typical invisibility of Black perspectives and storylines in school literature collections undermines the importance and centrality of Black worldviews (Boutte, 2002). Counternarratives are crucial because of the prevailing ideologies and negative stereotypes about African Americans in society, in general, in the media, and in the curriculum (Perry et al., 2003).

Commonly Asked Questions About CRP

Anticipating commonly asked questions and comments about CRP, I have provided responses below.

1. *What do I do if I have a racially diverse classroom that includes students of color and Whites? In other words, does CRP work for them?* (As an aside, I do wish that K–12 teachers would ask the reversed version of this question about the Black students in their classes (e.g., "What should I do if I have Black students in my class and the instruction is irrelevant to them?"). It is not surprising that performance trends favor students from mainstream and/or White ethnic groups and disadvantage Black students.)

    Recognizing that schools are not neutral and that they reflect someone's culture, it is important to note that much of the content in school curricula is currently culturally relevant to White students. For all students, it is important for them to develop cultural competence—competence in their own culture (mirrors) and competence in at least one additional culture (and, ideally, competence in many cultures). I suggest that most topics discussed in schools can be tailored to many cultural groups. Readers may find it helpful to look at examples of multiple perspectives provided in Chapter 3 on critical literacy. For example, if families are being studied, students and parents can contribute information and stories about their own familial backgrounds.

2. *Can we do that (examples presented in this book) in our classrooms?* Yep! There is nothing that is presented in this book that cannot be presented and related to curriculum standards. However, *how* you choose to implement the ideas presented in this book is crucial. As noted in Chapter 3, do make sure that you can provide a rationale for what you are teaching. Also, share your ideas with your administrators and parents/guardians. Typically, parents or administrators will not complain if students are succeeding and engaged in school.

3. *This all sounds good, but I have to teach the standards and follow pacing guides/ curriculum for my district.* Remember that one of the dimensions of culturally relevant teaching is academic achievement, and so one goal is to ensure that students are learning. Culturally relevant pedagogy is just a method for doing so. In fact, the examples shared in this chapter will demonstrate that CRP teachers often teach much more than is listed in narrow curricular standards and pacing guides. By the way, judging from the longstanding outcomes of Black children, the standards *are not currently being taught*. They may be *covered*, but, obviously, students are not learning. CEEEAAS teachers are not limited by curriculum standards. Their teaching is much broader and more organic, building from the children's culture and needs. However, I mention the standards in examples so that readers can see that standards are being taught.

4. Many of the examples you use show African American teachers. *Does this mean that White teachers or other teachers of color tend to be less effective?*

Absolutely not! As evidenced in the literature (e.g., Compton-Lily, 2004; Cowhey, 2006; Ladson-Billings, 1994/2009; Milner, 2010), a number of examples of White, Latino, Asian, and Native American teachers who use CRP exist in the literature. The findings indicate that it is not the teacher's race that is a determining factor on how well they teach African American students. It has more to do with the color of their ideologies and beliefs. Thus, any teacher who has the wiliness to do so (Hilliard, 1992) will seek information and work to figure out how to be successful teaching African American students. As Woodson (1933/1990) pointed out in his classic, prophetic work, the role of White educators is not to "save Black people," but to help them help themselves. That is what teachers who engage in CRP do. The teachers featured in this book happen to be Black and White teachers because they were the ones with whom I had opportunities to work closely.

Examples From Elementary School

Although the examples that I share focus on individual teachers, the effect of culturally relevant teaching can be magnified if it is a whole-school effort. However, in the meantime, teachers who refuse to let African American students suffer yet another day, week, month, or year (while waiting for the rest of the teachers to join in) can use CRP to continue to work toward ensuring that, in their classrooms, *the children are well.*

Afros, Waves, and Razorblades—If Schools Were Like Barbershops—Mr. Edward Hill, Third-Grade Teacher

Edward Hill, a third-grade teacher, decided to engage his classroom of all-African American male students in extended study of one of the oldest and most prevalent, male-dominated institutions in Black communities—the barbershop. Although most of Mr. Hill's students had been intimately familiar with the Black barbershop experience since their first haircuts at age 1, he wanted his students to also understand and respect the vast sources of knowledge, resources, and guidance that exist among African American males, from many walks of life. He explains:

> I see the present and the future, the old and the young, bound together in one place—the barbershop. As I look into little boys' eyes, I wonder to myself if they realize the importance of the assembled men in front of them. These various men of the community are who they could become— respected and valued members of the community. In spite of the harshness black men face outside the barbershop walls, little boys sit in the presence of potential hope.

> (Boutte & Hill, 2006, p. 312)

Rationale for Focusing on Black Barbershops

The African American barbershop has a long and distinctive heritage in the US, as old as the history of the Africans in America. Its history reveals a fascinating social institution that has played a significant role in the lives of Black men. For most of the 20th century, within racially segregated African American communities, this fundamental social institution was a central location for meaningful association, dialogue, and learning among men (Wilkinson, 2002). Historically, this intriguing, male-dominated territory has served as a "classroom," a recreational center, and a social setting for exchanging viewpoints and debating about local and national events. Topics of conversation have ranged from community issues to economic and political realities and the "troubles of the world." The African American barbershop is a sample of a cultural institution—its survival tells a strong story of the history of men in a land that has not always treated them kindly. The interaction among men—fathers, sons, uncles, and friends—has constituted an important foundation for manhood, friendship, community building, and intelligentsia (Wilkinson, 2002). Within the hallowed walls of the barbershop, men's jobs, roles, and responsibilities serve as an elevator that transports many men above their menial Monday through Friday routines. Men both young and old look forward to the "barbershop" experience, the lessons learned, the exchanges made, and the empowerment received. The barbershop is a place where many young African American males have real pride and joy. This is a place where their talents, opinions, and skills are recognized and appreciated. They are seated in a place where men can discuss and exchange the best and worst of their professional and personal selves. In the barbershop, a young African American male is not viewed as a "boy," but rather as a young man. This important distinction is typically overlooked in most classrooms.

To sit and observe this quiet, overwhelming presence of men is astonishing. Week after week, young African American males share the experiences of membership of brotherhood, a community, and an engaging, inquiry-based classroom. The African American barbershop is a classroom overflowing with lessons of academia and life. The barbershop serves as an alternative to the traditional school classrooms by offering important lessons, information, guidance, and values. What is most instructive is how Black males who are considered "slow" in school can interact with extreme skill, analysis, and quick-wittedness in the barbershop. In many cases, the same males who are considered to be lacking self-esteem or hyperactive in classrooms are regarded as smart and respectful in the barbershop. In the midst of the voluminous body of literature and statistics that convey that Black males are not experiencing success in schools, it makes sense to question why males who are labeled "at risk" in school are transformed in barbershops. What underlying structures and assumptions empower the same males who are pervasively labeled negatively in schools? Although Mr. Hill could have just as easily chosen to focus on the Black church—another longstanding, powerful institution from which schools could learn and in which Mr. Hill is intimately involved—he decided to focus on a place where the source of power centers around Black males. As Black males are often excluded in schools, devalued, and not seen as sources of wisdom (Hopkins, 1997), it was important for Mr. Hill's all-male students to explicitly observe Black men's performance in a setting where they felt empowered. He wanted to document strategies used in barbershops that facilitated the maintenance of men's dignity and confidence. Importantly, the men and boys were respected and understood by the barber and other customers. Not surprisingly, Mr. Hill found that implicit aspects of Black culture (see Box 1.4 in Chapter 1) are embedded in the very nature of many Black barbershops.

A testament to the importance of Black barbershops in Black communities is that, when Senator Barack Obama was campaigning for presidency, he spent many hours visiting Black barbershops. Photos on the Internet abound, including one or two prints of him and the (now) First Lady, Michelle Obama, praying with the community or engaged in dialogue with customers.

Description of Mr. Hill's Classroom

Mr. Hill is an energetic, 30-something (but younger-looking) teacher. Enter Mr. Hill's all-male class, and images of African American males command your attention (see Figure 5.3).

FIGURE 5.3 Sample of Imagery in Mr. Hill's Classroom Affirming Black Males (Mirrors).

However, visitors are quickly diverted by Mr. Hill's commanding presence (he's more than 6 feet tall) and expectations that are taller than his height. Students begin the day by reading the newspaper, as Mr. Hill explains that an educated man is an informed man. The professional countenance of the third-graders is apparent, and visitors are greeted by students with a handshake and a welcome. Students are addressed as "Mister," and parents flock into the classroom that their sons enjoy and talk about so much. Interestingly, Mr. Hill is a graduate of an all-male, historically Black college (Morehouse) that has a long tradition of addressing young men with the respectful title "Mister"—the term itself is a counternarrative. The fact that Mr. Hill is also a thespian outside the classroom is evident by how he effectively uses his voice to engage students and by the verve generated as he weaves stories to convey the content to students. Mr. Hill is also very involved in his church and fraternity and spends much time outside the classroom "giving back" to the community. This value is, in turn, conveyed to students. Students are taught to work together for the betterment of all. Mr. Hill's class has 15 male students.

Eight of the fifteen children live in single-parent homes, three live with both parents, and the remaining four live with grandparents. Always reflecting on his students' reality (most of the students are from low-income backgrounds), Mr. Hill realized that, if his students followed the typical projected trajectory, many of them would eventually internalize the negative and limited stereotypes about Black males. Concerned that his students may not be aware of the many strengths of the Black community, he decided to immerse them in study of barbershops. He noted that all of his students were familiar with barbershops, which made the topic one that they could be experts on. So, they delved into their inquiry about barbershops. Enlisting the assistance of four education majors at Benedict College who were part of the "Call Me Mister" program, designed to increase the number of Black male teachers, the class set out to study the barbershop beyond what students already knew. Incidentally, the term "Mister" in the Benedict College program connotes the respect and honor of the teaching profession in the black community. Mr. Hill carefully selected barbershops that were well respected by the community, well utilized, and known for their rules of conduct, which did not tolerate lewd language or behavior. Over a 4-week period, students visited 10 barbershops (during and outside regular class time). They researched the history of the businesses, conducted interviews with barbers and customers, administered questionnaires, did extensive observations, kept copious notes, and learned the inside beauty and value of barbershops. Going beyond narrowly defined state standards, his students also learned about running a business, self-presentation, research, and technological skills. Observational and anecdotal notes were taken from the barbershops visited throughout the city. To point out the focus on academic achievement, the standards that Mr. Hill covered are listed below.

Standards Taught in Barbershop Unit

Social Studies: IV. Production, Distribution, and Consumption: Economics:

- 3:14 The learner will demonstrate an understanding of markets and the role of demand and supply in determining price and resource allocation. The student will be able to:
    - 3:14:2 give examples of goods and services that have increased or decreased in supply;
    - 3:14:4 name a wide range of job opportunities in South Carolina; and
    - 3:14:5 discuss the role of the entrepreneur in the state and local community.

Language Arts

The learner will:

- SC.ELA.3–C1.1 demonstrate the ability to face an audience, make eye contact, and use the appropriate voice level;
- SC.ELA.3–C1.2 demonstrate the ability to initiate conversation;
- SC.ELA.3–C1.5 begin giving brief presentations, demonstrations, and oral reports.

Additionally, the students administered questionnaires to all males in the third, fourth, and fifth grades at their school. A list of the interview questions that students developed and then asked barbers and customers is provided below.

Interview Questions Devised and Asked by Students

Questions for Barbers

- How long have you been a barber?
- What academic skills do you need to be a barber?
- Since you, the barber, set the rules, how do you maintain a positive environment?
- What types of rules do you have in the shop? Are they written or unwritten?
- What would you tell teachers to help them be successful in teaching African American males?
- How can a teacher create a learning community?

Questions for Customers

- What is the significance of the barbershop to the African American community?
- How can a classroom teacher create the same type of environment that the barbershop embodies?

Students enthusiastically videotaped and photographed customers, barbers, and community members to find out as much as possible about barbershops. Figure 5.4 shows students actively interviewing one of the barbers. Students explored literature on the topic as well. A listing of the text set that Mr. Hill used on Black barbershops is provided below:

1. Battle-Lavert, G. (1994). *The Barber's Cutting Edge*. San Francisco, CA: Children's Book Press.
2. Cole, K. (2001). *No Bad News*. Park Ridge, IL: Albert Whitman.
3. Mitchell, M. K. (2005). *Uncle Jed's Barbershop*. New York: Simon & Schuster.
4. Tarplay, N. A. (2003). *Bippity Bop Barbershop*. New York: Little Brown Books for Young Readers.

FIGURE 5.4 Andrè Wilson and Tordrey Price Interview Barber, Tracey Edwards.

Source: Reprinted with permission from Boutte & Hill, 2006

Table 5.1 provides a summative list of Mr. Hill's students' findings, which compared and contrasted barbershops with school settings. Readers should note inherent aspects of Black culture in the barbershop setting. For example, typical barbershop greetings are affirming to the young men and demonstrate community expectations of doing well in school. It is common for the barber to ask youth how they are doing in school.

In the final analyses, Mr. Hill found that the young men in his class learned more than he initially envisioned. The elements of collaborative learning became real when they worked together to write interview questions. His students engaged in critical thinking to create rather than duplicate prefabricated questions. For the students, economics, entrepreneurship, and investments became more than meaningless words that they looked up in the glossary, but rather inspirational principles that they can now incorporate into their thinking and lives. Mr. Hill observed as the young men, who were programmed by the doctrines of education to compete against each other, began to gain a mutual respect for each other intellectually and began to "pour into each other's cup of knowledge."

Another interesting finding of the inquiry unit on barbershops was that accountable talk and debate occur naturally in the barbershop and should be recreated in classrooms. As Otis, a regular customer in Jacobs' Barbershop since he was 4 years old, commented, "(If) we can't talk straight in the barbershop— where can we talk straight? There's a lot of chewing in here. You have to be sharp!"

Mr. Hill also collaborated with the music teacher at his school. She worked with the young men on researching barbershop quartets and the concept of harmony—a concept that complements the communal dimension of Black culture. Through this unit, these young men learned that harmony is two or more distinctly different notes that blend together. In African American barbershops, males work in harmony rather than unison—the same note made at the same time.

The barbershop inquiry reiterated Mr. Hill's tacit thoughts that learning for African American males has to include a connection with spirituality. One Saturday, the shop seemed almost like church. A customer began talking about God. Before anyone knew it, sermons were flying. "The only thing that was missing was the passing of the plate," remarked barber Chris.

The barbershop experience did not culminate with the standard multiple-choice test, where there is always a chance to guess some of the answers, or at least look for clues that would jog the memory. The inquiry process provided students with a more comprehensive assessment than essay tests, which provide an opportunity for students to camouflage their uncertainty in complex phrases, sentences, or sufficient regurgitation of teachers' words. Importantly, students learned that there is a wealth of information and wisdom in their communities.

At the beginning of the year, all students were at the 50th percentile in regard to required tests. In terms of tangible results of Mr. Hill's culturally relevant

TABLE 5.1 Structural Differences Between Schools and Barbershops

Barbershop	School
Hearty greetings—barber is familiar with regular customers	Teachers may or may not greet children or know them well
Social club—The barbershop serves as a haven for social learning and interactions with others	Students are encouraged to be quiet most of the day—even in the cafeteria. Working independently is encouraged for most of the day
Individualized attention when sitting in barber's chair and during group dialogue	Most of the day is spent doing large-group work, with little attention to individual students' needs
Wide range of relevant topics is discussed	Many irrelevant topics are discussed and presented in a decontextualized manner
Customers are treated like family—barber knows and discusses information about family members	Many teachers are unfamiliar with student's family
Barber typically has a long-term relationships with customers—beginning with first haircut at age 1	Most teachers have short-term relationships with students—9 months
Customers typically do not entrust their haircuts to new barbers with whom they do not have a relationship	Many students of color and students of poverty resist learning from teachers if they do not have a relationship with them
Customers can let barbers know when they are dissatisfied with haircut	Students' perspectives are often not solicited or heard
Barbershop captures and builds on aspects of Black culture such as communalism, oral tradition, verve, and movement (e.g., call and response, co-narration, dramatic storytelling)	School rewards Eurocentric ways of knowing and communicating (Delpit, 1995)—e.g., sequential speaking, "canned responses"
Debate skills are practiced. A broad range of topics is debated, and each person tries to present convincing arguments	School usually encourages "canned" responses and dialogues rather than critical thinking and questioning
There is culturally relevant literature (signs; magazines—*Ebony*, *Sports Illustrated*, local newspaper)	Predominant literature is Eurocentric (Banks, 2001; Boutte, 2002)
Culturally relevant music and sounds are played—e.g., local radio station, rhythm and blues	Most classrooms are sterile and absent of music or limited to "classical" or children's music
Barbershops are male-dominated spaces	Schools are female-dominated spaces

Source: Reprinted with permission from Boutte & Hill, 2006

teaching, at the end of the year, all 15 of the students exceeded all of the district's benchmark standards. Additionally, when students took the mandated state test, the Palmetto Achievement Challenge Test (PACT), which is required for the first time during the third-grade year, all students met or exceeded the state standard. The PACT has four categories: (1.) below basic (standard not met); (2.) basic; (3.) proficient; and (4.) advanced. Eight of Mr. Hill's students scored advanced; five, proficient; and two, basic. At the beginning of the year, six of the students qualified for the academically gifted program. By the end of the year, 11 of them qualified—three scored high enough to be identified at the state level. Lastly, Mr. Hill also received a promotion of sorts. He looped up with his students and now teaches fourth grade. Although the test results of the students are impressive, Mr. Hill aims to normalize high achievement for his students and to ward off the typical fourth-grade decline that has been noted among African American male students.

Commentary

It is important to note that, once Mr. Hill turned the students onto learning by making the information relevant, he was also able to normalize high achievement for the students in all subjects. Mr. Hill was able to pull off the barbershop inquiry project because of his relationships with the students, their families, the community, and his administrators. Mr. Hill cares deeply about the welfare of Black children.

Other teachers will find ways to connect Black students to learning in ways that make sense to them. Mr. Hill has since completed his doctoral degree, served as assistant principal and principal at two different schools, and pursued a career in the academy. He is now dean of a school of education at a historically Black college.

"Even When She Sick, She Want to Come to School"— Nichole Folsom, Second- and Third-Grade Teacher

Nichole Folsom's teaching exudes energy, verve, and African-centricity. Neighboring teachers become accustomed to Ms. Folsom's drumming on djembes to teach anything from letters of the alphabet, to place value, history, or you name it. Her students love coming to school and love learning. One parent lamented that her daughter never wants to miss school because of Mrs. Folsom. The parent explained, "Even when she sick, she want to come to school."

While Mr. Hill towers over 6 feet tall, Mrs. Folsom is less than 5 feet tall. Since I have known her, she has taught at three different schools, because she is often recruited by principals, because of her effectiveness in teaching Black students. Here, I will describe aspects of her teaching in two different settings—first, as a second-grade teacher in a school that enrolled 99 percent African American students—mostly from low socioeconomic statuses. In this setting, all of Mrs. Folsom's students were Black. The second setting was a third-grade class in which she was recruited to teach because of rapidly changing racial and socioeconomic demographics in a nearby school district. The school enrolled 80 percent African American students, and Mrs. Folsom had 22 students in her classroom (10 females, 12 males). All but two (one White and one Latino-American) of her students were African American.

Description of Mrs. Folsom's Classroom

As with most of the CEEEAAS teachers, I visited her classrooms often. Both classrooms had African-centric imagery, such as sculptures like those seen in Mrs. Strickland's class (Chapter 3, Figure 3.2). In the third-grade classroom, colorful Adinkra symbols are posted with the following words: "Strength," "Unity," "Compassion," "Cooperation," "Responsibility," "Readiness," "Loyalty," "Confidence," "Patience," "Greatness" (see Figure 5.5). These values are taught in her classroom.

Integrating African-centric ways of knowing and countering society's lack of respect for these values, Mrs. Folsom makes the Adinkra principles come to life. Consider a few examples below that occurred during daily routines.

FIGURE 5.5 Adinkra Symbols Posted in Ms. Folsom's Third-Grade Class.

- While most students are at tables of four to six children, four of the third-grade boys are engaged in writing a letter to the principal. Another boy gets Ms. Folsom's attention and complains that one of the boys would not let him put his name on the letter. Ms. Folsom compassionately asks the complainer, "Can you understand why he would be upset if you didn't help write the letter and wanted to sign your name?" The complainer acknowledges that he can understand the situation. Mrs. Folsom does not attempt to resolve the issue for them, but the message about taking responsibility for one's actions (or inaction, in this case) has been taught. The focus on working together is evident in the group letter-writing effort.
- The value of unity comes across strongly in each of her classrooms. If students are physically aggressive, Mrs. Folsom immediately reminds them, "We are family. We don't kick, hurt, or harm each other." On the issue of responsibility: "Don't tell what he was doing—talk about yourself."
- Leadership is another message that resonates strongly. Mrs. Folsom frequently asks the group: "You are what?" (pausing for a response). The students respond in unison, "Leaders!", to which Mrs. Folsom affirms, "Right, leaders!"
- It is rare that any management problems occur in Mrs. Folsom's classroom for more than a few minutes. When Mrs. Folsom stops to deal with a discipline problem, other children put their heads down and wait, while she privately speaks to the child or children involved.

Mrs. Folsom's interactive communication style builds on Black culture's communal strengths. She gets students' attention by saying the Twi word, "*agoo!*", and the children respond, "*amee.*" The term "*agoo*" is used when someone is about to enter a house or a room and wants to notify whoever is inside of his/her intention to enter. These words are uttered instead of knocking at a door or gate. The response could be "*amee,*" meaning "come in" or "you are welcome." To say "*agoo*" is to ask for permission from the gathering to speak. Borrowing from the culture of the Akan people in Ghana, normally, if there is a meeting of elders or the chief and his entourage, it is the linguist (a post not taken lightly, because one must be able to speak in very flowery language and mostly in parables) who shouts this alert, bringing the gathering to silence. When the floor responds "*amee,*" then it means you are given consent to express your view.

Because of Mrs. Folsom's never-ending verve, affect, and enthusiasm about teaching, even ordinary lessons are transformed into exciting learning experiences. In her third-grade classroom, students often work together in small groups. They choose the names of their "tribes."[3] Defying the belief that girls are not as mathematically inclined as boys, girls actively participate in the game of "Fast and Furious Math" that Mrs. Folsom devised. Students get together in teams and line up. Mrs. Folsom puts math problems on the board, and each group can confer and collectively see which team comes up with the answer first and writes it on the board. Pausing briefly for discussion of the problems as needed, the game continues with all children actively involved. Activities such as this capitalize on Black cultural dimensions such as verve, movement, and communalism. Students are not expected to sit still in their seats to do math.

I've watched Mrs. Folsom turn typically mundane topics such as place value and rounding into engaging tasks for the children. Mrs. Folsom uses a metaphor of people in a house to teach students where to place a comma. She tells students that only three people can be in each house (e.g., the three people may be ones, tens, and hundreds). Occasionally, when Mrs. Folsom lists large numbers (e.g., millions), students may say, with a little dread, "That's a big number!" Mrs. Folsom replies, "Are you afraid of those numbers?" The children (confidently and in unison) respond, "I'm not afraid of these numbers," and solve the problem, placing the comma in the right place. During one mini lesson, examples of numbers that children were asked to name place values for and to round to the nearest designated number (e.g., thousands) included:

- 7,245,872
- 23,442
- 2,685
- 65,824.

In each case, children enthusiastically rounded numbers, regardless of the size of the number.

Mrs. Folsom demonstrated the same type of teaching engagement in her second-grade classroom. Always using dimensions of culturally relevant teaching, Mrs. Folsom helps students develop cultural competence in many areas, including language proficiency (as shown in Chapter 4, in Figures 4.1 and 4.2 and in Table 4.3).

If readers look closely behind the picture of Mrs. Folsom in Figure 5.2, which shows the photos of all of the teachers featured in this chapter, a picture of Dr. Carter G. Woodson can been seen. Using songs, drumming, and poetry, Mrs. Folsom taught students more about Dr. Woodson than I knew at the time. Students also wrote essays and drew pictures that were posted in the hallway. Like Mrs. Strickland, mentioned in Chapter 3, Mrs. Folsom found ways to make history relevant to young children. As noted in Chapter 3, diaspora history is sorely missing in most classrooms for Black children.

Readers may be able to detect that the standards that were being taught were also posted, as Mrs. Folsom usually engaged her students in critically conscious discussions about what they were supposed to be learning in school and why.

In each of her classrooms, students said simple, but powerful, weekly affirmations that were posted on the bulletin board (Figure 5.6). The weekly affirmation for the week pictured in Figure 5.6 is as follows:

> Pride (by Alma Flor Ada)
> Proud of my <u>family</u>
> Proud of my <u>language</u>
> Proud of my <u>culture</u>
> Proud of my <u>race</u>
> Proud to be <u>who I am</u>

Such an affirmation can be used for students of different ethnicities and cultures as well. Believing that all children can succeed, Mrs. Folsom invites each student to contemplate a goal that they plan to work on during each week. Students write the goals on post-it notes and place them on the board as a reminder (see Figure 5.6).

Mrs. Folsom takes copious and ongoing notes of students' progress. She is not bothered by what school skills students do not know: Her goal is to ensure that all students make progress. For example, Mrs. Folsom later taught kindergarten students. None of her 19 students knew any of the required sight words at the beginning of school. By midyear, all but four of them met the criterion. Even the students who did not meet the criterion had made some progress.

Commentary

Mrs. Folsom can best be described as a conductor (Ladson-Billings, 1994/2009). All eyes are on her, and nothing happens in her classroom without her knowledge.

> *Conductors* believe that students are capable of excellence and they assume responsibility for ensuring that their students achieve that excellence. If we push the metaphor we can visualize an orchestra conductor who approaches the orchestra stand; all members of the orchestra have their eyes fixed on the conductor. Nothing happens without the conductor's direction. So

FIGURE 5.6 Weekly Affirmations and Goals in Mrs. Folsom's Second-Grade Class.

powerful can the personality of the conductor be that the audience and music critics describe the quality of the performance, even though the conductor did not play a single note.

(Ladson-Billings, 1994/2009, p. 26)

Like Mr. Hill, Mrs. Folsom's personal sense of drama serves as a catalyst to help propel her students to academic excellence. As was mentioned earlier, each teacher's style can and should be what makes sense to them.

Teaching and Caring for Our Children—Jennifer Strickland, Preschool and Kindergarten Teacher[4]

Mrs. Strickland was briefly introduced in Chapter 3 because of her strong focus on diaspora literacy. Mrs. Strickland's classroom is inundated with African-centric imagery, perspectives, activities, and resources. Numerous, positive images of African Americans greet children and parents each day. Imagery is thoughtfully selected, affirming, and far-reaching. Examples include an advertisement from Tuskegee Institute, with photos of graduates and other students, pictures of a university in the Virgin Islands, and a photo of an African American woman who started her own wedding magazine. Implicit in these images is the belief that students can and should reach far and wide.

Culturally relevant teaching is second nature to Mrs. Strickland, and high expectations are conveyed, both covertly and overtly. As she is a White teacher, Mrs. Strickland's African-centric approach takes some by surprise, but also encourages teachers from many ethnic backgrounds—including African Americans—who have shied away from affirming aspects of African and African American culture. From her diverse collection of children's books, which is heavily African-centric, to the candid and multiple-perspective lessons that she teaches about Africa, slavery, and contemporary life, Mrs. Strickland's approach represents the epitome of culturally relevant and emancipatory teaching. She believes in engaging her students in critical thinking—even preschool and kindergarten children. She is a complex thinker and a visionary who is informed on global and world issues; therefore, this ideology pervades her classroom. Based on extensive reading and experience working with African American students and families, Mrs. Strickland has developed her own model of teaching that goes beyond surface-level efforts toward addressing Black students' culture.

For instance, over the span of 1 year, Mrs. Strickland's kindergartners engaged in a discussion of the disproportionate number of Black males in the prison system, because of observations of her students' conversations and life experiences. She and the students perused magazines, analyzed photographs of men and boys, and discussed how African American males were portrayed in different magazines. Students began to notice negative depictions of Black males and females in some of the magazines, but also noticed the positive roles that they saw in other magazines, such as *Black Enterprise*. In the process, the dialogue about how people are portrayed led students to observe how clothing affects the images that people hold about others.

Familiar with the literature that documents that 80–90 percent of African American students speak AAL and benefit from specific strategies for learning SE (Linguistic Society of America, 1997; Perry & Delpit, 1998), Mrs. Strickland teaches children about AAL and applies strategies learned from the Academic English Mastery Program led by Dr. Noma LeMoine (1999), who directed the program in the Los Angeles Unified School District. Children also lead the morning activities in order to work on self-presentation skills, and Mrs. Strickland sits with the rest of the children while the leader "teaches."

Like other CEEEAAS model teachers, Mrs. Strickland ensures that students learn the academic skills that are supposed to be taught. In addition, teachers using culturally relevant instruction will ensure that information is taught beyond the surface level and start by connecting the content to the children. Equally important, students should exit classrooms and school with some sociopolitical awareness, as well as cultural knowledge about themselves and at least one other culture (Ladson-Billings, 1994/2009). Mrs. Strickland has been able to accomplish this complex task each day and is committed to the long-term success of each child.

Commentary

Mrs. Strickland typically speaks in a very soft voice. She possesses an unassuming, but powerful, presence. Because of her caring demeanor, children listen, and parents feel that she is approachable.

As a White teacher, she has taken the time to study her own cultural background and various social identities. Readers may want to do a quick refresher of the conceptual framework presented in Chapter 2 to recall the importance of knowing oneself as a teacher. This is true for all teachers, regardless of ethnicity; however, it is especially important when teaching cross-racially.

Mrs. Strickland was recruited to teach as an instructor at a historically Black college. She is currently teaching there, while also completing her doctoral degree.

Examples From Middle School

No Bad Hair Days—Cassandra Tyler, Middle-School Art Teacher

Mrs. Tyler's class is a stark contrast to Mr. Hill's in a number of ways. Her art class is smaller than most, and Mrs. Tyler teaches several classes of middle-school students each day. Whereas Mr. Hill can make his voice boom like thunder, Mrs. Tyler is soft-spoken, although she has no problem commanding the attention of her students. Mr. Hill is tall; Mrs. Tyler is short-to-average in height. Mrs. Tyler's teaching career spans more than 30 years, although she looks to be in her mid thirties. Her respect for Black culture is reflected in her in-depth study of, and continuing quest for, literature on the topic. Her collection of Black dolls is extensive and also echoes her appreciation of Black culture.

Although the budget for art is limited, Mrs. Tyler's excellence in teaching is not deterred. She is an avid reader, is familiar with literature on African American students, and is an astute observer of their interests. In order to teach the standards and integrate art across the curriculum, Mrs. Tyler begins her work with students with relevant topics that they find engaging. One example is hairstyles. Mrs. Tyler notes, "Our hairstyle reflects our culture and style. After observing my students' and others' hairstyles, I started taking photographs to document their changing patterns" (Boutte & Hill, 2006, p. 321). Instead of framing students' preoccupation with hair as a problem, Mrs. Tyler figured out how to capitalize on students' interests. Figure 5.7 shows one of the hairstyles that inspired Mrs. Tyler's study of hair. The process that Mrs. Tyler used to teach about hairstyles is outlined below.

Mrs. Tyler began the inquiry process by affirming the students' culture (mirrors) and then ventured on to related global topics (windows). As an art

FIGURE 5.7 Mrs. Tyler Photographed Students' Hairstyles to Use When Teaching About Tessellations and Patterns.

Source: Reprinted with permission from Boutte & Hill, 2006

teacher, Mrs. Tyler introduced works of art that had hair themes and the Black artists who did the works.

Artwork Used by Mrs. Tyler

- *Three Generations*, Mauuk Hulis: A print that shows a grandmother sitting in a chair and a mother and daughter on each side of her braiding the grandmother's silver hair.
- *Three Generations*, Paul Goodnight: This print is like a collage that shows a grandmother with white hair. Her granddaughter is doing her hair, and the child's mother is braiding the child's hair.
- *Middle Passage*, Tom Feelings: These two pages from Tom Feelings's book, *Middle Passage*, show two enslaved Africans—one with manacles around his neck and a woman who is connected by chains to him. The woman sports beautiful cornrows and has her head upward in a powerful show of pride and self-possession. In the second picture, two people are shown adorned with African jewelry and beautiful patterns and symbols painted on their faces. These pictures show the African origin of many of the beautiful hairstyles worn today.
- *Full Set or Fill In*, Annie Lee: This print captures a scene in a beauty shop.
- *Extensions*, Annie Lee: This print shows three women having their hair done in a beauty shop—with hair extensions being added.
- *You Next, Sugar*, Annie Lee: This colorful beauty-shop scene captures much of the movement, verve, orality, improvisation, and other Black cultural activities that happen in beauty shops.

Books Used by Mrs. Tyler

Books about Black female hair (to affirm Black female hair) were shared with the students. Although these books are children's books, students enjoyed looking at the hairstyles.

- *Rapunzel* (African version), Fred Crump.
- *I Love My Hair*, Natasha Anastasia Tarplay.
- *Foluke: The Afro Queen*, Nefertari Hilliard-Nunn.
- *Nappy Hair*, Carolivia Herron.
- *Cornrows*, Camille Yarbrough.
- *Happy To Be Nappy*, bell hooks.

As a way of extending the coverage of hair, books about males, females, and other cultures were shared. This broadened the initial concept and demonstrated that both similarities and differences among humans should be valued. Sample books are listed below:

- *My Hair Is Beautiful Because It's Mine* (black males and females), Paula Dejoie.
- *Hair Designs* (females, multicultural, nonfiction), Margaret Caldwell.
- *Hats Off to Hair* (males, females, multicultural), Virginia Knoll.

Books Addressing Other Related Concepts Covered by Mrs. Tyler

- *Madame C. J. Walker* (history—to teach about the first Black female millionaire who earned her money selling hair products), A'Lelia Perry Bundles.
- *Black Hair: Art, Culture, Style* (nonfiction discussion of Black hair, including works of art), A'Lelia Perry Bundles.

Extending the Discussion to Related Science Concepts

Because Mrs. Tyler is an avid reader, she came across ideas for extending her unit when reading a chapter that was written by Lisa Delpit (2002). The next three sections share some of the ideas that she was able to use in her classroom.

- unit on the chemical content of hair dressing and popular hair and makeup products;
- names, properties, and other purposes of chemicals;
- process of testing products.

Extending the Focus to Mathematics

- *Ethnomathematics*: Mrs. Tyler and her students examined the work of Dr. Gloria Gilmer, an ethnomathematician who studies patterns and tessellations in African braiding.[5]
- Mrs. Tyler and her students took photographs of the students' hairstyles (boys' and girls'; see Figure 5.7). Hair patterns were related to patterns in baskets, quilts, and other crafts.
- The students studied patterns in hairstyles in works of art (sculptures and prints).
- Students estimated the amount of hair needed for various styles and monetary issues such as the cost of hairstyles. Discussion ensued about the length of time hairstyles will last and the cost-effectiveness of styles.

Extending to the Study of History and Social Studies

Students engaged in research to study the history of hair among humans. Some of the things that they discovered are listed below.

- Hair has interested humans since the dawn of history.
- Mrs. Tyler shared a website from the Delpit (2002) chapter that traces hairstyles through history.[6] Information about hairstyles in Africa, China, Rome, and around the world is included on the website.
- Sumerian noblewomen dressed their hair in a heavy, netted chignon, rolls, and plaits around the head, or let it fall thickly over the shoulders. They also powdered their hair with gold dust or scented yellow starch and adorned it with gold hairpins and other ornaments.
- Persian nobles curled their hair and beards and stained them red with henna.
- Egyptian noblemen and noblewomen clipped their hair close and, later, for coolness and cleanliness in the hot climate, they shaved their heads with bronze razors. On ceremonial occasions and for protection from the sun, they wore heavy, usually black, wigs. These were in short curly shapes or long and full, in curls or braids, and were adorned with ivory-knobbed hairpins, fillets, fresh flowers, or gold ornaments.
- Babylonian and Assyrian men dyed long hair and beards black and crimped and curled them.
- Greek people used curling irons, and some women dyed their hair red or blue, or dusted it with red, gold, or white powder.
- The "forefathers" of America wore white wigs.

Other Related Topics

- Bookkeeping/record keeping;
- marketing;
- small-business operation and entrepreneurship;
- chemistry, anatomy, biology (knowledge for giving proper facials for particular skin types and structures; proper hygiene);
- electrical currents (electrical apparatuses).

Mrs. Tyler, who has an extensive collection of Black dolls with various hairstyles, was able to build on her passion as well by sharing the dolls. By the end of the unit, Mrs. Tyler had addressed several art standards, as well as content in other subjects. Additionally, students were introduced to artists and artworks that probably would not have captured their interest without a familiar context.

In general, much of Mrs. Tyler's instruction starts with observation and knowledge of her students, as well as her belief in their potential. In the study of hair, student interest encouraged her to venture in depth with the theme. First, she sought to affirm and validate the beauty of Black hair. Anyone who has delved into the politics and issues surrounding hair in the Black community (from both inside and outside forces) can appreciate the need to counter culturally invasive and assaulting messages about Black hair. Even though there has been considerable appreciation for the beauty of Black hair within the Black community in recent years, innuendos and intimations about "good" hair and "bad" hair still are alive and well among many Blacks (Collison, 2002). Pronouncing that Black hair is a topic worthy of study in school and making it an integral part of the course of study, as opposed to a peripheral add-on, served as a counternarrative in itself.

The text set and artwork on Black hair served as a strong counternarrative, as did photographing the children's hair. Too often, Black females' elaborate hairstyles that are worn with pride go unnoticed by educators or are regarded with disapproving comments, whereas White females' new perms are complimented (Boutte, LaPoint, & Davis, 1993). As students proudly posed for photos or called her attention to other students' creative styles, Mrs. Tyler was able to demonstrate the cultural legacy of hairstyles in the African diaspora via African sculptures and prints by renowned artists such as Tom Feelings. Prints showing intergenerational hairstyling routines and women congregating in beauty salons reiterated the beautiful and affective process of "doing someone else's hair." While "sistahs" are getting their hair *fried, dyed, and laid to the side* (borrowing a proverbial phrase commonly heard in Black salons), there is also an unspoken, communal bonding process taking place.

The communal spirit built in beauty shops parallels that of barbershops for males. Amid the braiding, cutting, coloring, straightening, curling, and weaving, little girls learn about womanhood in its many possibilities. In schools, Black female students rarely see Black female teachers or administrators. So, it is not surprising that, in schools that are dominated by White female teachers, the cultural memory and accompanying significance of "getting yo' hair did" is unknown, unacknowledged, and overlooked as an important part of one's being. In thinking about this unit, Mrs. Tyler was well aware that, too often, Black female students will learn that hairstyles labored over and praised at home receive little or no notice at school and in society, outside one's community.

Congruent with one of the tenets for culturally relevant teaching, Mrs. Tyler helped her students make connections between their community, national, and global identities (Ladson–Billings, 1994). Recognizing that she needed to take students beyond their own worldviews and current skill levels, she ventured into content areas and perspectives beyond art and Black culture and was careful to include males as well. In the final analysis, the project served as an important segue to further study in science, math, and history. It should be emphasized that, although the learning process was engaging, it was also rigorous and academically based. Working with other content teachers on the unit and consulting outside resources made it possible for teachers to see learning connections and possibilities that may have gone unnoticed or been labeled pejoratively as extracurricular or related arts. As a student from another classroom who viewed a PowerPoint presentation summarizing the unit commented, "I didn't know that you could learn all of that about hair!" Yes, that and much more (See Majors, 2001, for example).

Commentary

Mrs. Tyler had a career of caring and teaching African American students—giving hope to many and opening up a world of possibilities to her. The unit shared here is one of many of her efforts to make learning meaningful to Black students. Quiet and steadfast, her teaching has positively impacted untold numbers of students. Anyone who knows Mrs. Tyler will immediately understand that teaching was a calling for her, and that she understood one of the purposes in life. While others complained about what the Black students could not do, she demonstrated what could be done. She recently retired, but is still quite busy ensuring that the world will be a better place for her grandchildren and other Black children.

This unit on hair is so important. I cannot begin to count the number of school instances where I have heard White teachers make culturally assaultive comments about Black hairstyles. One only has to ride around a Black neighborhood for a minute to know that hair is on the minds of people—multiple beauty shops, barbershops, and hair stores. These provide opportunities to learn about and from Black people. In these spaces, rich conversations and dynamics occur (Majors, 2001). Although Ms. Tyler did not visit the beauty shops, in the way that Mr. Hill visited barbershops, teachers would benefit from doing so—more than once—or at least watching movies (e.g., *Beauty Shop* or *School Daze*) or reading books about the politics of Black hair. This unit would lend itself to discussion of the ownership of hair stores as well. Another resource that readers may find useful is the website of the ethnomathematician Ron Eglash.[7]

Indie Arie's song "I Am Not My Hair" would also be a wonderful counter-narrative and complement to this unit.[8]

Importantly, culturally relevant teachers such as Mrs. Tyler and the other teachers featured in this book pose an important subtextual question: "What happens if students are not engaged in school?" They look beyond their own classrooms and try to re-envision futures full of possibilities rather than full of dread, low achievement, high-school dropout, unemployment, and the like. Mrs. Tyler worried that, if the girls were not educated, then their possibilities would likely be greatly narrowed. For her, this was not an option.

Other Examples of Middle-School CRP in the Academic Literature

Although the examples shared in this book can be tweaked and extrapolated to different grade levels, some readers may benefit from seeing other examples. Two resources are listed below.

- Milner (2010) features a middle-school, White, male science teacher who uses CRP, in his book. Milner, H. R. (2010). *Start Where You Are, but Don't Stay There: Understanding Opportunity Gaps, Diversity and Teaching in Today's Classrooms.* Cambridge, MA: Harvard Education Press.

- Irvine and Armento (2001) provide field-tested units for elementary and middle levels in language arts, mathematics, science, and social studies. Irvine, J. J., & Armento, B. J. (2001). *Culturally Responsive Teaching: Lesson Planning for Elementary and Middle Grades*. New York: McGraw-Hill.

High-School Examples

Preaching and Poetry—Mr. Nathaniel Bonaparte, High-School English Teacher

Classrooms have their own distinct flavors that are mediated through teachers' personalities, experiences, and interpretations (Ladson-Billings, 1994/2009). So, whereas Mrs. Tyler's class has the quiet undertones of a soft melody, Mr. Bonaparte's class has spiritual overtones, reflecting his other occupation as a minister. Mr. Bonaparte, who is of average height and slight build, had been teaching for 5 years when he became involved with CEEEAAS. Mr. Bonaparte taught in a school that was 100 percent African American, and most of the students were from lower socioeconomic backgrounds. The school was identified as an "A+ school" (a euphemism for a failing school).

Capitalizing on his strength and passion as a minister, one day he entered the classroom dressed in a graduation gown (simulating a minister's cloak), stood at the podium, and began reciting James Weldon Johnson's "Go Down, Death (A Funeral Sermon)." Knowing that students in his class attended church regularly, he instructed them to respond in a call-and-response manner, a common African American church tradition. In the following, student responses are in italics—typically stated in a sing-song manner.

> Weep not, *weep not*
> She is not dead; *no!*
> She's resting in the bosom of Jesus. *Yes!*
> Heart-broken husband—weep no more
> Grief-stricken son—weep no more; *no more*
> Left-lonesome daughter—weep no more; *no more*
> She only just gone home. *Yes.*

Once he had completed the first rendition, a student pleaded to read the poem and to wear the gown. After the student finished, Mr. Bonaparte then read Emily Dickinson's "Because I Could Not Stop for Death," using his best English accent. Instead of the sterile feel of the classroom, the sermon generated an emotionally charged excitement level among the students. Parts of the sermon being dramatized could be heard throughout the classroom. In small groups, students looked for examples of personification in both poems. They also discussed death as the common literary theme. They ended by writing a paragraph outlining the major differences between the two authors' personification of death and why the poems are so different. Students were expected to understand perspective and context. Students left the class reciting and playacting verses from the various poems. Meanwhile, Mr. Bonaparte had taught the standard that he set out to teach: "E1-R2.3—Demonstrate the ability to compare and contrast universal literary themes as they are developed in works in a variety of genres."

Each year, Mr. Bonaparte struggles with ways of generating student interest in topics most remote to them. To do so requires that he, like the other CEEEAAS teachers, focus on what he knows about Black culture in general, his students specifically, himself as a teacher, and the content. This is the ongoing tension that teachers seeking to teach in a culturally effective manner will face.

Mr. Bonaparte's classroom is decorated with culturally relevant imagery, including African artifacts, positive pictures of Black people, books, and other resources. He builds on the semantic features of AAL by posting a word of the day on a poster on which he has used his considerable artistic skills and drawn a very muscular, super-hero-type figure with what looks to be a black and yellow Sphinx's crown. Students write the words on the poster and use them daily. For example, one day, when I visited his classroom, the word of the day was "Debonair." The student wrote the following definition, "suave, urbane; affable, graceful, charming, and smooth; carefree."

Although Mr. Bonaparte does not use a booming voice like Mr. Hill, his friendly and spiritual countenance and caring manner command respect from the students. Like Mrs. Folsom, Mr. Bonaparte teaches character development. For instance, he has a mahogany African cane with the images—*see no evil, speak no evil, hear no evil.* To teach respect for speakers and their audiences, when students are engaged in dialogue, the person holding the cane is supposed to *see no evil* (not be sidetracked by others who are trying to distract the speaker), *speak no evil* (speak respectfully), and *hear no evil* (not listen to naysayers or negative comments).

Teaching students to learn collaboratively and expecting them to teach each other and take responsibility for each other, Mr. Bonaparte uses daily affirmations. Because he teaches several sections of English classes, some years he has to use different affirmations for different classes, depending on how they resonate with the students. He keeps the same affirmations until they no longer seem to resonate with students. Hence, sometimes, students may have two or three different affirmations. Students jointly contribute to the creation of the affirmations and participate in a call-and-response manner. These "class creeds," such as the one below, help keep the focus on education and unity.

Teacher:	What are we here for?
Students:	We are here to learn.
Teacher:	How do we learn?
Students:	Together!
Teacher:	If you don't know . . .

Students:	Ask somebody!
Teacher:	If you know . . .
Students:	Help somebody!
All:	We meet our end
	We sink or swim
	We rise or fall
	Together

Commentary

Mr. Bonaparte is dedicated to teaching. His teaching provides an excellent example of how teachers' personalities do not have to be compromised in order for them to use CRP. For example, during one of the CEEEAAS roundtable discussions, the group read two articles that considered using aspects of pop culture in the classroom:

- Alexander-Smith, A. C. (2004). Feeling the Rhythm of the Critically Conscious Mind. *English Journal*, 58–63.
- Mahiri, J. (1998). Streets to Schools: African American Youth Culture and the Classroom. *The Clearing House*, 71(6), 335–338.

Mr. Bonaparte and the group liked the articles in general and saw possibilities; however, when I played a song by Jay-Z, "Girls, Girls, Girls," to discuss possibilities for critical literacy discussions (e.g., how the lyrics could be used to critique misogyny; why students find the song compelling; the lyrical genius of Jay-Z; classroom implications), Mr. Bonaparte found the explicit lyrics (though beeped out in the song and not printed in the accompanying PowerPoint) offensive and not appropriate for him to use in classrooms. I do not know where Mr. Bonaparte currently stands on the issue of using hip-hop in classrooms and I certainly understand the problems and politics surrounding using explicit lyrics in school. Nevertheless, I appreciated Mr. Bonaparte's strong knowledge of self and of what makes sense for him. That is what culturally relevant teaching is about—knowing how to connect to students in a manner that makes sense to you as the teacher.

Effective teachers such as Mr. Bonaparte are highly recruited and needed. Mr. Bonaparte now teaches in another district.

Making Connections Between Students' Community, National and Global Identities—Edwina Hicklin, High-School Social Studies Teacher

Mrs. Hicklin teaches at the same high school as Mr. Bonaparte (100 percent African American students, mostly from lower-socioeconomic-status backgrounds). Her classroom is very literacy-rich and cultural. Visitors are greeted by global images (e.g., a poster that says, "Celebrate Africa"; Egyptian imagery and information; world maps; a framed, blown-up picture of currency from Iraq; a large *World Almanac*; posters of Paul Robeson, James Baldwin, Wilma Rudolph) that reinforce cultural competence. A large poster with the Preamble to the U.S. Constitution is posted in the front of the classroom over the chalkboard. The first paragraph of the Declaration of Independence is also posted on the other side of the Preamble. All historical documents are critically discussed.

On the board, the date is posted, along with a handwritten statement of standards being taught on any given day. Sociopolitically conscious posters are displayed, with people from different ethnic, age, and religious groups, such as one that says:

> . . . His beliefs don't match ours.
> *So what?*
> His values aren't normal.
> *Who cares?*
> His clothes look funny.
> *Doesn't everyone's?*
> His accent is odd.
> *You have one too.*
> Did you ever stop to realize . . . people who you stereotype . . .

Students' projects on current world events, with newspaper clippings and students' personal illustrations, are posted along with the rubrics for the projects. One project that was posted looked at economics globally, from different cultural standpoints.

A timeline of Africans coming to the US wraps around much of the top portion of one of the walls. Mrs. Hicklin's classroom is very student-centered. She begins lessons by posing questions of engagement that draw students into the lesson (e.g., "What type of technology do you use most frequently?" "Does your most frequent technological mode differ from or compare to the technology that is used by the majority of Americans?"). Questions such as these are used to open discussions about specific cultural practices and equity issues surrounding the economics of prepaid cellphones versus plans. Discussion would continue with connections throughout the world, often using pictures of daily lives in other nations. Typically, Mrs. Hicklin culminates these mini units by allowing students to work on a 2–3-day project in which they observe personal and cultural practices with their families and record their observations in their journals. Examples from journals are shared in class and often lead to related topics of study. Classmates are expected to take notes when others are reporting and later to apply the five themes of geography to at least three of the countries that they heard about in their classmates' presentations. Often, students create collages, videos, and so forth, which explains the abundance of informational, student-created posts on the walls of the classroom. As a daily grade, each student answers the question, "How did I see me or someone I know personally in today's lesson and/or research?".

Throughout class, students engage in group and individual activities, and Mrs. Hicklin poses thought-provoking questions for which there are no right or wrong answers. She seeks input from students on how they best learn about geography (e.g., students complete the statement, "I wish I could . . ."). Mrs. Hicklin encourages students to talk about their home lives, families, friends, and extracurricular activities, to get ideas of what her students are interested in learning. A variety of student posters on different assignments can be seen everywhere (e.g., American clothing versus African clothing). It is clear that Mrs. Hicklin shares the ownership of the classroom with the students, and that the students love learning about geography and social studies. For everything that she teaches, Mrs. Hicklin focuses on helping students make connections between their community and national and global identities.

Mrs. Hicklin also shares aspects of her life with her students (e.g., her children and things that she does outside school). Although the subject matter lends itself to this, many teachers make social studies and geography mundane topics and, hence, lose interest in the topic. Not so in Mrs. Hicklin's classroom. It exudes energy and vibrancy—very much like the world does.

Commentary

Mrs. Hicklin loves teaching, and so her students love school. She is able to adeptly multitask and seemingly be in more than one place in the classroom at a time. Like Mrs. Folsom, all eyes are on her in the classroom, and students hang on her every word. By now, readers should not be surprised that Mrs. Hicklin was recruited to teach at middle school in a nearby district. I have no doubt that she continues to teach in a manner that is culturally relevant, as it is second nature to her.

Simply the Best! Mr. William Lenard, High-School Mathematics Teacher

"He's the best teacher I ever had!" exclaimed one of Mr. Lenard's ninth-grade students, who was quickly echoed by others. Mr. Lenard's ninth-graders, from low-income backgrounds, eagerly come to his ninth-grade algebra and math tech classes. Teaching at the same school as Mrs. Hicklin and Mr. Bonaparte and having only taught for 3 years when he began working with CEEEAAS, Mr. Lenard is indistinguishable from many of his students in his youthful appearance. Although math is a subject that many high-school students dread, Mr. Lenard's students love the subject. After teaching for 1 year, Mr. Lenard received the principal's award for the huge gains that ninth-graders made in math. Using culturally relevant methods, the end-of-year examination scores rose from 49 percent passing to 71 percent passing. After his second year, the passing rate increased to 78 percent.

Mr. Lenard's classroom is best described as highly energized. Having played baseball in college, he coaches the high-school baseball team and has been known to run across the classroom or to stand on his desk while teaching. Needless to say, students find his teaching style engaging.

Following the tenets of culturally relevant mathematics, Mr. Lenard takes a standard math concept, such as teaching about functions, and relates it to something that his students understand (Matthews, 2003; Rousseau & Tate, 2003). Once he has demonstrated the relevance of the concept to students, they transfer the skill to similar problems and willingly attempt other problems. At the beginning of one class, Mr. Lenard queried, "How many of you have bought or sold someone a 'burnt' CD?". Noting that his students often had burnt CDs, his question of engagement immediately caught their attention, and he mentally noted that he could use this opportunity to teach them about the ethical concerns of selling and buying burnt CDs. Capitalizing on the students' undivided attention, Mr. Lenard gives the following two-part definition of function:

- a rule that establishes a relationship between two quantities—an input and an output;
- a rule that, in most cases, can be represented by equations or algorithms.

Although the students do not fully understand what a function is yet, they realize that it can have something to do with buying or selling burnt CDs. Next, he introduces the function form:

$$f(x) = x$$

Contrast Mr. Lenard's approach with a typical algebra lesson where an equation is introduced in a decontextualized manner, and students are expected to immediately start working on the equation, with no understanding of why. Mr. Lenard also introduces the standards that he will be teaching.

Mr. Lenard continues by asking students to write a function to project the profit that a person can make from selling burnt CDs, if they are selling them for $5 each and they had to spend $15 to buy burnable CDs and $10 to buy CD cases. He asks them to (a) identify the rate at which each CD will be sold, and (b) identify the costs needed to start the business. He explains that profit is the amount of money made after the cost of starting the business has been deducted.

The lesson concludes by asking students to determine three ways that selling burnt CDs can be detrimental to the music industry. Hence, Mr. Lenard has: (a) made the lesson relevant, (b) taught a new skill, and (c) facilitated students' thinking beyond their own perspectives (considering the larger ethical issues of selling burnt CDs). Because Mr. Lenard contextualizes math, students' anxiety levels are reduced, and they view math as doable and useful. This is evident in concrete ways, such as significant increases in the passing rates of students on the end-of-year tests.

Commentary

Mr. Lenard has a talent for figuring out how to make math relevant to his students. Even though he is a math teacher, he recalls being turned off math in middle school because of the way it was taught. Using this memory as an impetus, he engages students. Mr. Lenard knows that mathematics is not the same everywhere. As explained by Ladson-Billings:

> There are those who suggest that mathematics is "culture free" and that it does not matter who is "doing" mathematics; the tasks remain the same. But these are people who do not understand the nature of culture and its profound impact on cognition.
>
> (1997, p. 700)

Many teachers are building on new literacies that youth find engaging, such as hip-hop (Paris, 2012). The two links below show examples of teachers using hip-hop in math classrooms.

* www.youtube.com/watch?v=OFSrINhfNsQ
* www.youtube.com/watch?v=t2uPYYLH4Zo

Mr. Lenard was recruited to teach in a majority White school district and later became an assistant principal. He is currently teaching math at a high school in a school district with a rapidly growing African American population.

Yo—Whassup? William Boyles, High-School Science Teacher

Mr. Boyles was not a CEEEAAS teacher. I met him a few years after working with the other CEEEAAS teachers. However, he taught at the same high school that Mrs. Hicklin, Mr. Lenard, and Mr. Bonaparte did—though not at the same time. Mr. Boyles has been successful teaching science using hip-hop pedagogy in a number of school settings. Importantly, he has documented the impact of his teaching, as can be seen in Figure 5.8, which shows how his classes outscore other courses using conventional methods of teaching science. Recently, I asked a student at the high school where he taught if she knew him. She excitedly said that she did, though she had not been taught by him, but wished that she had. Her friend who had him, she reported, said he was great!

The following audio and video links will allow readers to hear more about his teaching:

* www.youtube.com/watch?v=pZ0EtxR0JCc
* www.blogtalkradio.com/allthingseducation/2013/06/13/hip-hop-science

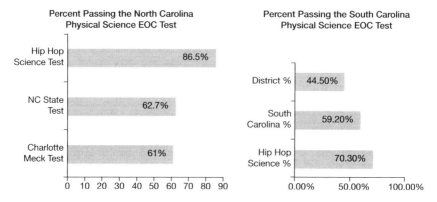

FIGURE 5.8 Mr. Boyles' Outcomes for Hip-Hop Science Classes in Two Different Schools/States.

Commentary

As Dr. Joyce King, distinguished professor and president of the American Educational Research Association in 2014, is fond of saying, "Not everyone has to do the same thing [to be effective]" (personal communication). It should be clear from the examples presented so far that that is indeed true. Mr. Boyles followed his passion and interests and used them as avenues for engaging students in science teaching and learning. He and Mrs. Folsom traveled with Dr. Susi Long and me as one of the teachers in a Fulbright–Hays delegation to Sierra Leone (mentioned in Chapter 3). He quickly taught the students there some of the hip hop science lyrics, much to their delight.

Readers may also find it useful to look up work by Dr. Chris Emdin at Teachers College (Emdin, 2010). A preview to his work can also be found online.[9]

Mr. Boyles has taught at another school and is now an assistant principal at a middle school in Texas. He is also completing his doctorate degree.

Charlease Kelly-Jackson, College Instructor and Teacher for a Summer Program for African American High-School Students[10]

Like many scholars studying culturally relevant science, Mrs. Kelly-Jackson wanted to know, "How can science teachers enable all students to study a Western scientific way of knowing and at the same time respect and access the ideas, beliefs, and values of non-Western cultures?" (Brayboy & Castagno, 2008, p. 743). Her intent was not to supplant the "science curriculum." Rather, she sought to add multiple perspectives, critiques, and counter-stories that required attention to particular cultural contexts.

Mrs. Kelly-Jackson's interest in learning how to teach science more effectively to African American students led her to venture into culturally relevant teaching. Her openness to feedback indicates that she views herself as a learner who recognizes that becoming a culturally relevant teacher is an ongoing journey. As will become evident, her first efforts focused primarily on engaging students (with little or no emphasis on critical and sociopolitical consciousness). With an unspoken and commonly espoused goal of increasing the number of African American scientists, she sought to increase students' critical thinking skills by demonstrating the interdisciplinary nature of science and defying the notion that science learning is boring and irrelevant to real-life settings. She also wanted students to learn scientific terminology that could be used in dialogue with other scientists and to understand science content. Balancing her expectation for students to learn the course's content with the realization that students did not find the mundane memorization of science vocabulary engaging, she reasoned that the study of cells would lend itself to interesting and relevant activities. Being resourceful, Mrs. Kelly-Jackson found and adapted a cell analogies collage.[11] The activity challenges students to make original analogies between cell structures and everyday objects and experiences. To learn the vocabulary words for the chapter on cells, students were asked to use personal references to develop analogies. Mrs. Kelly-Jackson spent time explaining analogies and giving examples (e.g., "The nucleus is like a brain, because it controls and coordinates the activities of the whole cell in the same way the brain controls and coordinates activities of the body"). Students were asked to select at least 10 words from the chapter's vocabulary list (see below) and use analogies to relate the words to a theme of their choice:

- cell wall
- chromatin
- cytoskeleton
- mitochondrion
- lysosome
- rough endoplasmic reticulum
- microvilli
- microtubules
- desmosomes
- centriole
- nucleolus
- flagellum
- ribosome
- nuclear envelope
- plasmodesmata
- intermediate filaments
- gap junctions
- tight junctions.

At first, Mrs. Kelly-Jackson's students showed little enthusiasm, but, when they were able to bring their own interpretations, they became invigorated. They found magazine and newspaper pictures of everyday objects that had personal or cultural references and also had a similar function (or use) as each cell structure or organelle. Students used a wide variety of themes such as: (a) "Let the Cell Say Amen" (see Figure 3.3); (b) "What's a Cell to a Cello?"; (c) "CEO and Cells"; and (d) "Willy Wonka and the Chocolate Factory." This activity implicitly and explicitly taught students the strategy of creating an inventory of their interests and passions and relating it to what they were learning. In many ways, it validated the students' worldviews and experiences, and they began to see science as less remote and the terminology as less convoluted.

Below are the examples that one of Mrs. Kelly-Jackson's students used for her collage. Because of her strong religious beliefs and social identity, she decided to use Christianity as her theme. As seen in Figure 5.9, she titled her collage, "Let The Cell Say Amen."

1. Chloroplast = pastor: The chloroplast converts energy of sunlight into chemical energy that the plant can use, as the pastor converts the nutrients in the Bible into a Rhema (word that is spoken) for the followers.

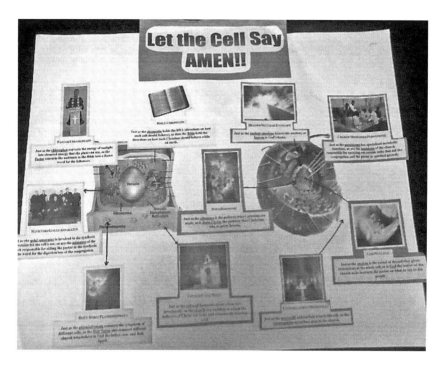

FIGURE 5.9 Analogies Poster Developed by One Student Who Related Religious Principles to Concepts About Cells.

2. Chromatin = Bible: The chromatin holds the DNA (directions on how each cell should behave), as the Bible holds the directions on how each Christian should behave while on Earth.

3. Nucleus = God: The nucleus is the center of the cell that gives instructions to the whole cell, as God is the center of the church and instructs the pastor on what to say to his people.

4. Cell wall = church: The cell wall keeps the plant cell intact structurally, as the church is a building where the believers of Christ can come and structurally worship God.

5. Microvilli = congregation: The microvilli add surface area to the cell, as the congregation adds surface area to the church.

6. Golgi apparatus = ministers: The golgi apparatus is involved in the synthesis of proteins for the cell's use, as ministers of the church are responsible for aiding the pastor in the synthesis of the word for the digestion/use of the congregation.

7. Plasmodesmata = Holy Spirit: The plasmodesmata connects the cytoplasm of different cells, as the Holy Spirit connects different churches who believe in God, the Father, Son, and Holy Spirit.

8. Ribosome = Jesus: The ribosome is the pathway where proteins are made, as Jesus Christ is the pathway that Christians take to get to heaven.

9. Nuclear envelope = Heaven: The nuclear envelope houses the nucleus, as heaven is God's home.

10. Peroxisome = church ministries: The peroxisome has specialized metabolic functions, as the ministries of the church are responsible for carrying out certain tasks that aid the congregation and the pastor in spiritual growth.

In terms of overall outcomes for this chapter and for the freshman science course at the historically Black college where Mrs. Kelly-Jackson taught, her efforts helped improve student achievement, engagement, and interest. To hear students who had historically experienced little success in science exclaim their interest in taking other coursework was its own reward. Even more importantly, Mrs. Kelly-Jackson has noted that her efforts to engage students culturally and actively over the past 4 years have resulted in increased vocabulary scores and critical reasoning. For example, students' test scores from this chapter ranged from 75 to 90 percent, instead of the typical 60–85 percent when analogies were not used as an instructional strategy.

Commentary

Viewing the cell collage activity through the lens of the three dimensions of culturally relevant teaching (academic achievement, cultural competence, and critical consciousness), this activity produced mixed results. Academically, according to the records, students increased their passing rates on the vocabulary tests and are now more likely to integrate the vocabulary into their discussions and to understand scientific terminology. Yet, this is a very cursory level of achievement, and I do not want to leave the impression that culturally relevant teaching can be reduced to a bag of pedagogical tricks or one-time activities. An isolated activity cannot meet the larger goal of reversing students' unfavorable view of science or increasing the likelihood of pursuing careers in science. The activity can serve as a rudimentary introduction to the notion that students can view concepts through their own cultural and personal lenses. Yet, this notion has to be probed through ongoing dialogic exchanges and opportunities to read and act on their lived experiences and worlds (Freire, 1970/1999). Students can explore who they are, what they already know, and how this applies to science in their personal spaces. Importantly, they will need opportunities to examine whose ideologies, knowledge, and worldviews are represented in the content and standards and whose are not. I will discuss this later after examining all three activities. Although Mrs. Kelly-Jackson engages in a series of interesting and engaging activities in her classroom, taken alone, they may seem to be loosely connected and would benefit from a cohesive CRP framework that extends beyond definitions of academic achievement that are narrowly defined by mastery of the chapter's vocabulary. So, what about increasing the students' cultural competence? Many African American students have had little or no exposure to information regarding scientists in the African diaspora. Whenever possible, Mrs. Kelly-Jackson provides powerful counternarratives by using scientists of color (and females), so that students understand that science is not the purview of White men and also learn of strong science legacies among the people of the African diaspora. Readers may refer to the set of guidelines for examining biases that were stated in Chapter 3: Cultural information that is presented should not be fragmented, presented on the periphery of the unit, or glossed over (Boutte, 1999). A good place to start developing deep cultural competence for Black students is to explore scientific funds of knowledge in students' own communities and spaces. Discussion on cells can also include the work of scientists such as Dr. Ernest Just (Black Inventor Online Museum, 2010; Hayden, 1970), whose work has not been amplified in most science books. Dr. Just sought to understand the world of the cell and sought to find "truth" using scientific methods and inquiry, challenging the theories of leading biologists of the 19th and 20th centuries. His scholarship contributed to scientific understanding of the process of artificial parthenogenesis and the physiology of cell development. CRP should not be narrowly defined as teaching only within the classroom setting, but should keep larger global perspectives and relevance to real-world events as important considerations. Students who are faced with daily inequities are likely to identify with Dr. Just's experiences with racism and prejudice, which ultimately led him to leave the United States and study in Europe in 1930. Comparisons and contrasts between various eras can also be discussed. Dialogue regarding the different epistemological stances and the idea of "truth" can be critically explored. Doing so will require teachers such as Mrs. Kelly-Jackson and other science educators to suspend the typical coverage of topics in favor of the uncovering of multiple perspectives. Yet, given the realities of classrooms, educators often fear that dialogues on interrelated issues not included in the standards will detract from student learning. In Mrs. Kelly-Jackson's case, we can see that this was not the case, and the academic outcomes of students increased. More importantly, students actually liked Mrs. Kelly-Jackson's classes and enjoyed learning about science. As Mrs. Kelly-Jackson continues to develop her CRP skills, she can begin to help students increase their sense of agency as scientists. This can lead to inquiry efforts that address ethnoscientific problems in their communities and in the world, such as investigating the relationship between zinc levels and prostate cancer in African American males.

Mrs. Kelly-Jackson—Example 2: DNA Extraction Activities

This series of activities was done with a group of African American high-school students as part of a summer program designed to increase students' awareness of, and interest in, science-related disciplines and careers. The DNA extraction activity introduces students to various biological techniques. The activity integrated technology by having students visit the DNA Extraction Virtual Lab.[12] The website provides students with a general idea of the process of extraction and its importance in biotechnology. Students followed links from the virtual lab to a link named, "How to Extract DNA From Anything."[13] This activity was completed in class using various items, such as chicken liver, strawberries, green split peas, and/or broccoli. Because most of the students were familiar with crime scene investigation (CSI) television shows (e.g., *CSI: Miami*, *CSI: Crime Scene Investigation*, and *CSI: NY*), the idea of studying DNA biotechniques connected to their lives on some level. The television shows allowed students to see how practical applications of DNA technology are used in our daily lives, from medical applications to forensic evidence. Additionally, students are familiar with talk television shows such as *Maury* (Povich) or *Divorce Court*, which use DNA samples to determine paternity. This prior knowledge is useful when students are introduced to the concept of ABO and Rh blood typing, invaluable tools in the fields of medicine and criminology.

For this activity, students tested four synthetic blood samples to identify the ABO and Rh blood types. The activity introduced students to different blood types and how blood types are inherited. To reinforce students' knowledge and to show cultural relevance, students identified and researched a selected blood disorder or condition (i.e., thrombosis and sickle cell). From their engagement in scientific inquiry, the product of this assignment was a PowerPoint presentation that included: (a) causes; (b) diagnosis; (c) symptoms and complications; (d) data and statistics, with a special focus on how it relates to African American populations; (e) tips for healthy living (again with a focus on the cultural relevance); and (f) the cost to society.

Commentary

Typical for initial ventures into culturally relevant teaching, an underlying subtext of the activity is for students to have "fun" and to be actively engaged. Some aspects of all three dimensions of CRP are evident, but can be prodded. This unit lends itself to the possibility of investigating genealogy studies that are being conducted by *National Geographic* (2014) researchers and others who collect mitochondrial DNA and/or Y chromosomes. This can lead to very complex dialogues on genetics and history (e.g., how African Americans' genealogies were affected by the European slave trade and related ethical issues). Such possibilities being opened up could lead young scientists (students) to pursue efforts that may be useful one day in providing African Americans with more information about their African lineage, which was systematically destroyed during the slave trade. A critique of Nobel Prize winner James Watson's scientific work, in light of his recent racist statements about Africans and Blacks being intellectually inferior (Associated Press, 2007), could also be reexamined regarding the role that his beliefs may have played in research questions and conclusions. A dialogue on the topic helps make "scientists" less remote and also allows for examination of the relationship to research, questions posed, methods used, and biases. Seeing science as a human and cultural construction is key. Charles Drew's discoveries (Black Inventor Online Museum, 2010; Lonesome & Huggins, 1990; Love & Franklin, 1997; Whitehurst, 2001) relating to the preservation of blood can serve as a counternarrative to discussing only White scientists. By separating the liquid red blood cells from the near-solid plasma and freezing the two separately, Drew found that blood could be preserved and reconstituted at a later date. His system for the storing of blood plasma (blood bank) revolutionized the medical profession. He also established the American Red Cross blood bank, of which he was the first director, and he organized the world's first blood bank drive, nicknamed "Blood for Britain." Sociopolitically, students can discuss the historical irony surrounding Dr. Drew's death. While driving to a science convention, he fell asleep and was seriously injured in rural North Carolina. It was 1950, in the South, and Dr. Drew was not admitted to an "all-White" hospital. Students can research the details of his death to determine the role that racism played. Some sources indicate that Dr. Drew needed a transfusion and was denied one; others disagree and say that he was not admitted to the White hospital, but was admitted to a "mixed-race" medical facility (Black Inventor Online Museum, 2012). Dialogue, inquiry, and critical analyses on this topic position students as teachers/learners, which is the hallmark of culturally relevant science teaching. It also connects science to other disciplines, such as history in this case, and can propel students to take reflective action to address global problems in their communities and in society.

Mrs. Kelly-Jackson—Example 3: Integumentary System

Mrs. Kelly-Jackson was able to see numerous possibilities for making the study of the integumentary system accessible to her university freshmen biology students. Given the sociopolitical nature of skin color, studying the integumentary system lends itself to a discussion of melanin (different levels of melanin by racial groups, skin tones, and benefits). As science is conceived as a socially and culturally constructed discipline, the inclusion of non-Western, indigenous, or other racial/ethnic traditions of knowing is important in culturally relevant science classrooms (Lee & Buxton, 2008). For example, Mrs. Kelly-Jackson's discussion of skin and hair led to the discussion of Madame C. J. Walker's (2014) development of Black hair products, as well as the politics of Black hair. As noted in Mrs. Tyler's unit on hair, chemical names of specific hair dressings, the impact that chemicals have on hair, as well as the safety and potential dangers of inadequate testing, can be included. Even in racially integrated classes, through scientific inquiry, students can examine their own personal hair-/skin-care products, including testing, marketing, and ingredients for different types of skin and hair. Although African American students can certainly serve as experts and informants on Black hair, educators will also need to spend some time studying Black hair in order to present information in a culturally informed manner. It is important to note that, in culturally relevant classrooms, conventional methods and assessments are used when appropriate. For example, Mrs. Kelly-Jackson consulted the following website, and students tackled mini and mega quizzes on the topic: www.zoology.ubc.ca/~biomania/tutorial/skin/outanc19.htm. In this example, not only did this unit allow students to understand the basics of the integumentary system as one of our body's systems, but they were able to connect the concepts to their daily living experiences and worldviews as well. Many students were excited to learn more about Madame C. J. Walker (Altman, 1997) and realized that she played a role in their learning about science and science ethics. Most of the students surmised that Ms. Walker tested her products either on herself or family and friends and understood that her products were not tested to the extent products are tested today. The healthy discourse students had about product testing was refreshing, especially as they discussed their homemade hair-/skin-care products. In the end, students had a better understanding about skin and hair and the ethics and safety of product testing. They also were able to see how culture is related to modern-day science, which was the underlining goal of the unit.

Commentary

As in the first two activities, Mrs. Kelly-Jackson uses the textbook curriculum as a source of ideas so that she can address the course's objectives. Yet, as she thinks about Hoya's conception of curricula, she understands that the unit can be revisioned based on students' interests. At some point, Mrs. Kelly-Jackson may consider allowing students to peruse the syllabus and textbook to determine particular areas of interest where they can engage in in-depth study. Small-group inquiries into subjects may help students start to transform the view of science as a pre-set and non-dynamic subject. Allowing them to engage in "scientific processes" (not necessarily standard processes) will be an important part of capturing students' voices and promoting critical consciousness. Here, students can learn that many worldviews can and do coexist. That is, they can come to understand that the textbook is one of many ways of knowing, and that theirs provide other epistemologies. Hence, they can become proficient in the "mandated" ways of knowing, alongside their cultural ideas, beliefs, and values (Brayboy & Castagno, 2008). From a critical point of view, contradictions between various epistemologies do not have to be reconciled. The following section suggests sample topics that may stimulate provocative dialogue and research by students and teachers. The topics are difficult, and educators should be willing to position themselves as learners, as addressing many of the issues will require consulting several sources and a willingness to accept non-resolution as a possibility for future study.

Problematizing Science as "Factual" and Uncovering Scientific Racism

Probably the most difficult and surprising revelation for teachers and teacher educators who engage in CRP work is that they have to move beyond the typical neutral, apolitical stance in science and actively address oppression. This dimension is more than many teachers bargain for or are ready to address. Yet, unless they do so, hegemonic principles and Eurocentric knowledge and ways of knowing are unintentionally privileged and reinforced. In culturally relevant science classrooms, the assumption is that science involves inquiring into one's own world. Hence, science content is not decontextualized from students' and teachers' everyday experiences. Overall, Mrs. Kelly-Jackson's activities and engagements sought to tap into students' interests; however, a key part of CRP is addressing power relations. Because science, like other subjects, is cultural (Lee & Buxton, 2008), the way that we think about science in the US inevitably reinforces existing power relations in society. That is, Western and European knowledge is privileged in textbooks and classrooms (Barton, Ermer, Burkett, & Osborne, 2003; Davis & Martin, 2008; Ryan, 2008). A CRP framework lends itself to potentially interesting discussions and inquiries in classrooms regarding why the worldviews of some groups are marginalized and devalued. It gives educators a chance to reexamine science content and to problematize the widespread Eurocentric bias in the production and evaluation of scientific knowledge (Davis & Martin, 2008; Gould, 1981; Joseph, 1987). Difficult sociopolitical concepts such as scientific racism can be explored, and students and teachers can begin to uncover inaccurate and incomplete information in the science literature.

Scientific racism can be defined as the use of scientific methods to support and validate racist beliefs about African Americans and other groups based on the existence and significance of racial categories that form a hierarchy of races that support political and ideological positions of white supremacy.

(Davis & Martin, 2008, p. 14)

Many students of color recognize the existence of scientific racism, even if they do not overtly name it. This tacit and/or cultural knowledge may manifest itself as resistance to science as is currently taught (Boutte, 2002; Kohl, 2007). Notwithstanding, science educators will need preparation for leading discussions on scientific racism and other sociopolitical realties. Admittedly, this dimension of culturally relevant teaching is typically not addressed, because of educators' discomfort and/or little preparation. CRP is openly political, whereas conventional teaching is not. Helping educators see the political nature of conventional teaching, which privileges Eurocentric culture and positivist epistemologies, is a formidable task.

To illustrate the Eurocentric nature of science, consider the typical "linear" steps for the "scientific method" as a framework for investigating the natural world. "Within this tradition, Jean Lamark is credited with discovering a theory of evolution, Watson and Crick discovered the structure of the DNA molecule, and Boyle discovered gas laws" (Barba, 1995, p. 56). The step-driven scientific method is presented as a single way of investigating the world, rather than it being open to multifaceted possibilities (Boutte, 1999). According to this line of reasoning, if a scientist or group of people does not follow the step formula, the results are typically not considered "scientific." Yet, for thousands of years, Native Americans of the Southwestern United States, South America, and Central America have cultivated corn. Each year, the biggest and best ears of corn were saved by the harvesters and used as seeds the following year. The tradition of sowing only genetically superior seeds resulted in the improvement of corn, from stubby little weeds into the current version of well-formed ears of corn (Barba, 1995). In this example, Native Americans followed a scientific process (identified the problem, collected information about which ears of corn were the best, formed the hypothesis that planting the biggest seeds would result in an improved plant, conducted experiments in plant growth for thousands of years, and passed on the findings orally to their children). However, Native Americans are not viewed as the founders of genetics research, because they did not keep written records of their research or present findings for peer review in the "scientific" community. Credit for the discovery of genetics research is given to Gregor Mendel in many science textbooks. Sociopolitically, culturally relevant teaching would question whether Mendel alone discovered genetics research and would explore evidence of others who had previously discovered this. A Eurocentric view of science, which insists on keeping copious notes, writing reports, and the like, dismisses and overlooks the research of generations of Native Americans (Barba, 1995).

Here, it becomes obvious that science is not "objective," "neutral," or "factual." Like all disciplines, it represents the worldviews of the writers of the (science) texts. Why would a Native American or other student of color find this version of science credible, especially when Eurocentric worldviews dominate the texts and discount other versions?

Current science content, which is dominated by discoveries attributed to White males, also omits contributions from women, whose work was frequently claimed by White male colleagues or husbands (Barba, 1995; Ryan, 2008). There are numerous other examples beyond the scope of this chapter, but a few examples follow:

• Onesimus was an enslaved African man who shared information from Africa about the smallpox vaccine with his master.
• Maria Aimee Lullin's discoveries regarding honeybees were published under her husband's name, François Huber.
• Rosalind Franklin's contribution to the discovery of deoxyribonucleic acid (DNA) was credited only to Watson and Crick.
• There are countless unrecorded instances that demonstrate how scientific contributions of women and people of color were deliberately omitted from "scientific" records, and false information was conveyed to generations of students.

Dialogue on such topics reframes science from being static to dynamic and intimates that, as more accurate and complete information is uncovered, the knowledge base in science should reflect these changes (Kuhn, 1996). Additionally, as students learn to *read the world*, they can start to look for examples of science in everyday occurrences. Traditionally, science content has focused on "received" knowledge, which is dominated by Eurocentric thought. Hence, the focus has too often been on giving the right answer rather than on problem solving and problem posing (Freire, 1970/1999). CRP acknowledges that the history of science and science teaching has been oversimplified. Hence, it seeks to explore science from various ages and civilizations throughout human history. Given the backdrop of "traditional" approaches, culturally relevant science aims to include voices and worldviews that have been silenced and excluded from the curriculum (Barton et al., 2003; Brayboy, & Castagno, 2008; Keane, 2008; Ryan, 2008). This does not mean negating or excluding information from Eurocentric or Western worldviews, but it does mean substantively including other worldviews, as opposed to occasional or fragmented instances. Without culturally relevant science approaches, not only will a variety of worldviews be omitted, but existing hegemonic power structures will be reinforced (Ryan, 2008). From a critically conscious perspective, students will move beyond false binaries and dualistic and/or essentialist views that suggest that there is only one way of knowing science (Fleer, 2008). Hence, when they come to understand that science is also about people's relationships to others and to the phenomenal world, many perspectives (even contradictory or oppositional ones) can coexist (Fleer, 2008; Keane, 2008).

Conceptually, culturally relevant science defies the assertion that there is a singular or normative scientific worldview. It recognizes that there is a wide range of scientific skills and ways of knowing that people display in their lived experiences within diverse communities. Pedagogically, Fleer (2008) recommends that teachers use a "double move" approach, in which they have in mind the everyday practices, traditions, or concepts of their students, as well as the Western scientific concept(s) that they want students to acquire. "Having both in mind (double move) allows teachers to be respectful and mindful of the practice traditions, while at the same time seeking pedagogical ways of giving more meaning to Western scientific concepts" (Fleer, 2008, p. 785).

It is particularly important for science educators to rethink their approaches for teaching science, as many students consider it irrelevant to their lives (Barba, 1995; Boutte, 1999; Lee & Buxton, 2008). Additionally, females and students of color (with the exception of Asian Americans, as a group) tend to do less well than White males in science (Boutte, 1999). Although no cultural group is monolithic, the inclusion of culturally syntonic considerations for diverse learners is suggested. That is, attention should be given to seeing if the instruction, curriculum, and assessments are attuned to the students' cultural worldviews. Culturally syntonic examples can include making sure that the imagery in textbooks and classrooms reflects the students, the use of culturally familiar role models, or classroom activities that build on the communication strengths of the students: for example, oral tradition for African American students (Barba, 1995; Lee & Luykx, 2005).

Overall Commentary About Mrs. Kelly-Jackson

It is commendable that educators such as Mrs. Kelly-Jackson have the presence of mind and commitment to believe that high achievement is possible for African American students. The expectation that educators will be able to transform their classrooms overnight is unreasonable and unfeasible. It is important to recognize the hugeness and complexity of what educators on the frontline are up against: the status quo, which has built-in reinforcements to protect itself. So, I applaud Mrs. Kelly-Jackson's efforts, while acknowledging her plans to delve deeper and continue to be vigilant about addressing issues of equity, power, and culture. Her initial efforts focused on individual activities, which primarily emanated from the textbook. As culturally relevant teaching is a bridge to mainstream and other ways of knowing, not all activities/lessons included in classes are expected to focus only on students' respective cultural groups.

It should be emphasized that students may not remember all of the names of Black scientists and inventors—or even what they accomplished. However, they will have the knowledge and understanding that Black people made substantial contributions and are not missing from the field of science. The work that Mrs. Kelly-Jackson does is important for interrupting the pervasive scientific racism that exists in school curricula. Both Mr. Boyles and Mrs. Kelly-Jackson recognized that students were not motivated to learn vocabulary words that would be helpful for other science concepts.

Mrs. Kelly Jackson has since earned her doctoral degree and is no longer an instructor at a small university. Dr. Kelly-Jackson is now an assistant professor at a university.

Conclusion

There is much work to be done in the classrooms of Black children. These examples should offer glimmers of hope. Readers will note that the teachers often sought resources beyond the district's or school's curriculum. Understanding students and developing strong relationships and respect are foundational to the process (Bonner, 2009). In this chapter, I have tried to capture a deep sense of centering culture, critical consciousness, and achievement in classrooms for Black students. An important goal for teachers is to find ways to normalize high achievement for African American students, so that they will realize and regain their historical legacies of achievement. To do so requires becoming familiar with the context, students, and their cultures. Often, additional reading will be necessary, as well as deconstructing, reconstructing, and reframing teaching. Educators will also need to engage in an ongoing process of countering pervasive and long-held disbeliefs that African American students are brilliant and capable.

Although our focus has been on African American students (whom I do not consider to be monolithic, by the way), the same process is required for other cultural groups. Educators will also benefit from positioning themselves as teachers and learners (Freire, 1970/1999), viewing students as a source of information and letting them research topics of interest. Collaboration with other educators will likely make the process more interesting and insightful, as well as less threatening. The process of culturally relevant teaching is a dynamic and ongoing process. It is a continuous quest, not a destination, and so educators will need to remain open to refining and transforming their thinking. It is hoped that teachers engage in CRP, not solely to reduce the "achievement gap" or as a trend, but because it is an ethical and educational imperative that all students be effectively taught, in light of pervasive and persistent educational outcomes for Black students.

Although sporadic and not widely documented and circulated, there are numerous examples of teachers who are successfully teaching African American students (Boutte, 2012; Boutte & Hill, 2006; Ladson-Billings, 1994/2009; Howard, 2008; Milner, 2010; Morris, 2004). Despite an incredibly pessimistic backdrop that describes the academic and social problems that African American students face in ways that make it difficult for the public to realistically envision reversing this predicament in a sustained or large-scale manner (Buendia, 2011), there are substantive attempts to fundamentally reverse the negative legacies bequeathed to Black students and to counter the pervasive disbelief that widespread social and academic success for African American students is possible. Such efforts do not narrowly define success by test scores, although they certainly are directed toward increasing the overall academic performance and long-term success of African American students.

Key Points From the Chapter

1. Many of the examples included in this chapter are from teachers who were involved with the Center of Excellence for the Education and Equity of African American Students (CEEEAAS). Other examples are from the literature.
2. Three types of knowledge/skill are needed to effectively teach African American students: (1.) deep content knowledge, (2.) strong pedagogical content knowledge, and (3.) strong CRP.
3. CRP is instruction that uses students' cultures and strengths (cultural capital) as a bridge to success in school achievement.
4. CRP focuses on: (a) academic excellence that is not based on cultural deficit models of school failure, (b) cultural competence that locates excellence within the context of the students' community and cultural identities, and (c) critical consciousness that challenges inequitable school and societal structures.
5. CRP is not prescriptive, and the basic tenets are elastic enough to be addressed across K–12 grades and different content areas.
6. Commonly asked questions about using CRP have been posed and answered.
7. Examples of CRP in elementary, middle, and high school have been presented across several content areas.

Activities

1. Plan a lesson that addresses the three dimensions of CRP (academic achievement, cultural competence, and critical consciousness).
2. In classes where students are from different ethnic backgrounds, let students research topics from their respective cultural backgrounds, as well as from the backgrounds of others. Examples used in Mrs. Hicklin's class should provide ideas for doing this.
3. Reflect on one of the teachers' use of CRP. What would you add or change? How can you extrapolate to your own classroom?

Resources

1. Institute for the Study of the African American Child (https://isaac.wayne.edu/index.php). Provides information about a biennial conference on African American students and other resources.
2. Video: *Culturally Responsive Teaching* (36 minutes). Produced by the National Association for Multicultural Education.
3. Long, S., Hutchinson, W., & Neiderhiser, J. (2011). *Supporting Students in a Time of Core Standards: English Language Arts, Grades PreK–2*. Urbana, IL: National Council of Teachers of English. Provides thoughtful examples of teachers from different ethnic groups using culturally relevant teaching.
4. Kinloch, V. (2010). *Harlem on Our Minds: Place, Race, and the Literacies of Urban Youth*. New York: Teachers College Press. An excellent and engaging look at Black urban youth (high school) and their literacies.
5. Morris, J. E. (2009). *Troubling the Waters: Fulfilling the Promise of Quality Public Schooling for Black Children*. New York: Teachers College Press. Provides wonderful examples of elementary educators' effective teaching of Black children.

Notes

1. CEEEAAS was conceptualized and founded in 2002. Initially, it was funded by the South Carolina Commission on Higher Education. Additional funding was received from CEEEAAS's revenue, the South Carolina State Department of Education's African American History Program, and the U.S. Department of Education. Several school districts supported CEEEAS by funding graduate courses that were offered to PreK–12 teachers.
2. Portions of the description of CEEEAAS classrooms and teachers were included in the following article, which is used here with permission: Boutte, G. S., & Hill, E. (2006). African American communities: Implications for educators. *New Educator, 2*, 311–329.
3. This terminology seems to work for Mrs. Folsom's focus on unity and organization among the group.
4. Portions of the description of Jennifer's classroom and teaching were included in the following article, which is used here with permission: Boutte, G. S., & Strickland, J. (2008). Making African American culture and history central to teaching and learning of young children. *Journal of Negro Education, 77*(2), 131–142.
5. Retrieved May 21, 2015 from www.math.buffalo.edu/mad/special/gilmer-gloria_HAIRSTYLES.html
6. Retrieved May 21, 2015 from www.queensnewyork.com/history/hair.html
7. Retrieved May 21, 2015 from www.ccd.rpi.edu/Eglash/csdt/african/CORNROW_CURVES/cornrow_homepage.html
8. Retrieved May 21, 2015 from www.youtube.com/watch?v=E_5jIt0f5Z4
9. Retrieved May 24, 2015 from www.youtube.com/watch?v=wuG6BMfMT-Y
10. Portions of the description of Mrs. Kelly-Jackson's classroom and the accompanying commentaries were included in the following article, which is used here with permission. Boutte, G., Kelly-Jackson, C., & Johnson, G. L. (2010). Culturally relevant teaching in science classrooms: Addressing academic achievement, cultural competence, and critical consciousness. *International Journal of Multicultural Education, 12*(2), 1–19.

11. Retrieved May 21, 2015 from www.accessexcellence.org/
12. Retrieved May 21, 2015 from http://learn.genetics.utah.edu/content/labs/extraction/
13. Retrieved May 21, 2015 from http://learn.genetics.utah.edu/content/labs/extraction/
    howto/

References

Altman, S. (1997). *The encyclopedia of African American heritage.* New York: Fact on File.

Apple, M. W. (1992). The text and cultural politics. *Educational Researcher, 21*(7), 4–11.

Associated Press. (2007). DNA scientist is condemned for racial comments: Nobel laureate offers apology for remarks. Retrieved November 20, 2014 from www.boston.com/news/world/articles/2007/10/19/dna_scientist_is_condemned_for_racial_comments/

Banks, J. A. (2001). *Cultural diversity and education.* London: Allyn & Bacon.

Barba, R. H. (1995). *Science in the multicultural classroom: A guide to teaching and learning.* Boston, MA: Allyn & Bacon.

Barton, A. C., Ermer, M. L., Burkett, T. A., & Osborne, M.D. (2003). *Teaching science for social justice.* New York: Teachers College Press.

Black Inventor Online Museum. (2010). Ernest Just. Retrieved November 21, 2010 from www.blackinventor.com/pages/ernestjust.html

Black Inventor Online Museum. (2012). Charles Drew. Retrieved May 21, 2015 from http://blackinventor.com/charles-drew/

Bonner, E. P. (2009). Achieving success with African American learners. A framework for culturally responsive mathematics teaching. *Childhood Education, 86*(1), 142–146.

Boutte, G. (1999). *Multicultural education. Raising consciousness.* Atlanta, GA: Wadsworth.

Boutte, G. S. (2002). *Resounding voices: School experiences of people from diverse ethnic backgrounds.* Needham Heights, MA: Allyn & Bacon.

Boutte, G. S. (2012). Urban schools: Challenges and possibilities for early childhood and elementary education. *Urban Education, 47*(2), 515–550.

Boutte, G. S., & Hill, E. (2006). African American communities: Implications for educators. *New Educator, 2*, 311–329.

Boutte, G., Kelly-Jackson, C., & Johnson, G. L. (2010). Culturally relevant teaching in science classrooms: Addressing academic achievement, cultural competence, and critical consciousness. *International Journal of Multicultural Education, 12*(2), 1–19.

Boutte, G. S., LaPoint, S., & Davis, B. D. (1993). Racial issues in the classroom: Real or imagined? *Young Children, 49*(1), 19–23.

Boutte, G. S., & Strickland, J. (2008). Making African American culture and history central to teaching and learning of young children. *Journal of Negro Education, 77*(2), 131–142.

Brayboy, B. M. J., & Castagno, A. E. (2008). How might Native science inform informal science learning? *Cultural Studies of Science Education, 3*(3), 731–750.

Buendia, E. (2011). Reconsidering the urban in urban education: Interdisciplinary conversations. *Urban Review, 43*, 1–21.

Castagno, A. E. (2009). Making sense of multicultural education: A synthesis of the various typologies found in the literature. *Multicultural Perspectives, 11*(1), 43–48.

Collison, M. N.-K. (2002). *It's all good hair: The definitive guide to styling and grooming black children's hair.* New York: Amistad Press.

Compton-Lily, C. (2004). *Confronting racism, poverty, and power: Classroom strategies to change the world.* Portsmouth, NH: Heinemann.

Cowhey, M. (2006). *Black ants and Buddhists: Thinking critically and teaching differently in the primary grades.* Portland, MN: Sternhouse.

Davis, J., & Martin, D. (2008). Racism, assessment, and instructional practices: Implications for mathematics teachers of African American students. *Journal of Urban Mathematics Education, 1*(1), 10–34.

Delpit, L. (1995). *Other people's children. Cultural conflicts in the classroom.* New York: The New Press.

Delpit, L. (2002). No kinda sense. In L. Delpit & J. K. Dowdy (Eds.), *The skin that we speak: Thoughts on language and culture in the classroom* (pp. 33–48). New York: The New Press.

Emdin, C. (2010). *Urban science education for the hip-hop generation.* Rotterdam, Netherlands: Sense.

Fleer, M. (2008). A cultural-historical reading of "culturally sensitive schooling": Thinking beyond a constructivist view of science learning. *Cultural Studies of Science Education, 3*(3), 781–786.

Freire, P. (1970/1999). *Pedagogy of the oppressed.* New York: Continuum.

Gould, S. J. (1981). *The mismeasure of man.* New York: W. W. Norton.

Hayden, R. C. (1970). *Seven Black American scientists.* Reading, MA: Addison-Wesley.

Hilliard, A. G. (1992). Behavioral style, culture, and teaching, and learning. *Journal of Negro Education, 61*(3), 370–377.

Hopkins, R. (1997). *Educating Black males: Critical lessons in schooling, community, and power.* New York: SUNY Press.

Howard, T. (2008). Who really cares? The disenfranchisement of African American males in preK–12 schools: A critical race theory perspective. *The Teachers College Record, 110*(5), 954–985.

Irvine, J. J., & Armento, B. J. (2001). *Culturally responsive teaching: Lesson planning for elementary and middle grades.* New York: McGraw-Hill.

Joseph, G. G. (1987). Foundations of Eurocentrism in mathematics. *Race and Class, 28*(3), 13–28.

Keane, M. (2008). Science education and worldview. *Cultural Studies of Science Education, 3*(3), 587–621.

King, J. E. (1994). The purpose of schooling for African American children. In E. R. Hollins, J. E. King, & W. C. Hayman (Eds.), *Teaching diverse populations / Formulating a knowledge base* (pp. 25–56). New York: SUNY Press.

Kohl, H. (2007). I won't learn from you! Confronting student resistance. In W. Au, B. Bigelow, & S. Karp (Eds.), *Rethinking schools. Teaching for equity and justice* (pp. 165–166). Milwaukee, WI: Rethinking Schools.

Kuhn, T. S. (1996). *The structure of scientific revolutions* (3rd ed.). Chicago, IL: University of Chicago Press.

Kunjufu, J. (2010). *There is nothing wrong with Black students.* Chicago, IL: African American Images.

Ladson-Billings, G. (1994). *The dreamkeepers / Successful teachers of African American children.* San Francisco, CA: Jossey-Bass.

Ladson-Billings, G. (1994/2009). The dreamkeepers/Successful teachers of African American children. San Francisco, CA: Jossey-Bass.

Ladson-Billings, G. (1995). But that's just good teaching! The case for culturally relevant pedagogy. *Theory Into Practice, 34*(3), 159–165.

Ladson-Billings, G. (1997). It doesn't add up: African American students' mathematics achievement. *Journal for Research in Mathematics Education, 28*(6), 697–708.

Ladson-Billings, G. (2002). I ain't writin' nuttin: Permissions to fail and demands to succeed in urban classrooms. In L. Delpit (Ed.), *Skin that we speak* (pp. 107–120). New York: The New Press.

Ladson-Billings, G. (2011). Boyz to men? Teaching to restore Black boys' childhood. *Race Ethnicity and Education, 14* (1), 7–15.

Lee, O., & Buxton, C. A. (2008). Science curriculum and student diversity: Culture, language, and socioeconomic status. *The Elementary School Journal, 109*(2), 123–137.

Lee, O., & Luykx, A. (2005). Dilemmas in scaling up educational innovations with nonmainstream students in elementary school science. *American Educational Research Journal, 42*(3), 411–438.

LeMoine, N. (1999). *English for your success.* Maywood, NJ: Peoples Publishing.

Lewis, C., James, M., Hancock, S., & Hill-Jackson, V. (2008). Framing African American students' success and failure in urban settings: A typology for change. *Urban Education, 43*(2), 127–153.

Linguistic Society of America. (1997*). LSA resolution on the Oakland "Ebonics" issue.* Retrieved February 28, 2005 from www.lsadc.org

Lonesome, R., & Huggins, N. (1990). *Charles Drew.* New York: Chelsea House.

Love, S., & Franklin, J. H. (1997). *One blood: The death and resurrection of Charles R. Drew.* Chapel Hill, NC: University of North Carolina.

Madame C. J. Walker. (n.d.). The official website. Retrieved November 21, 2014 from www.madamewalker.net/

Majors, Y. J. (2001). Passing mirrors: Subjectivity in a Midwestern hair salon. *Anthropology & Education Quarterly, 32*(1), 116–130.

Martin, D. B. (2007). Beyond missionaries or cannibals: Who should teach mathematics to African American children? *The High School Journal, 91*(1), 6–28.

Matthews, L. E. (2003). Babies overboard! The complexities of incorporating culturally relevant teaching into mathematics instruction. *Educational Studies in Mathematics, 53*(1), 61–82.

Milner, H. R. (2011). Culturally relevant pedagogy in a diverse urban classroom. *The Urban Review, 43*(1), 66–89.

Milner, H. R. (2010). *Start where you are, but don't stay there: Understanding opportunity gaps, diversity and teaching in today's classrooms.* Cambridge, MA: Harvard Education Press.

Morris, J. E. (2004). Can anything good come from Nazareth? Race, class, and African American schooling and community in the urban South and Midwest. *American Educational Research Journal, 41*(1), 69–112.

National Geographic. (2014). The Genographic Project. Retrieved November 25, 2014 from https://genographic.nationalgeographic.com

Noguera, P. A. (2001). Racial politics and the elusive quest for excellence and equity in education. *Education and Urban Society, 34*(1), 18–41.

Paris, D. (2012). Culturally sustaining pedagogy. A needed change in stance, terminology, and practice. *Educational Researcher, 41*(3), 93–97.

Perry, T., & Delpit, L. (Eds.). (1998). *The real Ebonics debate: Power, language, and the education of African-American children.* Boston, MA: Beacon.

Perry, T., Steele, C., & Hilliard, A. III. (2003). *Young, gifted, and Black. Promoting high achievement among African-American students.* Boston, MA: Beacon Press.

Pritchy Smith, G. (1998). *Common sense about uncommon knowledge: The knowledge bases for diversity*. Washington, DC: American Association for Colleges of Teacher Education: Publications.

Rousseau, C., & Tate, W. F. (2003). No time like the present: Reflecting on equity in school mathematics. *Theory into Practice, 42*(3), 210–216.

Ryan, A. (2008). Indigenous knowledge in the science curriculum: Avoiding neo-colonialism. *Cultural Studies of Science Education, 3*(3), 663–702.

Whitehurst, S. (2001). *Dr. Charles Drew, medical pioneer*. Makato, MN: Child's World.

Wilkinson, D. (2002). African American barbershops. Retrieved December 15, 2004 from http://members.aol.com/scottcomuseum/african_american.htm

Woodson, C. G. (1933/1990). *The mis-education of the Negro*. Trenton, NJ: Africa World Press.

6

FAMILIES AND COMMUNITIES

Looking with Different Lenses

Proposition 10.1 There is much wisdom and beauty among Black families and in
    Black communities.

And how are the children's communities, homes, and families? These are often places
of refuge and love. This does not mean that Black families, homes, and
communities are not faced with trials and tribulations, just as are they are in other
ethnic groups. Nevertheless, there is a powerful and affirming socialization taking
place in African American communities that could be instructive to schools (Boutte
& Hill, 2006). This chapter illustrates how educators can build on the strengths
found in the Black community to teach African American students effectively.
Absent from many teacher education programs is an emphasis on developing an
inside understanding of students' communities and recognizing and illuminating
existing best practices that differ from mainstream conceptions. Rarely is wisdom
from African American communities sought and used in the quest for best practices for educating African American students. Paradoxically, whereas schools
consistently rank Black students on the lower tiers of education, these same students
often experience success in their homes and communities. A close examination
of some of the structural aspects of institutions within the Black community that
view Black culture as a strength rather than as a deficit may be instructive.

This chapter will provide suggestions for engaging parents and community
members. Before moving forward, reflect on the following questions.

1. Why are the parents of children in the CEEEAAS teachers' classrooms
   (Chapters 4 and 5) actively involved in their children's school experiences?
2. What does it mean to advocate for and with Black parents, families, and
   communities, and what knowledge is it necessary for educators to possess in
   order to do so?

3. What roles can educators play in joining grassroots efforts (e.g., educational, social) among families and community members in Black communities?
4. How can educators build bidirectional relationships with families and communities that focus on learning *from* as well as *about* students and families?
5. How can educators spend time in communities (e.g., places of worship, restaurants, community centers, homes) to build relationships and learn about the wisdom in students' lives and about community resources (businesses, institutions, agencies, people) available to support students (tutoring, sponsors for field trips, mentoring in and out of school)?
6. How can educators learn to build on family and community resources to construct meaningful curriculum?
7. How can educators ensure that collaborative dialogues are sustained?
8. How can educators connect the content to Black families and communities so that students are engaged by, and feel connected to, the lesson(s)?
9. What resources, sages, and wisdom exist in Black families, homes, and communities?
10. Are there misconceptions and fear about Black families, homes, and communities that educators need to address?
11. How can school meetings (e.g., parent–teacher association, school improvement council, parent conferences) be more meaningful and less contrived?

Assumptions

1. There is much wisdom to be found in Black homes, families, communities, and traditions.
2. Educators should consider the cultural capital that students bring from their homes and communities. Each community has its own style of discourse, stories, symbols, rituals, and routines that can inform educators. Their utilization can shift educators from positioning Black communities as pathological to viewing them as resources and sources of information. This will require educators to position ourselves as learners and approach the learning setting with the query, "What can I learn from this community?" Careful and respectful examination of institutions that students engage in daily can shed much light on how educators can infer relevant best practices for our classrooms.
3. The nature of home and community visits needs to be rethought. That is, we educators must examine our positionality as we enter homes and communities. Although we do not want to romanticize families and see only strengths and not challenges, missionary efforts that attempt to "save" African American children from themselves and their culture should be avoided.
4. There is a tremendous amount of variation among Black families and communities.

5. Educators have to recognize, acknowledge, and affirm the strengths that students bring to school—regardless of students' economic, academic, or social circumstances. In addition, although educators should use students' cultural capital as a starting point for teaching and learning, schools also have an obligation to extend students' knowledge and understandings beyond their own worldviews. As many non-mainstream communities may not spend exorbitant amounts of time doing so, schools could complement communities by providing global dimensions to students' knowledge bases.

6. Neither teachers nor parents are responsible for all that is good or bad in school or education. As educators, we cannot overlook deeply entrenched structures, policies, and practices still prevalent today, not only in schools, but also in the nation as a whole. It is important to understand and examine the causes of inequality in the first place.

7. Parent–teacher relationships should be true partnerships. That is, they should be bidirectional. Invite parent and community input for school activities, practices, policies, and issues.

8. The process of building strong relationships takes time and is an ongoing process. Both successes and failures can be expected.

9. In general, it is assumed that most parents care for their children. Caring looks different in different environments. Some parents may show they care by being present in schools. Others may show caring by providing a home or making sure that children arrive at school each day. There is no universal way of caring.

10. Instead of blaming parents for "not being involved," educators should focus on the space that we have control over—our classrooms. This means that assignments that require input from parents will need to be adaptive. Educators can figure out creative ways of ensuring that students succeed, regardless of whether parents are "involved" or not.

11. The best way to involve families is to talk with them directly to find out what interests them and what ideas they have for being involved.

Ideas for Parent and Community Involvement

As the reader considers how to involve parents, it will be important to think about differences between traditional notions of parent involvement and culturally responsive ones. Table 6.1 shows a comparison of the two ways of thinking about parent involvement.

The remainder of this chapter shares a few ideas for involving parents and community members in culturally responsive ways.

Micro-ethnography

Reflecting back to Chapter 1 and the discussion about Black culture, it is recommended that readers begin to study the culture and community contexts of the

TABLE 6.1 Traditional Versus Culturally Responsive Parent Involvement.

Traditional family–school involvement	Culturally responsive family–school involvement
Information flows one way: from school to home	Information flows both ways: families and community members are partners in building curriculum
Schools make efforts to learn *about* families	Schools make efforts to learn, not only about, but *with* and *from* families
Attempts to learn about the community; attempts are largely based in school	Efforts to learn about the community are through teacher engagement *in* the community
Curriculum may be designed on a "one-size-fits-all" cultural model, often starting with what students *do not* know	Curriculum is tailored to the strengths and needs of students, because teachers know families and communities; curriculum starts with what students *do* know
Few collaborative discussions with parents to gain their insights for promoting student success	Families and community members are integral to school discussions about issues such as curriculum, testing, special education and gifted placements, coursework, disciplinary measures, etc.

Source: Boutte & Johnson, 2014

students whom they teach. In order to do so, the following recommendations are shared:

- Plan to spend *extensive* time in settings where students congregate (e.g., church, barbershops, certain restaurants). It will be important to visit these places often enough until the unfamiliar feels familiar. The goal is to try to get an insider's viewpoint of the settings and culture.
- Pay careful attention to how you felt in the setting. What did you learn that could be used as a bridge?
- Because we are cultural beings, cultural influences show up in the routines of our lives. Therefore, try to find out information about aspects of your students' routines (not private information, by the way). For example, what television shows or movies do they like? What types of literacy do they come in contact with (e.g., magazines, music, church)? What social organizations and extracurricular activities are they involved in? What makes them laugh? Cry?

First and Second Weeks of School

Many teachers are eager to begin the school year with exciting lessons that they have worked on during the year. However, more important than starting teaching standards on Day 1 is getting to know your students and developing a relationship with them and their families. This time should be thought of as an investment to ward off potential problems later in the school year. Villegas and Lucas (2002, p. 81) suggested the following ideas:

Things to Learn About Students' Family Lives

- Family life:
  - family makeup;
  - language use, mobility;
  - educational history;
  - childrearing philosophy and practices;
  - major activities;
  - labor history;
  - skills and knowledge used regularly.

- Social life:
  - use of leisure time;
  - favorite activities;
  - language use;
  - what students excel at (strengths);
  - interests, hobbies;
  - concerns.

- Community life:
  - demographic profile: economic makeup, racial/ethnic composition, linguistic makeup, patterns of language use, patterns of segregation;
  - formal and informal holders of power and influence;
  - available resources: businesses, institutions, agencies, people;
  - perceptions of school and school knowledge and participation in school.

Teachers can use some of the ideas discussed below to get information or use methods that make sense to them and the families whom they serve. Typically, written surveys will not yield the information needed. Some information can be gleaned from student files. If any question seems too sensitive or personal, it should not be asked. Only information that will be useful for informing instruction should be sought.

Community Exploration[1]

The activity may be done as a school project for teachers who are teaching in communities that they are unfamiliar with. Teachers are encouraged to undertake the exploration with sensitivity, creativity, and joy, to gather information and insights about the community. Appropriate safety precautions should be taken. For example, it makes sense to enlist the involvement of people who live in the neighborhood (e.g., parents) to accompany the group. It is always a good idea to be alert when in a new area. Make sure your cellphone is charged and available. Be sure that the school is aware that you are visiting the area.

As with the suggestion for the micro-ethnographic study of the community, more than one visit will be necessary. Perhaps the group may start by dining at a local restaurant or shopping in one or two of the stores. Below are possible things to note about the community:

- What city services, such as parks, did you observe?
- What standards of beauty or taste did you experience (in terms of home adornment, clothing, cars, etc.)?
- Is AAL used?
- What types of social services did you notice?
- What types of business seemed to be predominant in the area?
- What interesting places did your group investigate?
- How does this area compare with the area where you now live? What does it have that you do not, and vice versa?
- What was your most impressive or surprising finding or experience?
- How did this experience alter your perception of the community?
- What funds of knowledge exist in the community (e.g., cooking, religion, sewing, fishing)?
- How can these be used to inform your instruction, and how can these be related to the funds of knowledge at school?
- What else could you do now to further explore your students' lives and culture?
- As a teacher of students who live in this area, how would you determine what prior knowledge or schema you must build so that your students can be successful in your class?
- What is one thing you experienced or saw that you could use in the classroom?

An Example of Community Exploration and Using Information in Classroom Instruction

Two first-grade teachers, who taught in a predominantly Black school that was located in a historic district,[2] and Dr. Susi Long (university professor) engaged the first-graders in a study of the community (Long, Hutchinson, & Neiderhiser, 2011). Instead of using curriculum materials that contained remote information, students interviewed members of the community and used videos that were converted to a set of books that were used for literacy instruction in the classroom. Community members who were interviewed included a range of people (e.g., a nurse, a politician and business owner, a barber). Each community member also received copies of the books. In the process, the teachers and students found out more about the historic district, while also meeting literacy standards. Importantly, the children and teachers came to respect and understand the wisdom that exists in Black communities.

Family Literacy Book Club

Mr. Lamar Johnson (now Dr. Johnson) engaged parents of his high-school freshman English students in a year-long book club (Johnson, 2014). Parents and students engaged in dialogue around a multicultural book (*Mexican WhiteBoy*, by Matt de la Peña, 2009) to open up discussion about race and racism. Mr. Johnson was able to engage parents from different ethnic backgrounds in relevant discussions with their children. This idea could easily be extrapolated to creating a family literacy movie, science, math, or social studies club, or the like.

Community Mirrors in the Classroom

Like the classrooms of teachers whose teaching has been showcased in this book, educators should take care to ensure that classroom settings reflect families and communities. From posting photographs of familiar sights, signs, and people to recording oral histories of families, efforts should be made to enhance connections between schools and homes. Families can be invited to share their stories about various issues covered or can come to teachers' classes to listen to students' stories and projects.

On Open-Door Policies

Most schools profess to have an open-door policy; however, when parents show up unexpectedly, many teachers experience discomfort. Teachers should reflect beforehand on what to do if parents show up. How can they be involved? As a teacher, I always had an array of possible activities to involve parents when they showed up—from asking them to join in on whatever we were doing, to reading to a group of children or supervising a learning center, to helping on the playground. As a parent, I have gone to some classes and felt totally welcomed. For example, whenever I dropped in on my daughter's ninth-grade biology class, the teacher would not miss a beat. She would greet me, hand me a book, and tell me what page they were on. Once, I showed up on a day that the class was dissecting pigs. Yes, you guessed it: I was invited (made) to participate. In other cases, I have gone to classrooms, and the teacher did not even acknowledge me. I would find a seat and have to ask for a book. It felt very unwelcoming—even to me, an educator, who is familiar with the school terrain. I can only imagine what it must have felt like for non-educators.

Other School Personnel

It is important for schools to ensure that all personnel are welcoming to parents—regardless of the parents' educational level, appearance, etc. They are there at the school, so welcome them. Professional development on working with parents should include office and other school personnel. Everyone in the school should be respectful and welcoming.

PTA, Open Houses, and Large Group Meetings

It is probably worth faculty discussing ways to make large meetings more inviting for parents. Also, parents should be surveyed as well. Perhaps, welcoming and culturally relevant music could be playing in the background. Teachers can use these opportunities to display children's work or to put out sample books being used in the classroom and ask for feedback from parents. Slideshows of students engaged in various activities could play before and after the business of the meetings.

Parent–Teacher Conferences

The best advice is for teachers to be prepared and to know the students. These conferences are usually short, so they need to be efficient, yet responsive. Some teachers find it useful to let the parents/guardians have a few minutes at the beginning of the meeting to express any concerns. Be sure to have something positive and sincere to say about the students and have concrete examples to share. It is important to remember that both the teacher and parent/guardian want what is best for the student. A plan of action should be jointly devised to resolve any challenges that the student is facing. If a student is having problems, teachers should not wait until scheduled meetings to talk to parents.

Using Technology to Communicate With Parents

Most parents have access to 21st-century technologies (e.g. texting, emails), and so these can be used to make quick contact with parents. Teachers may also set up social media pages to communicate with parents and students.

Advocating for Black Parents

Some parents may not know how to navigate school policies. For example, Black students are disproportionately placed in special education classes and tracked throughout their school careers. As mentioned before, both teachers and parents should have the students' best interests in mind. Therefore, it may be useful to engage advocates to help parents understand their rights. During individual education program meetings, parents are in the room with a group of educators (e.g., speech pathologist, school psychologist, principal, teacher, sociologist). Schools should be aware of the power differential. If parents are not familiar with the policies, teachers may want to encourage parents to bring an advocate. This person does not have an adversarial role, but can help parents fully understand their options and the implications for the students. Importantly, parents need to know that they have a voice in the proceedings and outcome of the meeting.

Engaging Community Sages

One of the advantages of teachers' familiarizing themselves with the community and some of the key players there is that teachers can enlist the assistance and support of community sages (wise people in the community) when needed. As seen in Chapter 5, with the barbershop project, most community members care about the welfare and education of Black children. Teachers should develop relationships with key players and seek their guidance and help as needed. For example, most Black churches, fraternities, sororities, universities, and other social groups would willingly tutor or mentor students in need, thus providing the necessary individualized attention that some students may need. These community members are also likely to know of resources that may be available to help families who are struggling, financially or otherwise.

Conclusion

Without strong parent–teacher relationships, many children's chances of success are greatly reduced (Boutte, 1999). As no one approach works for all parents, teachers should engage in a wide range of outreach possibilities. Concern for students should be holistic rather than narrowly focused on academic outcomes alone. What is most important will be how educators choose to see Black students and their families and communities. If we look through the lenses of the larger societal views, it is likely that Black families will be seen negatively. However, if we look through culturally relevant lenses, we see the beauty, wisdom, and humanity that exist in most Black communities, families, and homes.

Key Points From the Chapter

1. There is much wisdom in Black homes and communities.
2. Teachers should engage in in-depth study of, and immersion in, Black culture and communities in order to better understand their students.
3. Teachers need to learn about and from Black students, families, and communities.

Activities

1. Reflect on the following mini-case (Boutte, 1999):

    Miss Mack is an African American parent of six children under 14 years of age. She is a welfare recipient who lives in a housing project. She speaks fluent AAL. She loves her children very much. Her oldest child, Baby, is a ninth-grader. Baby's teacher sent a note home to all parents encouraging them to volunteer in the classroom. As Miss Mack's other children are in school, she visits Baby's classroom.

    School is just beginning when Miss Mack arrives, and many parents come in the office, sign the visitors' book, and proceed to their children's classrooms. Other than for Open House or PTA meetings, Miss Mack has never visited her children's classrooms. Miss Mack is nervous and does not know what to do or where her son's class is. The secretary in the office does not greet or smile at Miss Mack, but looks at Miss Mack with disdain and then turns her head and returns to work. After a few minutes of waiting, Miss Mack stutters, "Ah wanna volunteer." Without getting out of her seat, the secretary looks at her, frowns, and says, "What?" Miss Mack nervously repeats, "Ah wanna volunteer in my son's class." "*Who* is your son?" asks the secretary, looking at Miss Mack with disapproval. (Miss Mack is wearing a snug-fitting, brightly colored outfit and has on heavy makeup.) "Baby," replies Miss Mack. The secretary laughs and says, "What is his *real* name?"

    The dialogue continues in this manner for a few moments, and, finally, the secretary tells Miss Mack how to find her son's classroom. After leaving the office, Miss Mack is so embarrassed that she goes home instead of visiting her son's class as planned.

    •   What misconceptions is the secretary operating on, and what changes need to be made in office procedures for welcoming parents?
    •   How can schools become more inviting to all parents?

2. Make a list of community "sages" who can visit your classroom. You may find it helpful to do an inquiry project to find out historical sites in the neighborhood as well. The project can simultaneously be used to teach curriculum literacy, history, mathematics, and other standards.
3. Try to find out pressing issues in the community and see if you can contribute to ongoing grassroots efforts.

Resources

1. López-Robertson, J., Long, S., & Turner-Nash, K. (2010). First steps in constructing counter narratives of young children and their families. *Language Arts*, *88*(2), 94–103.

2. Look at examples of activities and opportunities for families and communities that are offered by the Harlem Children's Zone (http://hcz.org/).
3. Subscribe to Black magazines such as *Essence* (www.essence.com/) *or Ebony* (www.ebony.com/) to keep your eye on the purse of Black community issues.
4. Tune in to Black radio shows such as the *Rickey Smiley Show* (formerly the *Tom Joiner Morning Show*) or the *Steve Harvey Show*.

Notes

1. A version of this activity was initially described in Boutte (1999). It was shared with me by Dr. Ronald Wilhelm, University of North Texas, P.O. Box 13857, Denton, TX 76203.
2. The community is listed on the National Register of Historic Places. Although many current residents are not aware of its rich history, several elders who live there know the history. The community has existed since the late 1800s and is in the heart of the city. By the early 20th century, it had evolved into a community of African American artisans, professionals (e.g., doctors), and social reformers. The neighborhood currently has approximately 200 primarily residential buildings, blending Victorian architecture, bungalows, and new homes and townhouses (of late). At one time, it was home to a large housing project for low-income families. More than half of these were torn down as part of a gentrification process, and newer townhouses and a gym facility were built (www.columbiacvb.com/listings/Waverly-Historic-District/17222/).

References

Boutte, G. (1999). *Multicultural education: Raising consciousness*. Atlanta, GA: Wadsworth.

Boutte, G. S., & Hill, E. (2006). African American communities: Implications for educators. *New Educator, 2*, 311–329.

Boutte, G. S., & Johnson, G. (2014). Community and family involvement in urban schools. In H. R. Milner & K. Lomotey (Eds.), *Handbook on urban education* (pp. 167–182). New York: Routledge.

De la Peña, M. (2009). *Mexican WhiteBoy*. New York: Ember.

Johnson, L. L. (2014). *Who let the elephant in the room? Analyzing race and racism through a critical family literacy book club*. Unpublished doctoral dissertation, University of South Carolina—Columbia.

Long, S., Hutchinson, W., & Neiderhiser, J. (2011). *Supporting students in a time of core standards: English language arts, grades PreK–2*. Urbana, IL: National Council of Teachers of English.

Villegas, A. M., & Lucas, T. (2002). *Educating culturally responsive teachers. A coherent approach*. New York: SUNY.

7

REVISIONING THE TEACHING OF AFRICAN AMERICAN STUDENTS

Proposition 7.1 Through reflective action and collaboration, educators can play an important role in reversing negative performance trends and low expectations of African American students.

Proposition 7.2 Teaching African American students can be joyful and hopeful.

The purpose of this book is to liberate, inspire, mobilize, and educate people about African American students. It is by no means exhaustive, but may be considered to be a primer of sorts. It provides enough information to launch thoughtful praxis around educating African American students. Throughout this book, readers may have encountered many difficult and unfamiliar topics. It is important to know that we get better at anything with practice and experience, so keep working on developing your knowledge bases and it will become comfortable to you.

At any rate, tensions in teaching should be welcomed. As we reflect on the larger theme of this book, "And how are the children?", readers should remember that many, perhaps most, African American students encounter tensions on a daily basis, in school and in society. They do not have the option of not dealing with oppression and other issues. So, if the children can do this on a daily basis, surely we, as educators and adults who are charged with protecting the children, can endure discomfort for short periods of time in our learning spaces and classrooms.

Based on my three decades of experiences with teachers in K–12 schools around the country, I realize there is a need for examples of what to do in classrooms. The difficulty in writing a practitioner's guide to educating African American students is that recommendations are viewed as prescriptive. I have emphasized throughout this book that the intent is to provide some guidance and, hopefully, some level of scaffolding for teachers. Activities suggested in this book should be critically considered and tailored to teachers' respective classrooms.

There is a voluminous amount of information in this book. It is hoped that it can be used as a resource. However, it is suggested that teachers select one or two strategies or activities and build from there. Otherwise, it could be overwhelming and cause inaction—thus not meeting the needs of the children. If you are a teacher educator, the PowerPoint presentations on the companion website should be helpful for developing lectures on key points in each chapter.

I hope that it has become apparent that Black students have been, and are currently being, miseducated and undereducated. Likewise, we, as educators, have also been miseducated and undereducated about African and African American history, language, and culture. As information is power, my expectation is that we will have the courage to make a meaningful and transformative difference in the lives of children. In addition, we can do this with enthusiasm, as many examples of successful teachers of African American students have been shown.

More than three decades ago, Dr. Ron Edmonds (1979) posed the compelling question:

> How many effective schools would you have to see to be persuaded of the educability of all children? If your answer is more than one, then I submit that you have reasons of your own for preferring to believe that basic pupil performance derives from family background.
>
> (www.lakeforest.edu/library/archives/effective-
> schools/HistoryofEffectiveSchools.php)

He explained:

> We can, whenever and wherever we choose, successfully teach all children whose schooling is of interest to us; we already know more than we need to do that; and whether or not we do it must finally depend on how we feel about the fact that we haven't so far.
>
> (Edmonds, 1979, p. 23)

There are numerous other success stories of schools, districts, and states demonstrating excellent achievement outcomes for African American students (Education Trust, 2011). In this book, I have provided copious examples showing that it can be done. Now, it is up to you to figure out what will work best in your respective educational spaces. Readers are encouraged to revisit examples in this book as needed. However, do not be limited by them.

Next Steps

Each reader will need to decide how to engage in praxis (reflective action) in her or his educational space. Although the range of actions will vary, inaction should not be an option. McClintock explains that inaction actually works against social justice, because schools are not neutral places (2000). As noted in Chapter 3, educators are either contributing to the status quo by using only conventional methods of teaching (which we know do not work for most Black students) or working toward transformative teaching (Freire, 1970/1999). Examples of possible actions (McClintock, 2000) that can be taken include:

- Educating oneself: Reading this book is a good start. Of course, one book is not a panacea for all of the problems facing Black children. It is important to continue building your knowledge base.
- Interrupting oppression: The strategies in this book will be helpful for doing so in your educational spaces.
- Interrupting oppression and educating others: Share resources with others when appropriate. Perhaps you can recommend professional development sessions at your school or in your district. It is important to note that one-time workshops are generally ineffective, and long-term professional development is suggested. Schools might start by focusing on small groups of interested teachers, rather than trying to do professional development sessions with everyone. Alternatively, professional development may be done by subject area or grade level, as one size does not fit all. This will allow for more depth and tailoring of the professional development sessions. If teachers at your school or in your district have expertise, they should be considered as leaders or co-leaders for the sessions.
- Collaborating with others: Work with others in a proactive manner. For example, you might develop a committee that focuses on educating African American students. The group can study school policies and practices, make recommendations for change, and develop a strategic plan for doing so. Remember to collaborate with parents and community members as well.

As you think about your praxis (reflexive action), think about the following issues or components:

- What are your goals?
- What are the dispositions/attitudes that will need to be addressed?
- What changes are needed in the physical environment, materials, instructional strategies, institutional changes, daily structures, and interactions with students, families, and colleagues, etc.? Be very specific.
- What more do you need to know to put this plan into action? What understandings need to be clarified?
- With whom should this information be shared (e.g., administrators, parents, students)?
- How will you know when/whether or not you have succeeded in achieving your goal(s)? If successful, how will these actions affect African American children, youth, families, and/or communities?

- How will you get buy-in? Think about key players, barriers, allies, etc. What is needed to sustain the efforts?
- What is your timeline?

Celebrating Ourselves as Teachers

Sadly, for a variety of complicated reasons, teachers forget why they went into teaching in the first place—for the children. One of the reasons is that teachers feel ill equipped to teach culturally and linguistically diverse populations. Hence, teaching becomes a dreaded career rather than one that teachers enjoy. The problem of teacher turnover is especially acute, with as many as half of new teachers in urban public schools quitting within the first 5 years (Nieto, 2003). Approximately, 24 percent leave within the first 3 years (Kaiser, 2011). In this book, I have tried to show that the teachers featured were joyful and hopeful and believed in the possibility of the Black child. So the question is: How can teaching become a profession that is rewarding for more teachers? Having the necessary tools (e.g., instructional strategies, knowledge of the complexities of teaching, dispositions) greatly reduces the apprehension that far too many teachers have about educating African American students.

I want to end this book by sharing an activity that I have used in my graduate course, "Educating African American Students." I call the activity "Culturally Relevant Rhythms." It builds on the fourth key principle of Black education (King, 2005), which states:

> The "ways of knowing" provided by the arts and humanities are often more useful in informing our understanding of our lives and experiences and those of other oppressed people than the knowledge and methodologies of the sciences that have been privileged by the research establishment despite the often distorted or circumscribed knowledge and understanding this way of knowing produces.
>
> (p. 20)

I use this to honor Black ways of knowing—music being one of them. As shared in Chapter 2, "Teachers are often simultaneously perpetrators and victims, with little control over planning time, class time, or broader school policies—and much less over the unemployment, hopelessness, and other 'savage inequalities' that help shape our children's lives" (Au, Bigelow, & Karp, 2007, p. x). So, I would like for us to celebrate ourselves for a moment, to claim our agency, and to begin to teach for the liberation of our students and ourselves.

Culturally relevant teachers recognize that teaching is a profession that should be respected and revered. It would be great if teachers received the "red carpet" treatment and respect that well-known celebrities and entertainers do. So, for a closing exercise, I want readers to envision themselves as a star, and their classroom as a stage. Like movie stars, each teacher has her or his own unique style and strengths. In most movies, the star of the show has his or her own theme music. Imagine yourself walking down the hallway of your school and having your "music" playing in the background.

For this activity, you will put together a multimedia presentation (e.g., using PowerPoint and music, video clips, imovie, prezi). Select theme music that represents the essence of your teaching and what you stand for or value. Be thoughtful about your musical selection and have fun with the activity. Four examples are posted on the companion website for this book. These were put together as a culminating activity for the course, "Educating African American Students." Each one was a 5–10-minute celebratory project. Some of the presentations used more than one song (see Hetlena Johnson's (business education teacher) multimedia presentation, which was a mini movie, with songs playing in the background such as "Oh Happy Day," "Control," "We Are the World," and "I believe I can fly"). Mrs. Johnson wove in pictures and videos of her teaching, quotes from readings that captured what she believed, photos of things that were important to her (e.g., her family, sororities, career), and audio recordings of her students. Her love of teaching is evident in the video. She summarized Ladson-Billings's (1994) ideas that the classroom teacher is powerful, and teaching is a social responsibility. She posed the penetrating question, "Yes, but why do you want to teach?" (Ladson-Billings, 1994, p. 95).

Others teachers used one song (see Ezetta Myers (high-school math teacher), who used Donnie McClurkin's song, "Yes You Can"). Dr. Myers told her own story of self-determination during her schooling, where she learned to excel and later earned a doctorate degree. Following her theme, she writes,

> Yes, I Can . . .
>
> Make a difference.
>
> Teaching is my calling.
>
> As someone made a difference in my life, I hope and pray that I make a difference in the lives of my students.

She included key beliefs grounded in the literature, with supporting audio quotes from her students commenting on her teaching and what they appreciated about her. She ended with, "I can, yes I can do anything. No matter what—if you can just conceive it, if you can believe it, then you can achieve it."

Jennifer Strickland, whom you met in Chapters 3 and 5, used Bob Marley's "Redemption Song" to convey her theme of "Teaching for Liberation." Photos of her students and families were included, as well as activities that demonstrated her use of critical and diaspora literacy.

Mrs. Kitty Faden, a Curriculum Resource Teacher, who views herself as a servant leader and who has excellent relationships with students, used Whitney

Houston's, "One Moment in Time," explaining, "Teaching—a profession of excellence, that captures moments in time within all cultures, which influence and affect the world." Using pictures of students throughout, on her last two slides she writes:

The Teacher in Me

My smile can lighten their day.
My teachings can inspire their week.
My/their wisdom stays with me/them throughout the year.
My example/model can change their lives.
I'm their teacher, they are mine!

Teachers

Teachers educate every known profession in the world.

Teachers who, in spite of adverse and challenging situations, and limited resources, go the extra mile beyond lesson plans in order to motivate and inspire students. They grab that ONE MOMENT IN TIME to teach and inspire children to be the BEST THAT THEY CAN BE! They're the STARS!

It is obvious that these teachers "believe in the possibility of the Black child" and in teaching.

Creating Your Own Culturally Relevant Rhythm

The idea is for you to create your "platform" (theme) in an engaging slide presentation (or mini movie). Choose a musical selection to play in the background of your show—this is your own little movie. To provide a context (in case you share it with others, later—e.g., other teachers, administrators, your students), it is helpful to address the following in your presentation (though none of these is mandatory, and you should be creative and showcase what is important and makes sense to you):

- subject and grade level;
- educational setting (size of school, teacher and student demographics, relevant issues);
- your theme—your presentation should reinforce your theme;
- your beliefs about students and how they learn;
- how your beliefs relate to the body of literature presented in this book, when possible;
- relationships with families and community or hobbies (what makes you you!).

Hopefully, this culminating project will help you focus on the role that you can play in improving the lives of the children you teach. It can also be used to inspire and energize you about teaching.

Conclusion

Returning to the guiding question for this book, "And how are the children?", it is my hope that, after reading about, reflecting on, critiquing, and beginning to take reflective action (praxis) regarding some of the ideas discussed in this book, readers will find ways to be strong advocates for Black students. The companion website provides additional information such as PowerPoint presentations that can be shared with others who have also read the book. It is not recommended that any part of the book be taken out of context, as having a full conceptualization of the issues is important.

If you have gotten through the end of the book, it means that you are interested in educating African American students (or that the book has been assigned for a class). Ask yourself: How do Black children in my classroom and school feel? What am I doing well, and what can I improve? Have I provided mirrors and windows for the students?

The strategies shared in this book are not exclusive to Black children. As the title of one of Ladson-Billings's articles summarizes, "But that's just good teaching!" (Ladson-Billings, 1995).

Too many teacher education programs do not provide information that will help teachers succeed in their efforts to teach African American students in liberatory ways. Hopefully, this book will be a useful resource. It captures information from a course that I teach on "Educating African American Students." Virtually all of the students leave the course energized in a way that they were not previously, because they feel as if they now have the conceptualization and tools to be effective in teaching African American students. I hope that readers feel this way and feel as one teacher, who had taken a break from teaching, did:

> I am ready to go back and teach now that I know what I am doing. I am energized and now want to try it all out in a classroom. There is so much that I have done wrong, but you have not made me feel bad about that. I am ready now to do some good on behalf of African American students!

As esteemed elder Maya Angelou (poet, author, and so much more) said, "Do the best you can until you know better. Then when you know better, do better" (2010, no pagination). Co-narrating this sentiment, Biggie Smalls (hip-hop artist) sang, "If you don't know, now you know!"

I leave you now to enjoy the sweet and liberating sounds of Sweet Honey in the Rock singing one of the liberation songs that was used during the Civil Rights Movement and loved by Ella Baker (human and civil rights activist), "We who believe in freedom cannot rest" (www.youtube.com/watch?v=U6Uus—gFrc).

Key Points From the Chapter

1. Culturally relevant teachers enjoy teaching.
2. Culturally relevant teachers have the necessary tools and dispositions to teach African American students effectively.
3. We need to reclaim the joy of teaching.

Activities

1. Devise a plan of action to begin ensuring systematic changes in your school—e.g., a professional development series on AAL, diaspora literacy, changes to allow greater access for Black students to gifted programs or to reduce disproportionality of special education placements, school suspensions, and expulsions.
2. Consider starting a book study group.

Resources

1. DuBois, W. E. B. (1903/1990). *The Souls of Black Folk.* New York: First Vintage Books/The Library of America Edition.
2. King, J. E. (2005). *Black Education: A Transformative Research and Action Agenda for the 21st Century.* Mahwah, NJ: Lawrence Erlbaum.
3. Perry, T., Steele, C., & Hilliard, A. III. (2003). *Young, Gifted, and Black. Promoting High Achievement Among African-American Students.* Boston, MA: Beacon Press.
4. Woodson, C. G. (1933/1990). *The Mis-education of the Negro.* Trenton, NJ: Africa World Press.
5. Woodson, C. G. (1919). *The Education of the Negro. An Essential Preface for Understanding the Mis-education of the Negro.* Brooklyn, NY: A & B Books.

References

Angelou, M. (2010). Maya Angelou quotes. Retrieved May 10, 2010 from www.goodreads.com/quotes/show/197836

Au, W., Bigelow, B., & Karp, S. (2007). Introduction: Creating classrooms for equity and social justice. In W. Au, B. Bigelow, and S. Karp (Eds.), *Rethinking our classrooms: Teaching for equity and justice* (2nd ed., Vol. 1, pp. x–xi). Milwaukee, WI: Rethinking Schools.

Edmonds, R. (1979). Effective schools for the urban poor. *Educational Leadership, 3*(1), 15–27.

Education Trust. (2011). Success stories. Dispelling the myth. Retrieved on August 1, 2011 from www.edtrust.org/dc/resources/success-stories

Freire, P. (1970/1999). *Pedagogy of the oppressed.* New York: Continuum.

Kaiser, A. (2011). Beginning teacher attrition and mobility: Results from the first through third waves of the 2007–08 Beginning Teacher Longitudinal Study (NCES 2011–318). U.S. Department of Education. Washington, DC: National Center for Education Statistics. Retrieved on October 16, 2011 from http://nces.ed.gov/pubsearch

King, J. E. (2005). *Black education: A transformative research and action agenda for the 21st century.* Mahwah, NJ: Lawrence Erlbaum.

Ladson-Billings, G. (1994). *The dreamkeepers. Successful teachers of African American children.* San Francisco, CA: Jossey-Bass.

Ladson-Billings, G. (1995). But that's just good teaching! The case for culturally relevant pedagogy. *Theory Into Practice, 34*(3), 159–165.

McClintock, M. (2000). How to interrupt oppressive behavior. In M. Adams, W. Blumenfeld, R. Castaneda, H. Hackman, M. Peters, & X. Zuniga (Eds.), *Readings for diversity and social justice* (pp. 483–485). New York: Routledge.

Nieto, S. (2003). *What keeps teachers going?* New York: Teachers College Press.

INDEX